THE VANGUARD RETIREMENT INVESTING GUIDE

Charting Your Course
to a Secure Retirement

Revised Edition

THE VANGUARD RETIREMENT INVESTING GUIDE

Charting Your Course to a Secure Retirement

Revised Edition

The Vanguard
Group of
Investment Companies

IRWIN
Professional Publishing®
Chicago • London • Singapore

This publication is designed to provide accurate and
authoritative information in regard to the subject matter
covered. It is sold with the understanding that neither the
author nor the publisher is engaged in rendering legal, accounting,
or other professional service. If legal advice or other expert
assistance is required, the services of a competent professional
person should be sought.

*From a Declaration of Principles jointly adopted by a Committee
of the American Bar Association and a Committee of Publishers.*

Irwin Professional Book Team

Publisher: *Wayne McGuirt*
Executive editor: *Amy Hollands Gaber*
Managing editor: *Kevin Thornton*
Senior marketing manager: *Tiffany Dykes*
Project editor: *Margaret Rathke*
Production supervisor: *Dina L. Treadaway/Carol Klein*
Manager, direct marketing: *Rebecca S. Gordon*
Prepress buyer: *Jon Christopher*
Compositor: *Wm. C. Brown Publishers*
Typeface: *11/13 New Aster*
Printer: *R. R. Donnelley & Sons*

◥◤ **Times Mirror**
◣◢ **Higher Education Group**

Library of Congress Cataloging-in-Publication Data
The Vanguard retirement investing guide : charting your course to a secure
retirement / the Vanguard Group of Investment Companies. —
Rev. ed.

    p.   cm.
Includes index.
ISBN 0-7863-0502-9; ISBN 0-7863-0624 (software version)
1. Retirement income—United States—Planning. 2. Mutual funds—
United States. 3. Investments—United States. I. Vanguard Group
of Investment Companies.
HG179.V367 1996
332.024'01—dc20   95–24870
Printed in the United States of America
1 2 3 4 5 6 7 8 9 0 DOW 2 1 0 9 8 7 6 5

A t some point in your life, you will probably retire. Whether you leave the work force at the tender age of 50 or enjoy your job so much that you cannot bear to walk away until you are 80, the fact is that virtually everyone eventually stops working to enjoy the proverbial fruits of their labors. Unfortunately, most people let their retirement just sort of happen, without giving any serious thought to what they would like to do during their "Golden Years" and where the money will come from to pay for their expenses over the rest of their life. The fact that you now hold this guide in your hands is a good indication that you are taking the issue of a secure retirement seriously.

This guide begins with a look at some hard realities. The long-term viability of the Social Security system is a mounting concern for the next generation of retirees, traditional pension plans that guarantee a retirement benefit are not nearly as popular with employers as they once were, and many people simply are not saving as much as they need to. At the same time that retirement benefits and savings are coming under pressure, retirees are living longer and spending more for travel, entertainment, and health care. It seems pretty clear that if retirement benefits are decreasing and retirement spending is increasing, a time of reckoning is inevitable.

Chapter 2 offers five simple strategies to engage these threats to your retirement security on your own terms, rather than waiting passively until you retire to find out that you have not saved enough. In conjunction with this savings plan, a detailed worksheet is provided in Chapter 3 to assist you in identifying (based on your personal retirement objectives and financial resources) how much you should be investing each month to achieve your retirement goals.

Of course, it is one thing to realize that you must save more to attain your retirement goals; it is quite another to actually decide how you will put together an investment program to reach your long-term goals. In this regard, Chapter 4 addresses some fundamental principles of investing, including a review of the three major asset classes—stocks, bonds, and short-term reserves—and how the potential risks and rewards of each asset class can impact a diversified investment portfolio.

Chapter 5 is dedicated exclusively to a discussion of mutual funds and how they may be used as a critical component of your retirement portfolio. As one of the nation's largest providers of pure no-load mutual funds and investment services, it is perhaps not surprising that The Vanguard Group believes the mutual fund concept is the most effective way to build your retirement assets. We believe the diversification, professional management, liquidity, and convenience of mutual funds represent an overwhelming advantage relative to other investment alternatives, and the remarkable growth of mutual fund assets over the past decade suggests that investors concur with this assessment. Indeed, one out of four households now invests in mutual funds.

Particular attention is given in Chapter 6 to the crucial decision of how much you should invest in each asset class, given your risk tolerance, financial circumstances, and retirement goals. The road to retirement is a gnarled path, and the allocation of your retirement assets will change as you make your way through the different stages of your life cycle. This guide provides a straightforward framework to make rational decisions about the composition of your retirement portfolio.

The growth of the mutual fund industry has created a confusing by-product: there are now over 5,000 funds to choose from, and deciding which funds are the most appropriate for your portfolio is an imposing task. Chapter 7 attempts to facilitate your fund selection process by outlining the different types of mutual funds within each asset class and the sources of information that are available to investors. This chapter includes a discussion on how to analyze the past performance of a fund and the extent to which this performance is likely to presage similar future performance. While this type of analysis will be critical in making your investment decisions, it should be clear that selecting any investment is an inevitably fallible exercise. You will not find a magic formula for picking "the best" mutual funds within these pages.

The final four chapters tend to be more technical; they focus on describing the various types of tax-advantaged retirement plans (Chapter 8), the benefits provided by the Social Security and Medicare systems and how you go about claiming these benefits (Chapter 9), guidelines on what options are available to you when you redeem your assets from a tax-advantaged plan (Chapter 10), and a number of other critical issues that you should consider as you approach the final years leading up to your retirement (Chapter 11).

It is important to understand that the discussion of the myriad of retirement issues broached in this guide are by no means exhaustive. Entire books have been written on many of the topics that are covered here in just a few pages, so you should not assume that everything you need to know about each retirement issue is contained within these pages. When in doubt, you should contact an investment professional or refer to a more definitive source on a particular topic to clarify any areas of concern.

In the final analysis, you may be surprised at how fundamental the retirement planning process actually is. Indeed, Vanguard is known for speaking plainly and candidly about investment issues, and this same philosophy was applied to the writing of this guide. Whatever you do, don't let anyone tell you that investing is too much trouble—or too difficult—to accomplish on your own. Just turn the page, and begin traveling down the road to a more secure and satisfying retirement.

The Vanguard Group
of Investment
Companies

CONTENTS

PART I

Save More for Retirement—Today

PART II

Make Your Retirement Investments Work for You

SAVE MORE FOR
RETIREMENT—TODAY

The Challenge of Saving for Retirement

I f you are like most people, you probably dream about retirement. Maybe you think about how much golf you will play. Maybe you fantasize about all of the exotic places you will visit. Or maybe you simply imagine how enjoyable it will be to sit in the shade and catch up on 30 years' worth of reading. Whatever retirement means to you, the chances are that you probably have not spent enough time planning how you are going to pay for all of that travel and golf. Whether you are 50 years old or 30 years old, preparing for your retirement should be your top financial priority.

At one time, the model for saving for a comfortable retirement was fairly straightforward and could be thought of as a "three-legged stool," with each leg representing a separate element of retirement savings:

1. Social Security—the foundation of your retirement benefits.
2. Employer pension plan—supplemental benefits to raise the comfort level of your retirement.
3. Personal savings—discretionary funds for a virtually worry-free retirement.

Today, this traditional model faces new challenges. As the baby boom generation ages, it is discovering that Social Security may not be able to maintain the same generous benefits that it has in the past. While new employer retirement plans are allowing employees to take greater control of their retirement planning, these plans also require considerably more vigilance on the part of the employee. What is more, improvements in longevity suggest that the chances of a relatively long retirement are quite high. And a longer retirement means that additional resources will be required to meet monthly expenditures, pay increased medical bills, and protect against inflation.

In short, personal retirement savings can no longer be considered discretionary, a mere incidental element in an otherwise solid retirement plan revolving around Social Security and an employer pension. Rather, additional retirement savings are now an indispensable component of your total retirement portfolio. In the remainder of this chapter, you will discover how changing demographics have adversely affected the prospects for Social Security and how the gradual decline of the traditional pension plan is adding to the challenge of retirement saving. You will also learn of some other factors that will threaten your retirement security and therefore demand a renewed emphasis on personal savings.

Storm Clouds Ahead for Social Security

While 45 years ago there were 16 workers contributing to Social Security for each recipient drawing benefits, today there are only about three workers for each recipient. Forty years from now, there will be only two workers contributing for each recipient.

As the first "leg" of the traditional retirement program, Social Security remains the foundation of retirement savings. According to financial planning experts, most retirees will need an income level equal to as much as 80% of their preretirement salary to maintain the same standard of living in retirement as they enjoyed while working. While Social Security benefits will likely replace only a small portion of this amount, Social Security offers a noteworthy advantage: benefits have generally kept pace with the rising cost of living. Equally important for many lower- and middle-income retirees, in many instances Social Security benefits are free of federal income taxes.

In general, Social Security benefits will replace a relatively smaller portion of the income of upper-income retirees. That is, if your earnings consistently have been in the top Social Security bracket, you can expect your benefits to equal only about 24% ($14,388) of the portion of your pay subject to Social Security tax ($61,200 in 1995). Employer benefits and personal savings will be needed to make up the difference. Figure 1–1 shows that the higher your income, the lower the percentage that will be replaced by Social Security after you retire. To make matters worse, as much as 85% of the benefits to higher-income retirees may be subject (under current laws) to federal income tax.

As if all of that bad news were not enough, there is growing doubt about the ability of the Social Security system to sustain current levels of benefits into the next century. A 1992 survey by the Gallup Organization found that one out of every two Americans believes that Social Security will not be able to pay them a benefit when they retire. Not surprisingly, older people were more confident, while younger people were more skeptical. Seventy-five percent of those polled by Gallup said they think higher taxes would be required to finance Social Security benefits beyond the year 2000.

Some experts believe that the public's concerns about Social Security are justified. One of those experts is A. Haeworth Robertson, chief actuary for the Social Security Administration in 1975–78, who asserts that the Social Security system will not be viable in its present form when the first group of baby boomers expects to retire in about 2010. Other experts, such as Robert J. Myers, chief actuary for the Social Security Administration in 1947–70, believe that relatively small changes in benefits and tax rates can be made to assure Social Security's long-term viability. Indeed, Social Security and Medicare face possible financial shortfalls for two basic reasons: (1) changing demographic patterns, and (2) spiraling medical costs. From a demographic standpoint, the baby boom generation (those born between the years 1945 and 1965) will retire just as a much smaller cohort of "baby busters" is working to meet Social Security payroll taxes. The consequence of this trend will be larger retirement payouts, with fewer workers to pay.

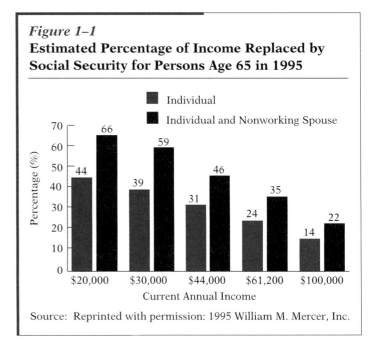

Figure 1–1

Estimated Percentage of Income Replaced by Social Security for Persons Age 65 in 1995

Source: Reprinted with permission: 1995 William M. Mercer, Inc.

Social Security and Medicare costs already total about 15% of taxable payrolls. (This is the amount contributed by employers and employees.) But the Board of Trustees of the program says that the benefits promised to retiring baby boomers will grow to a point where such payments may equal 48% of payrolls by the middle of the next century, under the most pessimistic official assumptions. Keeping both the promise to deliver current benefits and the promise to maintain Social Security taxes at reasonable levels may not be possible.

According to Mr. Robertson, "It seems clear that both promises will be broken since it will be virtually impossible to increase taxes enough to fulfill the benefit promises being made to the baby boomers."

At least for the time being, Social Security is taking in more money than it is paying out. In fact, the Social Security Trust Funds report a growing surplus that is projected to swell to

$3 trillion by the year 2019 and then decline as benefits are paid out to the retiring baby boomers. Yet critics contend that the surplus is illusory. The Trust Fund surplus is invested in US Treasury bonds; in essence, the excess money is being used to finance current federal expenditures. What this means, according to experts like Robertson, is that the government eventually will have to raise taxes in order to provide the Social Security system with the cash it needs to pay ballooning benefits.

What can you do as an individual to protect yourself as the nation wrestles with the impending problems of Social Security? All experts agree that you should be investing on your own. Robertson advises: "You should be saving personally and through employer-provided benefit plans, not only to supplement the Social Security benefits currently being promised, but also to make up for the shortfall that almost certainly will occur in such promised benefits."

The Decline of the Traditional Pension Plan

The number of traditional defined benefit plans paying premiums to the Pension Benefit Guaranty Corporation (a government agency guaranteeing pensions) fell from 105,000 in 1988 to 58,000 in 1995, a 45% decline. Many of these plans have been replaced with defined contribution plans, which do not guarantee a fixed pension at retirement.

Another challenge to retirement savings is the shift by employers away from traditional pension plans, the second leg of the retirement program. These traditional plans, often called defined benefit plans, pay workers a fixed monthly income at retirement, usually based on final average salary and number of years of service. Employers typically oversee the administration of the plans, including the investment management services that will assure benefits at retirement.

In recent years, the number of defined benefit plans in use has declined dramatically, with corporate restructurings and downsizings contributing importantly to the trend. Defined benefit plans are most common in manufacturing and other industrial sectors, and these parts of the economy were hit hard during the 1980s. In addition, employers have faced complex and burdensome government regulations that have driven up the costs of administering defined benefit plans. Costs have also increased as a result of soaring premiums charged by the Pension Benefit Guaranty Corporation to insure pension assets.

This confluence of events has led many companies to shed their defined benefit programs entirely. In some cases, companies have retained their basic defined benefit plans but have de-emphasized them somewhat, suggesting that these plans may continue to shrink in importance in future years. In other cases, companies have replaced their defined benefit plans with a lower-cost alternative: the defined contribution plan.

A defined contribution plan, unlike a defined benefit plan, does not guarantee workers a fixed pension at retirement. Instead, a specified amount of money is set aside each year for employees while they are still working. Put simply, in a defined contribution plan the annual contribution (the amount put aside for retirement) is specified, not the ultimate retirement benefit. So, the benefits that employees receive at retirement will depend on the amounts contributed on their behalf over the years, plus any investment earnings or appreciation (See Table 1–1).

In many defined contribution plans, both the employer and the employee contribute to the plan. For some of these plans, such as 401(k) and 403(b) retirement savings plans, employees contribute (on a pretax basis) the lion's share of the monies put aside for their retirement. They also decide how the monies invested on their behalf will be allocated. Defined contribution plans have one significant advantage in that they are portable. That is, when employees leave their jobs, they can usually take their accumulated savings with them. For many workers, the chance to control their retirement savings has brought about an enhanced sense of involvement in their future—and a much-needed appreciation of the importance of saving.

You should know that defined contribution plans are not a panacea for retirement programs. Some plans simply are not as generous as traditional defined benefit plans. Employer contributions to the plans may be lower, and workers may not be making up for the shortfall with their own savings. Most financial planners estimate that, in a defined contribution plan, total contributions (i.e., from both employer and employee) should equal at least 10% of annual salary over a 35-year working career. Saving at this rate, in combination with Social Security benefits, should provide a moderate level of retirement income.

Table 1–1
Defined Benefit Plan versus Defined Contribution Plan

	Plan Type	
	Defined Benefit	**Defined Contribution**
Type of benefit	Payments guaranteed at retirement	Guaranteed contribution, not guaranteed benefit
Source of assets	Usually employer only	Employer, employee, or both
Investment decisions	Employer only	Employer or employee
Examples	Pension	Money purchase pension, 401(k), 403(b), profit-sharing

Sounds easy, right? Well, don't relax yet. Raising your income to a higher comfort level, making up for possible shortfalls in Social Security benefits, retiring early, or simply putting aside a "travel the world" fund all require a higher savings rate—something in the area of 15% to 20% of your annual salary. The fact is few workers (or their employers) are saving at this level today. Indeed, many workers spend their accumulated retirement savings when they change jobs, rather than rolling over their assets into the new employer's plan.

The trend in favor of defined contribution plans over defined benefit plans seems likely to persist. Employers find the lower administrative costs appealing, and many employees prefer the flexibility and "portability" of benefits. What is not clear is whether Americans who have access to defined contribution plans are actually putting aside a realistic level of savings. In a nation that saves less than 5% of its disposable income each year, it seems very unlikely that many workers are saving the 15% to 20% of their salaries needed to ensure a comfortable retirement.

The Importance of Personal Savings

Saving is the essential element for future financial security. If retirement is to be longer—and costlier—an increased level of personal savings will be absolutely indispensable.

For some retirees, the "three-legged stool" they had expected to support them in their later years—Social Security, pension, personal savings—turns out to be not quite so sturdy. In fact, according to a nationwide survey conducted in 1992 by the Roper Organization, one in three retirees say that their standard of living is lower than they had expected. Changes in Social Security and pension plans, of course, are two important contributors to this situation. But why else do retirees feel so squeezed? For many, it comes down to some combination of three mitigating factors: (1) increased longevity, (2) early retirement, and (3) inflation.

Increased Longevity

Thanks to improved medical care and a heightened appreciation of the benefits of proper diet and exercise, Americans today can expect to live considerably longer than did previous generations. The increase in American life expectancy in this century has been astounding. In the year 1900, a newborn male could expect to live for 46 years, a female for 49 years. In 1994, the figures were 72 years for males and 79 years for females. If you reach the normal retirement age of 65, you can expect to live to age 80 if you are a male and to age 84 if you are a female. By the time the first members of the baby boom generation reach age 65 in the year 2011, life expectancies for retiring 65-year-olds could reach age 83 for men and age 88 for women, according to US Census Bureau projections. (See Figure 1–2)

One result of a longer life, of course, is higher medical bills. For example, the likelihood that you will need nursing home care increases dramatically as you get older. According to a recent federal study of nursing home utilization, about one in 25 men and one in 15 women between the ages of 74 and 85 live in nursing homes. For those age 85 and older, the figures for those residing in a nursing home increase to one in seven men and one in four women.

Early Retirement

At the same time that individuals are living longer, more people also are choosing to retire early. Although age 65 is generally regarded as the typical retirement age, currently more people leave the work force at age 62 than at age 65. What is more, only 16% of men over age 65 were in the work force during 1990, compared to 46% during 1950. There is every indication that this trend toward early retirement will continue, since surveys show that most working Americans plan to retire at age 60 and expect some 20 years of retirement.

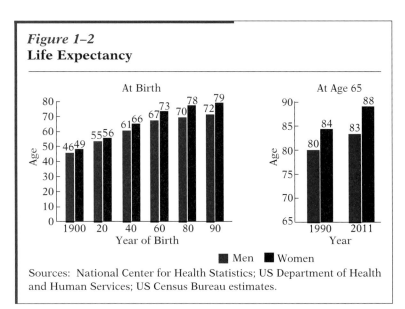

Figure 1–2
Life Expectancy

Sources: National Center for Health Statistics; US Department of Health and Human Services; US Census Bureau estimates.

The impact of these two trends—increased longevity and earlier retirement—seems clear. Americans on average will live longer after they have stopped working than their forefathers could ever have dreamed. As a result, many Americans could spend one-third or more of their adult years in retirement. Those extra years will provide more time for travel, visits with grandchildren, and many other endeavors that could not be accomplished during a busy working life. Of course, it goes without saying that these activities will require additional financial resources. So, you must either save more in anticipation of these additional retirement years, or stretch to get by on less than what you really need.

Inflation

A longer retirement also means more time for inflation (i.e., increases in the cost of living) to take its toll on your financial assets. Inflation reduces the purchasing power of your accumulated savings and of any fixed income payments that you are receiving during retirement, such as benefits from an employer pension plan. It may be useful to think of, say, a 4% inflation rate as a 4% annual tax on the entire value of your savings and investments.

During your working years, it may be possible to keep pace with inflation through salary increases, taking a second job, or perhaps by increasing your investment risk in the hope of boosting your "real" (inflation-adjusted) returns. Once you retire, however, you lose much of your ability to stay ahead of rising prices. Income tends to be fixed, and a limited time horizon makes it difficult to safely allocate a significant portion of your financial assets to more aggressive investments that might do better over the long run in keeping pace with inflation.

Since 1965, consumer prices have risen at a compound annual rate of about 6%. (The long-run average going all the way back to the turn of the century was about 3%.) Over some shorter periods, however, inflation has compounded at much higher rates. For instance, in the late 1970s inflation reached double-digit levels as consumer prices rose by almost 40% from 1979 to 1981. For most retirees, Social Security benefits are typically the only retirement income they receive that is indexed to inflation. Since employer pensions typically are not indexed to inflation, they are quite vulnerable to the inflation "tax."

It is important to understand that even seemingly insignificant rates of inflation can severely erode your capital over your retirement years. For example, as shown in Figure 1–3, assuming a relatively modest 4% inflation rate, income of $10,000 in today's dollars needs to increase to $14,800 in 10 years to maintain the same purchasing power. Over a 20-year period, income of $10,000 today would have to increase by 120%—to $21,900—to retain the same "real" value. If 20 years seems too long of a time horizon to contemplate, consider that on average many 65-year-olds retiring today will live at least that long. Many individuals will live even longer and will require still higher income growth to keep pace with inflation.

Many investors never fully grasp the importance of maintaining the so-called purchasing power of their investments. Another way to look at this issue is to consider the impact of inflation on a fixed yearly income payment. The payment could be from an employer pension plan, a bank certificate of deposit, or perhaps a government bond. Again assuming a 4% annual inflation rate, a $10,000 income payment in year one would be worth only $6,648 in year 10—an income decline of nearly one-third. In 20 years, the value of your income would drop by a staggering 56%, to $4,420. In essence, then, if your yearly income is not supplemented from some other source to make up for this erosion in value, you must reduce your yearly expenditures, which means less golf, fewer trips to visit the grandchildren, and so on.

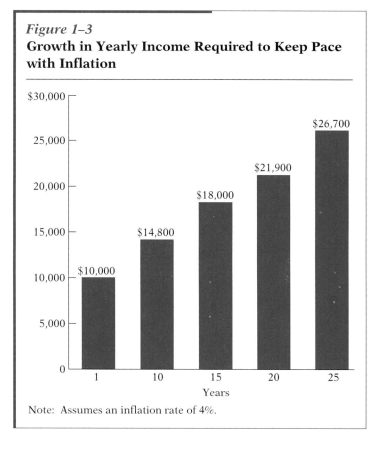

Figure 1–3
Growth in Yearly Income Required to Keep Pace with Inflation

Note: Assumes an inflation rate of 4%.

In fairness, the rate of inflation as it is tracked by the US Consumer Price Index (CPI) may not accurately reflect the actual impact of rising prices on retired individuals since retirees are generally not consumers of the total array of goods and services that comprise the CPI. For example, if you own your home, you are obviously unaffected by any increases or decreases in housing prices or rentals, both of which are included in the calculation of the CPI. On the other hand, retirees tend to be heavy consumers of services, and inflation in the services sector, particularly for medical care, has outpaced inflation for goods. Thus, in some cases, the effective inflation rate for a retired individual may be higher than the rate expressed by the CPI.

Final Thoughts

It should be clear by now that planning for retirement is not as easy as it was 20 years ago. The good news is that despite all of the hurdles that stand between you and a secure retirement, retirees say they generally are satisfied with their present circumstances. After decades of work, they have adapted well to a new lifestyle, if hardly an idle one. Most retirees stay busy with hobbies, part-time work, or community service. They finally have the time to cultivate new friendships, to travel, and to visit with family members. Many have learned the benefits of exercise and proper diet to help them stay healthy, and their personal horizons have expanded accordingly, particularly if they have sufficient financial resources to feel comfortable and secure about their later years.

But make no mistake about it: retirees will also tell you that they wish they had more discretionary income than they do. So, in pondering your own retirement situation, you should carefully consider whether your combined Social Security and pension benefits, plus any personal savings, will realistically meet your future retirement needs.

If after reviewing your retirement program you decide that you will likely need, say, an additional $10,000 in income each year to supplement your expected retirement benefits, you should consider carefully the following analysis. As shown in Figure 1–4, if you plan to spend the extra $10,000 each year over a 10-year period, you will need to augment your nest egg at retirement by more than $72,000, assuming a +8% annual after-tax return. If you will need the additional $10,000 each year for 20 years, you will have to begin your retirement with a supplemental nest egg of just over $106,000.

For a 45-year-old with 20 years until retirement, accumulating a $72,000 nest egg would require yearly investments of approximately $1,460, or $122 each month, assuming an annual return of +8%. Accumulating a $106,000 nest egg over 20 years under the same assumptions would require annual investments of approximately $2,145, or $179 each month.

These figures assume that you can defer taxes on your savings by investing through an employer pension plan or an individual retirement account. They also assume that you will fully exhaust your

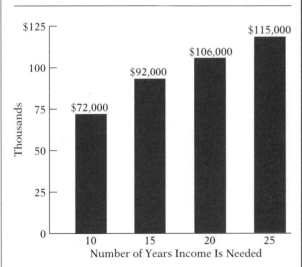

Figure 1–4
Savings Needed at Retirement to Provide $10,000 in Yearly Income

Note: Assumes a +8% return and an ending balance of zero.

savings throughout the duration of your retirement. If you will not be investing in a tax-deferred plan, or if you want to leave assets behind for your heirs, you will need to save even more money than is shown in the examples.

In the final analysis, concerns about Social Security, about the viability of traditional pension plans, and about inflation, longevity, and early retirement make planning for retirement a daunting endeavor. However, no amount of financial or retirement planning can proceed without first making the commitment *today* to put money aside for *tomorrow*. Individuals who have achieved financial security during retirement unanimously agree that small sacrifices during your working years will bear substantial rewards during your retirement years. To improve your prospects for a happy and financially secure retirement, you should begin by resolving to save more for your retirement—today!

A Model for Retirement Saving

W hether you are concerned about the future of the Social Security system, a change in your employer-provided retirement plan, or the impact of inflation during your retirement years, there are many compelling reasons to increase your personal retirement savings. But the fact is it takes discipline and motivation to sacrifice today and set aside money for tomorrow. This chapter outlines five strategies that should help you boost the effectiveness of your retirement saving plan and set your overall retirement program on the right course:

1. Adopt a steady savings plan.
2. Take advantage of compounding.
3. Diversify your retirement portfolio.
4. Take a long-term view.
5. Defer taxes whenever possible.

These strategies, of course, are merely a framework for you to follow as you begin saving for your retirement. You must provide the motivation and the discipline.

Adopt a Steady Savings Plan

To be certain of having sufficient assets during your retirement, you must be committed to maintaining a consistent savings program. There is simply no other option. To be sure, allocating a portion of each paycheck for retirement can be a challenge in today's uncertain economic times, but making precisely that commitment is essential to achieving your retirement goals. The excuse-proof method of gradually building your assets is to establish some form of monthly investment program.

Many companies offer employee savings plans that allow regular payroll deductions into a bank account or a mutual fund. If your employer does not offer direct payroll deductions, many mutual fund organizations will allow you to make direct payroll deposits into one of their fund offerings. Or you could arrange to

Learning to Save

A mericans currently save on average about 5% of their take-home pay. If you are in this group of "delinquent" savers, it may be because you have never formalized a game plan for saving.

have regular, automatic transfers made from your checking account to the fund company of your choice. In any event, the key is to eliminate the human element in making monthly deposits. Once the money makes its way into your checking account, you are liable to find some reason not to invest it.

As long as people have been saving for retirement, they have asked the question: How much should I save? Obviously, each individual's financial situation is unique; however, as a general rule most financial planners suggest putting aside at least 10% of your salary for retirement, more if you can afford it. (See Chapter 3 for more details.) The secret to a successful savings program is to change the way that you think about saving. The idea is to spend what you have left after saving, not save what you have left after spending. Here are some proven tactics that can help you start saving right away.

Pay Yourself First   Place retirement savings at the top of your list of monthly bills to be paid. There is nothing to be gained by waiting until the end of the month or the quarter before making your retirement contribution. But there is something to be lost—you might end up spending money that you otherwise would have saved.

Invest Automatically   Rather than writing a check each month, have your retirement contributions automatically deducted from your paycheck or from your checking account. The idea is that you can't spend what you don't have. You also eliminate the hassle of writing a check and then making the deposit, and you don't have to wait for the check to make its way through the mail before your investment begins earning money.

Split Your Next Raise   Make a deal with yourself to split your next pay increase. Keep part of the salary increase for yourself and earmark the remainder for your retirement savings. Say you receive a 6% raise; keep 3% for yourself and invest the other 3% for yourself as well—for your retirement, that is. You'll find that once you get past the first year, investing one-half of your raise gets easier each year thereafter.

Invest Any Bonuses or Tax Refunds   If you receive a bonus from your employer, invest it for your retirement. Since any tax refunds that you may receive are essentially "found money," use them to augment your retirement savings as well. As a compromise, split any bonuses or tax refunds between spending and saving, just as you would your raise in the previous example.

Take Advantage of Compounding

If you put off saving until later in life, time becomes your greatest enemy; if you begin saving early, time becomes your greatest ally. Year after year, any monies that you invest earn interest and dividends, and those earnings in turn generate additional earnings, and so on. This "magical" process is called compounding. The sooner you start saving for retirement, even if the amounts you set aside are modest, the greater the benefits you will receive from the power of compounding.

Suppose you need an additional $100,000 in retirement savings by age 65. As shown in Figure 2–1, if you wait until age 60 to start saving and earn a +8% annual return, you will need to save $1,352 per month to reach your goal. At the end of five years, you will have invested $81,000 of your own money, and you will have earned an additional $19,000. Conversely, if you start saving much earlier, say at age 35, you reap the benefits of compound earnings and need to save only $67 each month to reach your goal. At the end of 30 years, you will have invested a total of $24,000 of your own money, and earned an additional

Figure 2–1

Monthly Savings Needed to Accumulate $100,000 by Age 65

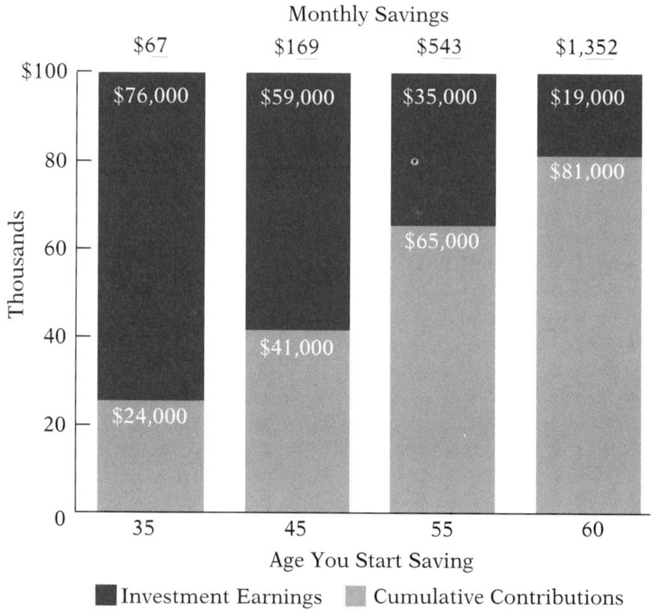

	Monthly Savings			
	$67	$169	$543	$1,352

Investment Earnings: $76,000 (age 35), $59,000 (age 45), $35,000 (age 55), $19,000 (age 60)

Cumulative Contributions: $24,000 (age 35), $41,000 (age 45), $65,000 (age 55), $81,000 (age 60)

Age You Start Saving: 35, 45, 55, 60

■ Investment Earnings ■ Cumulative Contributions

Note: Assumes a +8% average annual return.

$76,000. The difference in payments out of your pocket is a remarkable $57,000. It is not hard to see which scenario would be easier on your budget. By starting your investment program earlier, more of your retirement savings comes from compound returns and less from your personal savings.

If you start saving early you also will be less likely to feel "squeezed" as your retirement nears (at the same time that chil-

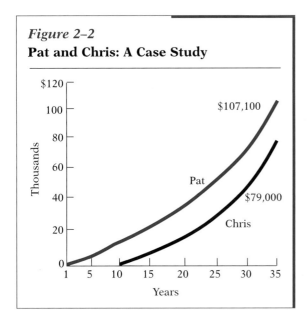

Figure 2–2
Pat and Chris: A Case Study

dren may be entering college). In fact, you may even be able to take it easy. Consider the example of Pat and Chris, each of whom is the same age and worked for the same employer over a 35-year period. Pat signed up for the company savings plan at age 30, invested $1,000 each year for 10 years earning an +8% annual return, and then stopped making contributions. Chris, on the other hand, waited until age 40 to begin saving for retirement, but then started contributing $1,000 each year for 25 years and earned the same +8% annual return. Which of the two would you guess has the most money now that they are ready to retire at age 65?

At first blush, there would seem to be no doubt that Chris must surely have the greater retirement assets. After all, Chris contributed $25,000 to the company savings plan over a period of 25 years, while Pat set aside only $10,000 over 10 years. But Pat's contributions were made earlier in the period, and they had a much longer time period in which to grow. As shown in Figure 2–2, at the end of the 35-year period the power of compounding transformed Pat's $10,000 in contributions into a total balance of $107,100. Chris's savings grew considerably as well, but with less time for compounding to work its magic, Chris's $25,000 in total contributions reached only $79,000.

The message is simple: The sooner you start saving, the easier it will be for you to reach your retirement goals. So get started on your savings program today, and take full advantage of the power of compounding.

Diversify Your Retirement Portfolio

Once you have committed yourself to a retirement savings program, the next step is to decide where to invest your contributions. It is difficult to encapsulate all of the issues involved in establishing a long-term investment program, but one principle stands clear: diversification. "Don't put all your eggs in one basket" is not merely a cliché; it is a serious observation about how your retirement savings should be allocated.

The first tenet of diversification is to eliminate what is called "specific security risk" by purchasing a broad array of investments rather than a limited selection of individual securities. A sensible retirement program should not be based on a single "hot stock" that promises double-digit returns. Indeed, buying one or two individual securities is probably closer to gambling than investing. If you have substantial savings, you might be able to compose a sufficiently diversified portfolio of individual securities on your own. But academic studies have shown that even holding 10 or 15 stocks in a portfolio may still provide a woefully inadequate level of diversification. For most investors, pooling their monies with other investors through mutual funds is probably the most sensible option.

The second tenet of diversification is to allocate your retirement assets among different types of securities. The three primary financial asset classes that should be included in most retirement portfolios are:

- Short-term reserves.
- Longer-term bonds.
- Common stocks.

Each asset class offers a unique combination of risk and return. And, since the risks of one asset class may complement the risks of another, it may be possible—by utilizing all three asset classes in your retirement portfolio—to achieve higher investment earnings while reducing your overall portfolio volatility.

Most first-time investors emphasize shorter-term investments, such as money market funds and bank certificates of deposit, that offer stable investment values plus current levels of income. Bank deposits, of course, are guaranteed up to $100,000 by an agency of the federal government; money market funds are not. You may also wish to include in this category short-term bond funds, which entail a slightly higher level of volatility risk but offer yields that typically have been one to one-and-one-half percentage points above those of money market funds. If you are saving through an employer-sponsored retirement plan, investment contracts offered by insurance companies also fall within this investment category.

In thinking about short-term reserves as an investment option, keep in mind that these securities are not risk free. Interest rates can vary precipitately—up or down—and the stability of your income payments is therefore always at risk. For instance, money market funds yielded close to 8% at the end of 1990, but by the end of 1993 yields had declined to about 3%. One final risk for holders of short-term reserves is inflation, which, over the long term, has consumed virtually all of the investment return earned by this asset class.

In the pursuit of higher investment returns, investors often look to longer-term bonds and bond funds, which historically have provided higher yields than short-term instruments. While the risk to your income stream is much lower in bonds than in short-term reserves (since your income is locked in for a longer period), your volatility risk in bonds is much higher. Bond prices fluctuate inversely with changes in interest rates (a phenomenon described as "interest rate risk"), and declining bond values may not always be offset by the accompanying higher yields. Inflation is also a risk for bondholders as well and historically has eroded a significant portion of the investment return from bonds.

Common stocks exhibit risk and reward characteristics that are quite distinct from those of short-term reserves and longer-term bonds. Stocks offer the potential for capital growth through rising stock market prices, and they often pay an income dividend as well. Over the long term, stocks have provided the highest returns of the three primary asset classes and have therefore been the best hedge against inflation. Yet the volatility risk of stocks, especially in the short term, can scare away many investors. While returns on stocks going back to 1926 (the modern history of the stock market) have averaged +10.2% annually, this period includes many years in which stocks incurred double-digit losses. Investing in the stock market, then, requires a long-term investment horizon and the fortitude to stay the course.

Surprisingly, the danger for most individuals is not that they will invest too aggressively for their retirement, but too conservatively. One study by the Wyatt Co., an employee benefits consulting firm, found that the cautious investment approach typically adhered to by employees in company-sponsored savings plans caused their portfolios to earn annual returns that were 1 to 3 percentage points less than those of the average professionally managed pension fund. Although this conservatism may be warranted for some investors, in many instances it reflects a fundamental lack of understanding about the relationship between investment risk and investment return.

In any event, by diversifying among all three of these asset classes, you can enjoy the benefits that each type of security

Figure 2–3
Investment Returns: 1926–1994

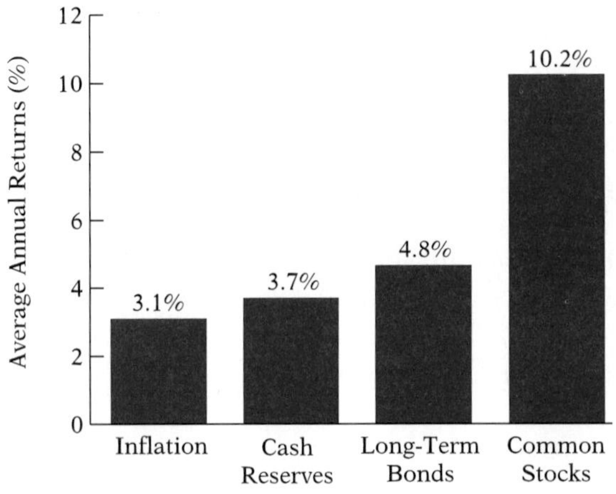

Source: © *Stocks, Bonds, Bills, and Inflation, 1995 Yearbook*™, Ibbotson Associates, Chicago. (Annually updates work by Roger G. Ibbotson and Rex A. Sinquefield.) Used with permission. All rights reserved.

Table 2–1
Risks and Rewards of Financial Assets

Investment	Potential Rewards	Primary Risks
Short-term reserves	Stable value and current income earnings	Inflation and income volatility
Longer-term bonds	Higher yields and stable income	Inflation and interest rate risk
Common stocks	Dividends and capital growth	Price volatility

offers, while mitigating some of their inherent risks. Table 2–1 provides an overview of the risks and rewards of each asset class. In seeking to strike a balance between maximizing your return while minimizing your investment risk, you should hold all three investment classes in your retirement portfolio. Over time, as your investment horizon and your financial circumstances change, your asset allocation—that is, your percentage invested in each asset class—will vary. Chapter 6 presents guidelines on how to arrive at an asset allocation that is suitable to your own financial situation.

Take a Long-Term View

The conservatism of employee retirement accounts relative to professionally managed accounts has to do with investors' tendency to place too much emphasis on short-term performance fluctuations. In assessing risk, even experienced investors may focus on short-term fluctuations in their investments and make hasty decisions that they soon regret.

The fact is most investors commit far too little of their savings to common stocks. And it is easy to understand why: the stock market can be extremely volatile, especially over shorter time periods. While it may take one year to earn a modest return of, say, +4% on a bank CD or a money market fund, it is not uncommon to gain or lose that much in one week—or even one day—in the stock market. The memory of October 19, 1987, when the stock market fell by more than −20% in a single day, still haunts many investors.

Common stocks, then, should be considered long-term investments, and their risks and rewards should be evaluated over a period of years, not days. Although common stocks can be quite volatile in the short run, the passage of time tends to smooth out the vagaries of stock market prices. What is more, seemingly lower-risk investments such as money market funds, bank certificates of deposit, or even long-term bonds may actually entail more risk to your retirement security than stocks. The reason is that, over time, the returns on bonds and short-term reserves have barely kept pace with inflation, giving investors no "real" growth in their assets. So, for investors who have the luxury of investing over an extended period, common stocks should comprise a significant portion of their portfolios.

Defer Taxes Whenever Possible

If time is your greatest ally where retirement investing is concerned, taxes are your greatest enemy. The longer you can shelter your assets from taxation and keep your investment earnings compounding on a tax-free basis, the sooner you will meet your retirement investing goals. How severe a bite do taxes take out of your investment return? Probably more than you would expect.

Assume that you are taxed at a marginal rate of 31%, and you earn an +8% annual return over 10 years on an initial investment of $10,000. At the end of 10 years, your initial investment will have grown to $17,114, after taking into account taxes on your earnings. Now consider the same set of circumstances, except this time assume that your initial investment is placed in an individual retirement account (IRA). Since taxes on an IRA are deferred until you begin to withdraw money during your retirement, your earnings compound at a higher effective rate. At the end of the 10-year period, your final account value in the IRA would be $21,589, more than 25% higher than for the taxable account. (With the passage of the latest tax package, the wealthiest individuals now pay a marginal tax rate of up to 39.6%, which further strengthens the case for tax-deferred investing.)

Of course, money that is growing on a tax-deferred basis in an IRA or other qualified retirement plan will eventually be taxed upon withdrawal. But even during your retirement you can make periodic withdrawals and continue to benefit from the tax deferral on your remaining balance. You should also know that all withdrawals from a qualified retirement plan are taxed as ordinary income, regardless of whether the gains in the account accumulated from income or from capital appreciation. What this means is that earnings that may have been taxed at the *capital gains* rate (28% in 1994) will instead be taxed at the *income* rate prevailing at the time the assets are withdrawn.

In addition to their tax-deferral features, many qualified retirement plans provide tax deductions on contributions by taxpayers in certain income brackets, or up to certain yearly limits.

These types of accounts include IRAs, 401(k) corporate savings plans, 403(b) savings plans for employees of public and nonprofit organizations, and Keogh and Simplified Employee Pension plans used by self-employed individuals and small businesses. (See Chapter 8 for more details on these plans.) The arithmetic of this feature is fairly straightforward. Assume that you are taxed at the 31% marginal rate, and you are eligible to make fully deductible contributions to an IRA. If you contribute $2,000 (the maximum allowable limit in any one year) to your IRA, the value of the tax deduction means that you effectively contribute only $1,380 (69% of $2,000), even though your IRA receives the full $2,000. Figure 2–4 illustrates how compelling this advantage becomes over time. The investor in the tax-deferred account contributes $1,380 (adjusted for a tax refund), but her account accumulates the full $2,000. The investor in the taxable account, on the other hand, accumulates only the $1,380 actually invested, since the contributions come from after tax dollars. At the end of 35 years, the difference in accumulated savings is a staggering $225,000 ($372,000 versus $147,000).

Once your assets are sheltered from taxes in a tax-deferred account, keep them sheltered as long as possible. As soon as you make a withdrawal, you immediately give up a portion of the proceeds to taxes and lose the advantage of further tax-deferred compounding as well. If you change jobs, for example, you might receive a lump-sum distribution from a company retirement plan. Unless the distribution is rolled over within 60 days into another employer-sponsored plan or an individual retirement account, you will owe taxes on the full amount of the distribution, plus a 10% penalty if you are under age $59\frac{1}{2}$. (For more information on withdrawal rules, see Chapter 10.)

The cost of taking money prematurely from a tax-advantaged plan is substantial. Nonetheless, many employees still do not take advantage of the rollover option.

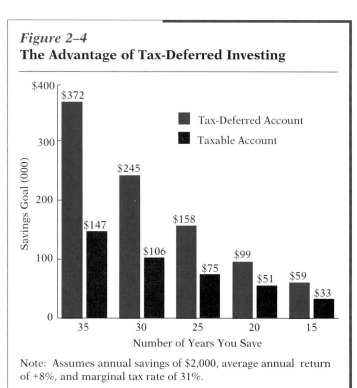

Figure 2–4
The Advantage of Tax-Deferred Investing

Savings Goal (000) / Number of Years You Save

Note: Assumes annual savings of $2,000, average annual return of +8%, and marginal tax rate of 31%.

A 1992 survey conducted by the Gallup Organization for the Employee Benefit Research Institute asked Americans what they would do if they left their jobs and received a cash distribution from a retirement plan. Sixty-one percent said they would continue to save the money for retirement in an IRA. The remaining 39% said they would give up their tax deferral, pay taxes on the money, and then use the proceeds to meet current spending needs (12%), pay off credit card or other debt (12%), or bolster their regular savings (13%). Spending retirement money to meet nonretirement financial needs may appear to make sense at the time, especially when you are young and retirement is decades away. But in the long run doing so will make it harder to achieve your retirement goals, especially with the extra burden of taxes and penalties that is incurred when you spend a retirement plan distribution.

Recognizing the importance of retirement savings, Congress has authorized generous tax breaks for tax-deferred retirement plans. To gain the maximum benefit from these tax breaks, participate whenever possible in tax-deferred programs, and insulate your savings from taxes and your own impulse to spend during your working years.

Final Thoughts

As you build your retirement nest egg, think about how much adhering to a disciplined savings program now will benefit you in your golden years. The reward of a well-planned retirement is financial independence. That means having the opportunity to enjoy your retirement to the fullest, including travel, community service, time with friends and relatives, recreational activities, and so on. If you follow the five strategies outlined in this chapter—adopt a savings plan, begin saving early, diversify your assets, invest for the long term, and defer taxes—you will be taking critical steps toward becoming an investor who will enjoy a more comfortable retirement.

Establishing a Retirement Savings Goal

Thus far, you have learned about the first two steps toward ensuring a successful retirement savings program. First, you must cultivate the discipline and the motivation to save. The uncertain future of both the Social Security system and the traditional pension plan should provide more than enough motivation; you must provide the discipline. Second, you must commit to a *long-term* savings plan, taking full advantage of compounding, diversification, and tax deferral. The third step in establishing a successful retirement savings program is to determine what your savings goal should be.

In Chapter 1, it was noted that most investors probably need to save at least 10% of their current gross salary to maintain their present standard of living. But individuals have different plans as to how they intend to spend their retirement, and a savings rate that is more than adequate for one person may fall woefully short of the retirement needs of another. In other words, before you can determine how much you should be *saving* each month for retirement, you first have to determine how much you are likely to *need* each month during your retirement. This chapter presents a worksheet that will help you to match your retirement demands of tomorrow with your retirement savings of today.

If you have purchased this guide along with the Vanguard Retirement Planner, you will probably notice some differences between the worksheet that appears in the guide and the worksheet that appears in the software. These differences arise because some of the calculating features of the software simply cannot be translated onto paper. As a result, if you are using the software you should ignore the worksheet instructions in the guide and instead follow the instructions in the Vanguard Retirement Planner user's guide.

Matching Retirement Needs and Savings

Whatever your approach to establishing a retirement savings goal, keep in mind that the validity of your retirement projection is only as good as the assumptions on which it is based, particularly the assumed investment return.

The worksheet in this chapter is divided into seven parts, designed to take you all the way from calculating your retirement income goal to determining the annual savings you should be accumulating to achieve that goal. You will need to provide some basic data, and you will also need to make several assumptions about future investment returns, your expected retirement age, and the expected length of your retirement. When you finish all seven steps of the worksheet, you will have determined the *percentage* of your annual income you should be saving each year for your retirement.

Once you have gathered all of the necessary data—and located a calculator—it should take you no more than 30 minutes to complete the entire worksheet. To keep the calculations as simple as possible, the worksheet has some general assumptions built in that may not precisely match your personal circumstances. This does not mean that the results of the worksheet are not useful. But you should be aware that your final savings goal will have to be adjusted up or down to reflect any discrepancies. In any event, here are the four broad assumptions in the worksheet:

1. You will retire at age 62 or older.
2. If you are married and both you and your spouse work, then you will retire at approximately the same time (within two to three years of each other).
3. Most of your retirement savings will be held in tax-deferred retirement plans, such as IRAs or company-sponsored 401(k) plans.
4. Your tax bracket during your retirement years will be about the same as that during your working years.

If you want to fine-tune your projections to adjust for these worksheet assumptions, you might consider retaining the services of a financial adviser. (Chapter 7 provides guidelines on how to obtain professional financial assistance.) If you have access to a personal computer, "The Vanguard Retirement Planner," Vanguard's proprietary retirement planning software program is also a useful tool to assist with fine-tuning your projections. If you did not purchase the software with this book you may call 1-800-876-1840 for more information about the program and how to obtain a copy.

Keep in mind as you prepare the worksheet that it is simply not possible to accurately forecast investment returns over extended periods or, for that matter, over shorter periods. Nonetheless, if your retirement is just a few years away, your final worksheet results should give you a reasonably accurate idea of your retirement needs. On the other hand, if you are in your 30s or 40s, your worksheet results will naturally be less reliable. The best way to plan for your retirement is to complete the worksheet several times assuming different investment returns, retirement ages, and so on. This method will give you at least some indication as to how sensitive your projections are to changes in your assumptions. You should also revisit your financial situation at least once a year, perhaps around tax preparation time.

Information You Will Need

Before starting the retirement worksheet, it will be helpful if you gather the necessary information in advance. If you are married, you will need this information for both you and your spouse. Married couples may prepare a combined worksheet if both spouses expect to retire within a few years of one another; otherwise, it is probably better to prepare separate worksheets. Here is the information you will need.

Current Income The first line of the worksheet requires your current salary on a gross (before-tax) basis. The worksheet uses your current income as a baseline for determining your income goal for retirement.

Social Security Benefits You will need to contact your local Social Security office to obtain an estimate of your Social Security benefits at retirement. Alternatively, you may call 1-800-772-1213 and ask for Form SSA 7004. Also, your employer may provide an estimate of your Social Security benefits on your annual benefits statements. When you ask for an estimate of your Social Security benefits, be sure to use the age at which you plan to retire (i.e., if you plan to retire at age 62, use estimated benefits for age 62, not 65).

Figure 3–1 gives a rough approximation of 1995 monthly Social Security benefits for a 65-year-old retiree. The estimates assume continuous employment during a working career and annual pay raises equal to the US average. (Chapter 9 provides additional information on Social Security benefits.)

Employer Pension Benefits If you are covered by a defined benefit pension plan—which pays a monthly income benefit at retirement and is typically based on years of service and your final average salary—ask for a "current dollars" estimate of your pension benefits at retirement. Your employer's estimate of your

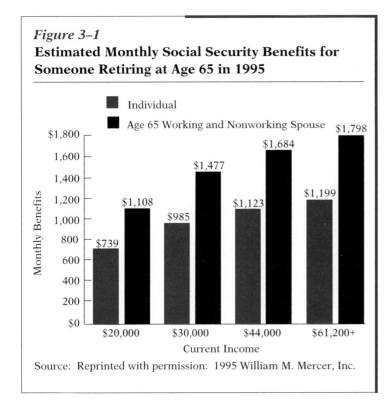

Figure 3–1
Estimated Monthly Social Security Benefits for Someone Retiring at Age 65 in 1995

Source: Reprinted with permission: 1995 William M. Mercer, Inc.

pension benefit will assume that you earn your current salary (with no cost-of-living adjustments) between now and retirement. Again, be sure that your pension estimate is for your expected retirement age.

Retirement Savings   You also will need a total of all your current savings earmarked for retirement. To determine this figure, start with your personal retirement savings, including any bank, mutual fund, or brokerage accounts. Add any assets in tax-deferred retirement savings programs, including individual retirement accounts, company 401(k) plans, or nonprofit 403(b) plans. Don't forget to count monies held in other employer-sponsored retirement plans, such as profit-sharing and other defined contribution plans. For more information on employer-sponsored retirement plans, see Chapter 8.

When you have calculated your total retirement savings, check to see that you have not double-counted any benefits in your employer-related retirement plans. For example, your employer plan may allow you to convert your savings into a fixed pension at retirement. In this case, to avoid overstating your retirement benefits, use either your current plan balance or the pension benefits estimate, but not both.

A Case Study

The best way to illustrate how the worksheet operates is to provide a real-life example of a couple planning for retirement.

Laura and David, a married couple in their 40s, have decided to start planning seriously for retirement. Laura, age 45, works at a local hospital and earns $30,000 per year. David, age 45, is an office manager earning $50,000 a year. Laura's employer provides a defined benefit pension plan. Assuming that Laura works until age 65, the hospital's plan will pay her an annual pension of $10,000, based on her current salary of $30,000. The hospital also offers a supplementary 403(b) savings program, to which Laura

Table 3–1
Profile: Laura and David Brown

Ages and Income		Current Benefits/Savings	
Laura's current age	45	Social Security	$24,000 per year
David's current age	45	Laura's pension	$10,000 per year
Annual joint income	$80,000	Total savings	$34,000
Expected retirement age	65	Current savings	$ 7,200 per year

contributes 4% of her salary ($1,200 in the current year). David's employer offers a defined contribution retirement plan, to which David and his employer will contribute $6,000 in the current year.

In aggregate, Laura and David currently are saving $7,200 per year for retirement—equivalent to 9% of their $80,000 joint income. Since they only recently began to save at this level, their current retirement nest egg amounts to just $34,000. Laura and David contacted the Social Security Administration and requested an estimate of their benefits based on David's likely retirement age of 65. Their combined annual Social Security benefits will total about $24,000 per year. Table 3–1 illustrates Laura's and David's current retirement savings profile.

As noted earlier, most financial planners estimate that you will need 70% to 80% of your preretirement income to maintain your present standard of living during retirement. At 70% of their current income, Laura and David would have a retirement goal of $56,000 a year (before taxes). But, as shown in Figure 3–2, they must adjust this estimate for the probable impact of inflation over the next 20-some years. Assuming a 4% inflation rate (the rate used in the worksheet), their yearly income goal would equate to $123,000 by the time they reach retirement. However, since inflation will likely continue throughout their retirement, by age 80 they could need yearly income of as much as $221,000 to maintain the same standard of living as they enjoyed in their first year of retirement.

Where will all of this income come from? During the first few years of retirement, Social Security and pension benefits will

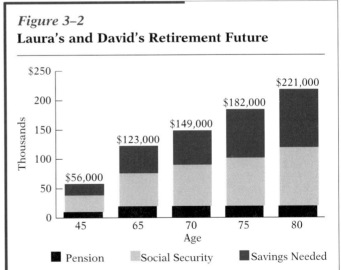

Figure 3–2
Laura's and David's Retirement Future

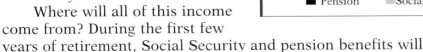

account for most of Laura's and David's retirement income. But while Social Security benefits will keep pace with the cost of living, Laura's fixed pension will not. So, as they move further into retirement, Laura and David will find themselves increasingly dependent on their personal savings to meet their income needs.

The Retirement Worksheet

Once you have determined your retirement goal, how much should you be saving today to meet this goal 20 or 30 years down the road? This worksheet is designed to help you answer exactly that question.

Part 1: Your Goals and Benefits

In the first part of the worksheet, you establish an income goal for retirement, summarize your current retirement benefits, and then calculate any shortfall that exists between your retirement goal and your prospective retirement benefits.

Line 1   Enter your current gross income.

Line 2   Enter your retirement goal. An appropriate goal for Line 2 is 70% to 80% of your current gross income. If you would like a higher standard of living during retirement than during your working years—say, to travel extensively—you should raise your goal to reflect your anticipated needs. Laura and David have a combined current gross income of $80,000, and they have set their goal at $56,000 (in *today's* dollars) in annual income, or 70% of their present gross income.

Line 3   Enter your estimated annual—not monthly—Social Security benefits based on today's income. For Laura and David, the figure is $24,000.

Line 4   Enter your current estimated annual benefits from defined benefit pension plans. For Laura and David, the figure is $10,000.

Line 5   Calculate any annual income shortfall (the amount of your retirement income that will have to come from personal savings) by subtracting the total of Lines 3 and 4 from Line 2. Laura and David subtract Social Security benefits of $24,000 and pension benefits of $10,000 from their goal of $56,000; the preliminary result is an annual income shortfall of $22,000, which must come from personal savings.

Line 6   Enter your current retirement savings from all sources. Laura and David have saved a total of $34,000 to date.

Table 3–2
Part 1: Your Retirement Income Goal and Benefits

	David and Laura	Your Own Situation
1. Your current income	$80,000	_____
2. Your retirement income goal (at least 70%–80% of Line 1)	$56,000	_____
3. Social Security benefits	$24,000	_____
4. Pension	$10,000	_____
5. Annual shortfall (Line 2 − Line 3 − Line 4)	$22,000	_____
6. Current retirement savings	$34,000	_____
7. Current annual savings	$7,200	_____

Line 7   Enter your current level of annual retirement savings. Laura and David are saving at the rate of $7,200 per year.

Part 2: Your Assumptions

Planning for the future requires that you make certain assumptions. In this part of the worksheet, you must estimate a future investment return for your retirement savings, along with the number of years that you expect these savings to last.

Line 8   Enter an assumed investment return. Your assumed return should be a whole number between 5% and 12%, and should be a *gross* (before-tax) return. To the best of your ability, you should select an investment return that reflects the proportion of your savings invested, or expected to be invested, in each asset class. When in doubt, be conservative in your estimate since picking too high a return will understate the amount of money that you need to save each year.

Because the worksheet assumes an inflation rate of 4% in its calculations, you should consider that fact as you determine your expected investment return. For example, short-term reserves and long-term bonds have historically provided returns barely above the inflation rate, while stocks have provided somewhat higher returns. (A reasonable range of investment returns for each asset class is shown in Table 3–3.) Laura and David choose an +8% annual return because the majority of their savings is invested in common stock mutual funds, with the balance in bond and money market funds.

Table 3–3
Making Your Assumptions

| | Investment Returns | Life Expectancy | | |
| | | Planned | | Couple |
Type of Investment	Reasonable Assumption for Worksheet	Retirement Age	Individual	of Same Age
Short-term reserves	4%– 5%	55	29	34
Long-term bonds	5%– 7%	60	24	30
Common stocks	7%–10%	65	20	25
		70	16	21

Line 9   Enter the number of years until your retirement. The earliest retirement age you can use with this worksheet is 62. The reason is that the worksheet assumes you begin receiving Social Security and pension benefits immediately upon retiring, and 62 is the earliest age at which Social Security benefits can begin. Laura and David plan to retire in 20 years when they reach age 65.

Line 10   Enter the number of years you expect your retirement savings to last. In essence, this figure is an estimate of how long you (and your spouse if you are married) will live. The worksheet accepts retirement periods of 15, 20, 25, 30, 35, or 40 years. While you obviously cannot predict how long you will live, it is possible to make reasonable assumptions based on life expectancy figures. For example, if you retire at age 65 and are single, you can expect on average to live an additional 20 years, until age 85. If you are married, either you or your spouse is likely to live an additional 25 years, until age 90. Table 3–3 illustrates some life expectancy estimates.

Keep in mind that life expectancy figures are averages and that you may live much longer or shorter than the averages suggest. For a more conservative approach, add five or more years to your stated life expectancy to determine your retirement period.

Table 3–4
Part 2: Your Assumptions

	David and Laura	Your Own Situation
8. Investment return	8%	
9. Years until retirement	20	
10. Retirement period (in years)	25	

For most individuals retiring in their early- to mid-60s, a retirement period of 25 to 30 years should be the norm. Laura and David plan to retire at age 65, and so choose 25 years.

Part 3: Retirement Factors

Based on the assumptions you made in Part 2 of the worksheet, you must now select several factors, or multipliers, that will be used to calculate your future retirement needs. These factors take into account your assumed investment return, the number of years you have until retirement, and the length of your retirement period. They also reflect a 4% inflation rate, which underlies all of the worksheet calculations.

Lines 11–15 Using your assumptions from Part 2 of the worksheet, select from Tables A through E in the Appendix the appropriate factors for each line. For example, because Laura and David have 20 years until retirement, they choose an inflation factor of 2.19 from Table A.

Table 3–5
Part 3: Retirement Factors

	David and Laura	Your Own Situation
11. Inflation factor (Table A)	2.19	
12. Savings needed for retirement (Table B)	16.49	
13. Inflation adjustment for pension (Table C)	4.96	
14. Investment growth (Table D)	4.66	
15. Current retirement savings factor (Table E)	.0150	

Note: See Appendix for Tables A through E.

Part 4: Your Retirement Income Needs

At this point, the worksheet turns from summarizing your goals and assumptions to calculating your retirement income needs.

Line 16 Multiply the figure you entered on Line 2 by the inflation factor you entered on Line 11, and enter the result. This calculation adjusts your retirement income goal (Line 2) for the impact of inflation up until your retirement. For example, Laura and David have a current retirement income goal of $56,000 a year, but, based on their inflation factor of 2.19 (which is derived from an annual inflation rate of 4%), by age 65 they will need about $123,000 each year to maintain the same standard of living. (All of the figures in the worksheet are rounded not only to keep the arithmetic simple, but also to emphasize the uncertainty underlying any projection of this sort.)

Line 17   Multiply the figure you entered on Line 5 by the inflation factor you entered on Line 11, and enter the result. This calculation adjusts your retirement income shortfall (Line 5) for the impact of inflation up until your retirement. Laura and David show a $22,000 shortfall today, but by retirement the shortfall will have grown to $48,000 due to inflation.

Line 18   Multiply the shortfall on Line 17 by the "savings needed for retirement" factor on Line 12, and enter the result. This figure indicates the level of savings that will be needed to make up the annual shortfall during retirement. For Laura and David, cumulative savings of $792,000 are needed to meet their projected annual shortfall during retirement. This sum may seem extraordinarily large, but keep in mind that it represents the savings they will need 20 years hence. A more realistic measure comes at the end of the worksheet when you calculate how much you need to save annually to reach that future dollar amount.

Table 3–6
Part 4: Your Retirement Income Needs

	David and Laura	Your Own Situation
16. Annual income goal at retirement (Line 2 × Line 11)	$123,000	_____
17. Annual income shortfall at retirement (Line 5 × Line 11)	$ 48,000	_____
18. Savings needed for retirement (Line 17 × Line 12)	$792,000	_____

Note: Figures in example are rounded.

Part 5: Inflation Adjustment

If you have an employer-sponsored fixed pension (Line 4), it will lose purchasing power throughout your retirement because of inflation. In this part of the worksheet, you calculate the additional savings needed to offset this inflationary loss. If you do not have an employer pension plan, you may skip to Part 6.

Line 19   Multiply the pension amount on Line 4 by the inflation factor on Line 11 and enter the result. This calculation translates the value of your pension today into its value at retirement (based on a 4% inflation rate). In the worksheet example, Laura's pension of $10,000 reaches $22,000 by the time she retires because of cost-of-living (inflation) adjustments.

Line 20   Multiply the figure entered on Line 19 by the "inflation adjustment for pension" factor on Line 13, and enter the result. This calculation indicates the additional savings you will need to offset the impact of inflation on your pension during retirement. In the worksheet example, Laura and David will need an additional $109,000 in personal savings to compensate for the fact that Laura's pension will not keep pace with inflation during their retirement years.

Table 3–7
Part 5: Inflation Adjustment

	David and Laura	Your Own Situation
19. Value of pension at retirement (Line 4 × Line 11)	$ 22,000	_____
20. Inflation adjustment for pension (Line 19 × Line 13)	$109,000	_____

Note: Figures in example are rounded.

Part 6: Value of Current Savings at Retirement

The final step in establishing your retirement savings plan is to estimate the growth in your current savings between now and your retirement.

Line 21   Multiply your current savings on Line 6 by the "investment growth" factor on Line 14, and enter the result. For Laura and David, based on an assumed annual investment return of 8%, their current savings of $34,000 will more than quadruple over the next 20 years, to $158,000.

Table 3–8
Part 6: Value of Current Savings at Retirement

	David and Laura	Your Own Situation
21. Current savings at retirement (Line 6 × Line 14)	$158,000	_____

Note: Figures in example are rounded.

Part 7: *Your Retirement Savings Goal*

With all of the prior steps of the worksheet completed, you are now ready to calculate a savings goal for retirement.

Line 22   Add your savings needed for retirement (Line 18) plus the additional money you need to offset the impact of inflation on a fixed pension (Line 20), and then subtract the value of your current savings at retirement (Line 21). Enter the net result. Laura and David need $792,000 to meet their annual income shortfall, plus $109,000 to make up for the impact of inflation on Laura's pension. Meanwhile, their current savings will grow to $158,000. Their net savings requirement at retirement is therefore $743,000.

Line 23   Multiply the net savings needed for retirement on Line 22 by the "savings" factor on Line 15, and divide the result by the current gross income figure on Line 1. This figure translates your *cumulative* savings needed at retirement into a percentage of your annual salary.

Line 24   Divide Line 7 by Line 1, and enter the result. This figure indicates the percentage of current income that Laura and David are saving in the current year.

Line 25   Subtract Line 24 from Line 23, and enter the result. This figure represents the annual increase in savings rate that Laura and David will require to meet their retirement savings goal.

Table 3–9
Part 7: Your Retirement Savings Goal

	David and Laura	Your Own Situation
22. Net savings needed for retirement (Line 18 + Line 20 − Line 21)	$743,000	_____
23. Percentage of annual income needed to meet retirement goal (Line 22 × Line 15 ÷ Line 1)	14%	_____
24. Current annual savings rate (Line 7 ÷ Line 5 ÷ Line 1)	9%	_____
25. Required increase in annual savings rate (Line 23 − Line 24)	5%	_____

Note: Figures in example are rounded.

The savings goal specified in the worksheet (Line 23) represents the annual percentage of income you must put aside for retirement from all sources. These sources include:

1. Your contributions to all employer-sponsored retirement programs.
2. Any employer contributions to such programs on your behalf.
3. Your personal retirement savings.

Remember that you should *not* include your employer's contribution to a defined benefit pension plan since these pension benefits are accounted for separately on Line 4.

As noted in the worksheet, Laura and David and their respective employers are already contributing $7,200 annually to retirement savings programs—equivalent to 9% of their current gross income. Thus, to meet their $11,200 (80,000 × 14%) goal in the current year, Laura and David need to boost their savings by roughly $4,000, or an additional 5% of their current gross income. As their salaries increase with the rate of inflation, the

Interpreting the Results

If you (and your employer on your behalf) are already saving the annual amount specified on Line 23 of the worksheet, then your retirement plan is on course.

amount that they put aside each year will also increase, even as the percentage of income (14%) remains the same. Of course, you may discover that you are currently saving more than the worksheet suggests. In that case, you may be able to retire with a higher standard of living. If you determine that you are saving too little, as did Laura and David, use the strategies outlined in the first two chapters to boost your savings to the requisite level.

When all is said and done, you may find that you simply do not have available monies to meet your annual savings shortfall. In this case, go back over the worksheet and review some of your assumptions. Perhaps your retirement goal entered on Line 2 is unrealistic given your present financial demands. Maybe the retirement age that you entered on Line 9 is unrealistic. Or perhaps you will need to invest your savings more aggressively in the hope of achieving a higher investment return (Line 8). Small changes to any one (or all) of these assumptions can have surprisingly dramatic results, especially if you are many years from retirement. For example, if Laura and David reduce their retirement goal to 65% of current salary instead of 70%, their required savings would drop from 14% of their salary to 11.4%. This adjustment would lower their personal savings shortfall from $4,000 in the current year to less than $2,000. Whatever you do, be especially cautious not to select an unrealistic investment return or retirement period.

Final Thoughts

If all of your worksheet assumptions seem reasonable and you are still showing an income shortfall, you should definitely consider increasing your retirement savings. Start with additional contributions to tax-deferred programs, such as an IRA or employer-sponsored savings plan. If your annual shortfall seems overwhelming, start small. Begin by saving an additional 2% of your current salary, and then increase that amount by another 1% or 2% each year until you reach your target. Before you know it, you'll be saving a significant portion of your current income and will be on your way to a comfortable retirement.

Whatever the savings goal recommended by the worksheet, you should recalculate the results several times using different assumptions. Over the years, continue to update your worksheet periodically as your personal circumstances change. Each time you complete the worksheet, scrutinize your assumptions carefully, and calculate the results under several scenarios to get an idea of the range of potential outcomes for your retirement future.

MAKE YOUR RETIRE-
MENT INVESTMENTS
WORK FOR YOU

Understanding the Basics of Investing

You now know that there are three critical variables that will determine the ultimate size of your retirement nest egg: (1) how soon you begin to save, (2) how much you save, and (3) how well your investments perform. The first two variables are controllable; after all, it is up to you when to start saving for retirement and how much money to put aside each year. The third variable—the rate of return on your investments—will be influenced by your investment selections, but it cannot be controlled. Returns in the financial markets are capricious and will vary widely and randomly from day to day, month to month, and year to year.

The unpredictability of market returns should not deter you from giving thoughtful consideration to the investments that you select for your retirement portfolio. The reason is that even small differences in investment return, when compounded over time, can have a tremendous effect on the amount of capital you accumulate for your retirement. So it is essential that you plan your investment portfolio carefully, taking into account the risk and reward characteristics of the various financial asset classes. For novice investors, this task may seem particularly daunting, but you will be well rewarded for your efforts. For experienced investors, familiar with the risk/return relationship, the temptation of high potential returns may lead to overly aggressive investment decisions, and saving for retirement becomes a perilous game of speculation.

This chapter attempts to eliminate some of the enigma of investing, to show that even novice investors can quickly master the basics and begin to develop a diversified portfolio that makes sense for them. The chapter begins with a discussion of the three primary types of financial assets—short-term reserves, bonds, and stocks—and then provides an overview of the fundamental relationship between risk and return, especially as it applies to each asset class. Finally, the chapter discusses some financial investment options that may not be well known to many investors, but nonetheless may add value to a diversified investment portfolio.

The Three Primary Financial Asset Classes

Numerous studies have shown that, over the long term, how you allocate your portfolio among the three primary financial asset classes will determine virtually all of your total return. The particular securities that you select within each asset class are largely insignificant.

Short-Term Reserves

Of the three primary asset classes, you are probably most familiar with short-term reserves. Whether in the form of bank money market deposit accounts, certificates of deposit (CDs), US Treasury bills (guaranteed by the US government), or commercial paper (issued by corporations), these instruments represent short-term IOUs of high-quality borrowers. (Money market mutual funds may hold any one or all of these securities.)

In exchange for the privilege of borrowing your money, the borrower agrees to pay you a stated interest rate over a predetermined time period. The lending period for "money market" instruments typically is less than one year, although small-denomination CDs can be of any maturity. When you purchase securities in the money market, there is very little risk that your investment will not be returned in full when the loan is due since you are lending the money for such a brief period. This low level of "principal risk" makes short-term reserves particularly attractive to retirement-oriented investors who are extremely risk averse. Unfortunately, this lower risk also means that short-term reserves tend to pay lower yields than longer-term fixed-income securities, such as bonds. In fact, historically short-term reserves have earned returns that barely exceed the rate of inflation.

Long-Term Bonds

A bond also represents a form of IOU, but with a longer repayment period. Bonds may be issued by the US government, corporations, or municipalities for periods up to 30 years. If you buy a 20-year bond, you have purchased a stream of 40 semiannual cash payments (your bond interest) spread out over a 20-year period. At the end of the 20 years, you will receive a final cash payment, which represents the return of your original investment (your principal).

Because you are lending the money for such a long period, there is uncertainty not only about the payment of interest, but also about the ultimate return of your original principal. For instance, if the borrower is a corporation, much can go wrong over a 20-year period that might jeopardize your investment. Even if you purchase a 20-year US government bond, where the full payment of interest and principal is virtually guaranteed, you are still "locked in," for better or for worse, to a fixed interest payment for 20 years.

What would be the "for worse" in holding a long-term bond? Well, assume you purchase a 20-year bond with a 7% coupon. If the general level of interest rates moves to, say, 8% immediately after you purchase your bond, you are still locked in to a 7% annual interest payment. You could, of course, sell your 7% coupon bond and purchase a new 8% coupon bond. But in selling your lower coupon bond you will receive a lower price than you originally paid when interest rates were at 7%.

This inverse relationship between interest rates and bond prices is called "interest rate risk." Using the previous example, it follows that if interest rates move to 6%, the price of your 7% coupon bond will increase since you are locked in to a higher income payment. Reflecting this interest rate risk, long-term bonds tend to provide higher yields than short-term reserves and should probably represent some portion of your retirement portfolio.

Common Stocks

Common stocks, the third major financial asset class, represent ownership in corporations. As an owner of a company's stock, you receive a proportionate ownership interest in all corporate profits paid out in the form of dividends, as well as any increase (or decrease) in capital value if the company's stock appreciates (or depreciates) in value. Of the asset classes discussed so far, only stocks offer both an income component *and* a long-term growth component.

Unlike interest payments, dividend payments are not fixed. In fact, companies often raise their dividend payments periodically, in some cases every year. Of course, companies may also reduce their dividends if they choose, but they usually do so only as a last resort when net cash flow dries up. Since stocks have no set maturity, as do bonds and short-term reserves, your investment may have bought you an infinite stream of rising cash dividend payments.

As you have probably guessed, there are some drawbacks to investing in common stocks. First, and most important to income-oriented investors, dividends are paid after a company meets all other financial obligations, including taxes, wages, raw materials, supplies, rent, and interest payments to bondholders. Thus, when a company experiences financial difficulties, common stock dividends are first in line to be eliminated. Second, the value of common stock shares fluctuates substantially, reflecting investors' changing perceptions about the prospects for the economy and for corporations themselves. Reflecting this high volatility risk, stocks historically have provided much higher returns than either long-term bonds or short-term reserves. For this reason, common stocks should represent a substantial component of most retirement investors' portfolios, although any holdings should be well diversified, not just one or two individual stocks.

An Overview of Risk and Return

Evaluating total return is a simple matter: A +10% return is better than a +8% return, but worse than a +12% return. Evaluating risk, on the other hand, is a complex matter involving three elements: principal, income, and inflation.

Now that you have some background on the general characteristics of each major asset class, you need to learn how to evaluate the trade-off between risk and return. To begin, you should be clear that this guide discusses investment return in terms of "total return," which takes into account any income earned (from interest or dividends) plus any capital change (appreciation or depreciation in the value of the asset). Studying the historical total returns of different financial asset classes provides a useful perspective on investing; however, you should never forget that "anything can happen" in the financial markets. In general, the longer the performance observation period, the more weight you can give to the returns.

The term *risk* evokes many different responses from investors. For instance, a major risk for retirement investors might be that the growth in their investments will not keep pace with the rate of inflation, reducing the future purchasing power of their assets. An investment, then, should be evaluated not only in terms of its "nominal" return (before inflation), but also in terms of its "real" return (after inflation).

But for most investors, risk can be summed up in one simple question: What is the possibility that I will lose money? In deciding among various investment options, it is hard to argue with the relevance of such a question. After all, it is difficult emotionally to watch the retirement savings that you have accumulated over the years decline in value, even if the decline may be only temporary. Unfortunately, investments with the highest potential returns tend to have correspondingly high levels of principal risk. In terms of principal risk, then, stocks, bonds, and short-term reserves fall along a continuum: at the far left lie the low-risk/low-return investments, such as short-term reserves; at the far right lie the high-risk/high-return investments, such as common stocks. Long-term bonds fall somewhere in the middle. Table 4–1 provides an overview of the risk/return relationship for each asset class.

Table 4–1
Risks and Returns of Financial Assets

	Short-Term Reserves	Long-Term Bonds	Common Stocks
Long-term total return potential	Low	Moderate	High
Inflation risk	High	Moderate	Low
Principal risk	Low	Moderate	High
Income risk	High	Low	Low

In addition to inflation risk and principal risk, investors must also contend with income risk. Retired investors who depend on the income from their investments to meet their daily living expenses are particularly vulnerable to any diminution in their level of income. Such income-oriented investors must maintain a delicate balance between assuring themselves of a stable and durable income stream, without unduly risking the value of their principal.

The Risks and Returns of Short-Term Reserves

Short-term reserves provide a safe haven for any monies that will be needed within a relatively short period of time. The long-term average annual return on short-term reserves has been about the same as the rate of inflation. As shown in Figure 4–1, a $1 investment in US Treasury bills on December 31, 1925, would have grown to $12.19 on December 31, 1994, equivalent to a +3.7% average annual return. However, after adjusting for an annual inflation rate of 3.1% over

Figure 4–1
Growth of $1 Invested in US Treasury Bills, 1926–1994

the same period, the final value of the $1 investment in today's dollars is just $1.46.

Obviously, the impact of inflation has been difficult to overcome for short-term investments, with inflation consuming nearly 85% of the long-term return on US Treasury bills. Looking at the 60 "rolling" 10-year periods since 1926 (1926–35, 1927–36, etc.), Treasury bills provided a *negative* real return (nominal return less the inflation rate) in 27 periods. In only nine periods did Treasury bills provide a real return in excess of +3%. With yields on short-term investments in the low single-digit range at the end of 1994, short-term reserves currently do not appear to be a very attractive alternative for retirement investors focused on long-term objectives.

Since the risk to both principal and interest is essentially zero in FDIC-insured bank CDs and US Treasury bills, most investors view these investment options as unequivocally safe. As noted earlier, however, the penalty for this level of security is lower investment returns that expose your assets to erosion by inflation. What is more, investors in short-term reserves incur the highest level of income risk. The extent of this income risk recently became all too obvious to many investors in short-term reserves, as short-term interest rates declined from 8% in 1990 to less than 3% in 1993, an income drop of more than one-half.

In sum, while short-term reserves provide peace of mind due to their safety of principal, their lower historical returns and high income risk make them unsuitable for all but a small portion of a long-term investment portfolio. Even for retired investors who may not be as concerned about achieving long-term growth, the low level of income stability in short-term reserves makes them a surprisingly risky investment option.

The Risks and Returns of Bonds

Over time, the returns on long-term bonds are largely determined by their coupon payments and the compounding of reinvested interest income. As shown in Figure 4–2, a $1 investment in long-term US government bonds on December 31, 1925, would have grown to $25.86 on December 31, 1994, representing an annual rate of return of +4.8%. Taking into account an inflation rate of 3.1% over the same period, the +4.8% nominal return translates to a +1.7% real return, and the final real value of the $1 investment drops to $3.09.

During the decades beginning in 1960 through 1975, high inflation rates were particularly costly for investors in long-term bonds, as rising interest rates caused bond prices to plummet, resulting in negative real returns. Interestingly, real average annual returns on bonds were negative in 33 of the 60 ten-year periods beginning in 1926. From the 1933–42 decade through the 1976–85 decade, not once did long-term government bonds provide a real return in excess of +2% annually.

In assessing the performance of bonds over longer-term periods—say, 10 years—your best indicator of possible future returns is the yield at the beginning of the period. For instance, with long-term US Treasury bonds yielding 6.5% at mid-1995, their return over the next decade may reasonably be expected to average about +7%. This rate of return would be well above the long-term historical average for bonds, and suggests that bond returns may be more competitive with stock returns in the years ahead than history might suggest.

As is the case with US Treasury bills and insured bank CDs, investors who hold long-term US Treasury bonds can be confident of receiving both their interest income payments and, upon maturity, their original principal. In this sense, US Treasury bonds offer an unparalleled degree of safety. However, if you own Treasury bonds and need to sell them prior to their stated maturity, the price that you receive per bond may not be the same as the price that you paid per bond. The reason, as noted earlier, is that bond prices change inversely with fluctuations in interest rates. Rising interest rates make existing bonds—paying a lower rate of interest—less attractive relative to new bonds—paying a higher current rate of interest. Thus, the prices of the lower-yielding

Figure 4–2
Growth of $1 Invested in Long-Term US Government Bonds, 1926–1994

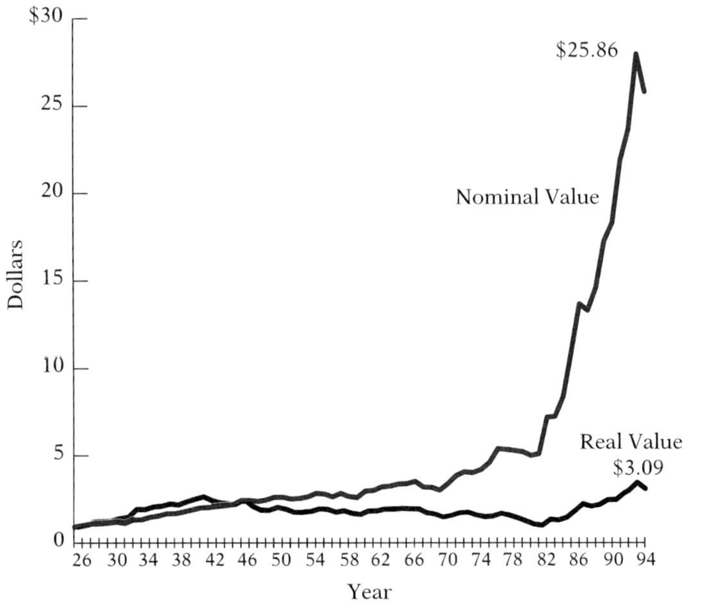

Source: ©*Stocks, Bonds, Bills, and Inflation, 1995 Yearbook*™, Ibbotson Associates, Chicago. (Annually updates work by Roger G. Ibbotson and Rex A. Sinquefield.) Used with permission. All rights reserved.

Table 4–2
Principal Volatility of Bonds

Bond Maturity (Years)	Value if Interest Rates Increase By					
	0.5%	1%	1.5%	2%	2.5%	3%
2	$991	$982	$973	$964	$955	$947
5	$979	$959	$940	$921	$902	$884
10	$965	$932	$900	$870	$841	$813
20	$949	$901	$857	$816	$778	$743

Note: Assumes $1,000 face value and 7% coupon.

bonds fall when interest rates rise. Conversely, falling interest rates make higher-yielding existing bonds relatively more attractive than new issues; thus, the prices of these bonds rise when interest rates fall.

Table 4–2 illustrates the effect of rising interest rates on the price of a $1,000 bond with a 7% coupon, assuming a range of maturities. You can see that the longer the maturity of a particular bond, the more severely its price reacts to a change in rates. For example, the price of a 20-year bond would decline by roughly 10% (from $1,000 to $901) if interest rates were to rise by one percentage point, and by 18% (from $1,000 to $816) in the event of a two percentage point rise. This principal volatility explains why rising interest rates—which typically accompany accelerating inflation—are so worrisome to bond investors. If you have a longer-term investment horizon, the price risk of bonds should be much less of a concern since income payments can be expected to offset to some degree the decline in principal. (Of course, if you hold a bond until its maturity, you will receive its full face value.)

Table 4–3 illustrates the effect of a *decline* in interest rates on the price of the same bond. The table suggests why the bond market was so favorable during the decade ending December 31, 1994, when 30-year US Treasury bond yields fell from 11.6% to 7.8%. This rate decline engendered a price increase of more than +40% for the full period, or an average annual gain of more than +3%. So, long-term bond investors benefited not only from a relatively high level of annual interest income, but from substantial price gains as well.

In combination, Tables 4–2 and 4–3 suggest that you can mitigate the principal risk in bonds by selecting a maturity level suitable to your needs and risk preferences. For example, a more conservative investor with a limited time horizon might prefer to

Table 4–3
Principal Volatility of Bonds

Bond Maturity (Years)	Value if Interest Rates Decline By					
	0.5%	1%	1.5%	2%	2.5%	3%
2	$1,009	$1,019	$1,028	$1,038	$1,047	$1,057
5	$1,021	$1,043	$1,065	$1,088	$1,111	$1,135
10	$1,036	$1,074	$1,114	$1,156	$1,199	$1,245
20	$1,056	$1,116	$1,181	$1,251	$1,327	$1,410

Note: Assumes $1,000 face value and 7% coupon.

steer clear of longer-term bonds. The table shows that intermediate-term bonds tend to be less sensitive to interest rate changes than long-term bonds, while the modest volatility of short-term bonds may make them a reasonable alternative for especially risk-averse investors.

While volatility risk should be your focal point as you consider bond investments, it would be unwise to overlook "credit risk." Credit risk refers to the risk that a bond issuer will be unable to honor its obligations with respect to the payment of income and, at maturity, principal. Here are the major bond quality ratings, as assigned by Standard & Poor's Corporation:

- An **AAA** rating indicates that the issuer is of unquestioned credit quality. This designation is given to only a few blue-chip corporations and municipalities. US government bonds are generally considered to be of better-than-AAA quality.
- Ratings of **AA** and **A** are assigned to highly secure corporate and municipal bonds.
- A **BBB** rating is the lowest investment-grade rating, and indicates that the issuer is creditworthy, with moderate risk to principal and income.
- Ratings of **BB and below** are assigned to lower-quality bonds that have questionable ability to meet annual interest payments or to repay principal at maturity.

In general, lower-quality bonds offer higher yields than higher-quality bonds. Since the credit quality of US government bonds is unequivocal, they typically provide the lowest available yields. Corporate issuers pay higher yields, reflecting the degree of uncertainty that they will be able to make timely payments of interest and principal. In choosing among bonds of varying quality, you have to decide whether the increased yield in a lower-quality bond is justified by the corresponding increase in credit risk. Retirement investors, particularly those who depend heavily on investment income, should generally limit their bond selections to investment-grade bonds (those rated BBB or higher).

Bonds can play an important role in your retirement portfolio. If you are a younger investor accumulating assets for retirement, long-term government and corporate bonds should provide a generous level of current income. Also, because bond returns tend to be less volatile than stock returns, including a bond component in your portfolio may reduce your overall portfolio volatility. Retired investors might also benefit from the income stability provided by intermediate-term and long-term bonds. In short, if you are seeking a relatively predictable level of current income, and can accept a reasonable level of interim volatility risk, bonds should be a key component of your investment portfolio.

One final caveat about bonds: most corporate issuers reserve the right to "call" (i.e., redeem) their bonds after 5 to 10 years from the original date of issuance. (US Treasury bonds are generally noncallable.) The company is likely to exercise this option only if it is in the company's best interests, which is usually when interest rates decline. When a bond is called, you are faced with the problem of reinvesting the proceeds, most likely at lower prevailing interest rates.

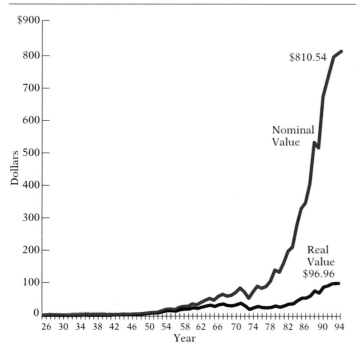

Figure 4–3
Growth of $1 Invested in Common Stocks, 1926–1994

The Risks and Returns of Common Stocks

Common stocks historically have provided the highest rate of return, as measured by the Standard & Poor's 500 Composite Stock Price Index, of any of the three major financial asset classes. Figure 4–3 shows how dramatically the value of an investment in stocks has grown over time. A $1 investment in the stock market on December 31, 1925, would have grown to $811 on December 31, 1994, reflecting an annual rate of return of +10.2%. Interestingly, about one-half of this return has been derived from reinvested dividends and one-half from rising stock prices. Unlike long-term bonds and cash reserves, the long-term returns on stocks have been comfortably ahead of the rate of inflation. Taking into account an annual inflation rate of 3.1% over the 1926–94 period, stocks have still provided a remarkable real return of +7.1%.

While the long-term average nominal return of +10.2% for stocks is exceptional, this figure conceals the dramatic volatility risk of common stocks on a year-to-year basis. Annual stock returns have ranged from a high of +54% in 1933 to a low of −43% in 1931, a staggering spread of 97 percentage points. More recently, in 1974, stock prices fell nearly 30%. And, during the "Great Crash" of October 19, 1987, stock prices plummeted more than −20% in a single day. Investors who sold their stock holdings during these market declines suffered major losses.

As a retirement investor, there are several features of investing in stocks that can make them more palatable if you are averse to volatility risk. First, the volatility of stock market returns declines dramatically as the holding period lengthens. The worst one-year period for stocks resulted in an astounding loss of −43%; the worst five-year period (1928–32) saw stocks decline an average of −13% annually. During this five-year period, an investment of $1,000 on December 31, 1927, would have declined to $514 on December 31, 1932.

But when evaluated over longer time periods, as shown in Figure 4–4, the volatility risk of stocks is much less extreme. Looking at the rolling 10-year periods since 1926, there were only two decades when stocks posted a negative return. The worst such period was from 1929 to 1938, when a $1,000 investment at the beginning of the decade declined to $915 at the end.

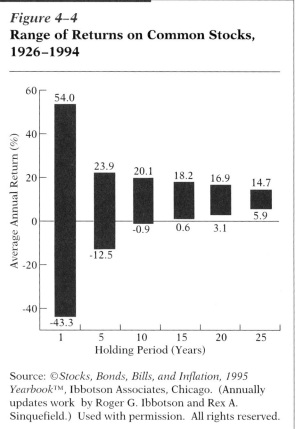

Figure 4–4

Range of Returns on Common Stocks, 1926–1994

Source: ©*Stocks, Bonds, Bills, and Inflation, 1995 Yearbook*™, Ibbotson Associates, Chicago. (Annually updates work by Roger G. Ibbotson and Rex A. Sinquefield.) Used with permission. All rights reserved.

In every other 10-year period—58 of them in all since 1926—stocks posted a positive return. Amazingly, over the rolling 15-, 20-, and 25-year periods going back to 1926, not once did common stocks provide a negative average annual return.

The primary reason that the stock market has been less volatile over longer periods, but has been dramatically volatile over shorter periods, is that stock prices in the short term are influenced by emotional factors, such as investors' hopes and fears about the economy, inflation, and the like. Over the long run, however, stock prices are determined largely by growth in corporate earnings, profits, and dividend yields. Where stocks are concerned, then, the longer your investment time frame, the less likely you are to be negatively impacted by the vagaries of the stock market.

A second way that you can minimize the volatility risk of stocks is to make regular monthly investments rather than an all-at-once commitment each year. By investing on a regular basis, regardless of market fluctuations, you buy more shares when stock prices are low and fewer shares when stock prices are high, virtually assuring yourself of a reasonable average cost basis for your cumulative stock purchases. This disciplined approach to saving, known as "dollar-cost averaging," eliminates the risk of investing all of your money at the market's high point. Of course, dollar-cost averaging does not assure you a gain on your investments; but it will mitigate the extent of any losses. (Chapter 6 provides more details on dollar-cost averaging.)

Common stock dividends are a third feature that make stocks an appealing investment alternative in spite of their short-term price fluctuations. Although dividend payments are not guaranteed—and may even be reduced in periods of financial duress—they have proved remarkably durable. Indeed, since 1926, dividends on stocks as a group declined in 9 years but increased in 60 years. (In one year, dividends were unchanged.) As shown in Figure 4–5, for the full period from 1926 to 1994, divi-

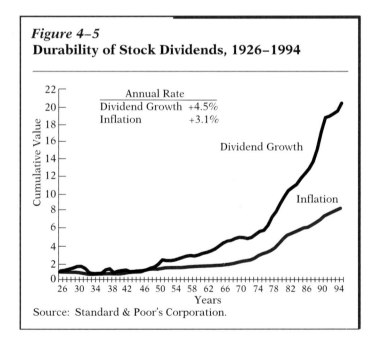

Figure 4–5
Durability of Stock Dividends, 1926–1994

Annual Rate	
Dividend Growth	+4.5%
Inflation	+3.1%

Source: Standard & Poor's Corporation.

dends have grown at an annual compound rate of + 4.5% compared with an inflation rate of + 3.1%, resulting in real income growth of +1.4% annually.

Finally, by combining stocks with long-term bonds and cash reserves, you can create a balanced portfolio that is tailored to meet your individual risk tolerance. Given the lower variability of returns on long-term bonds and cash reserves, the volatility of a balanced portfolio will be reduced. However, because the returns on bonds and cash reserves have been well below those of stocks, a balanced portfolio is likely to underperform an all-stock portfolio over time. In all, as you begin to construct your investment portfolio, you should be concerned with the volatility of the *overall* portfolio, rather than the volatility associated with any individual component.

Moving Beyond "The Big Three"

So far, this discussion of investments has focused exclusively on the three primary asset classes: short-term reserves, long-term bonds, and common stocks. In reality, the number of investment options extends well beyond these basic asset descriptions. This section begins by taking a look at another short-term reserves equivalent, then turns to two special types of bond investments—municipals and mortgage-backed securities—before concluding with a discussion of three important common stock subcategories.

Short-term reserves, long-term bonds, and common stocks are the three major building blocks of an investment portfolio; however, there are many ancillary investment options that may be worth considering.

Guaranteed Investment Contracts

Many employer-sponsored retirement plans offer Guaranteed Investment Contracts (GICs), sometimes called "Investment Contracts," as the primary form of short-term reserves. GICs have proved very popular in such plans, due largely to their guarantee of principal. They are not available to investors outside of these employer-sponsored plans.

The precise structure of GICs varies from plan to plan, but all share two common features: (1) they are issued by insurance companies (banks issue a version known as BICs), and (2) they pay a stated rate of interest over a finite period, typically two to five years. The insurance company underwriting the contract guarantees the payment of income and principal, and may permit early withdrawals at full value under certain circumstances (for instance, if you were to retire or leave the company). GIC rates generally are competitive with rates on bank CDs of compa-rable maturity, which is to say that GIC returns likely will lag the results of longer-term investment alternatives.

The problem with GICs is that the so-called guarantee is only as good as the financial standing of the insurance company issuing the guarantee. Assessing the credit quality of your plan's GIC investment offering will be difficult if it consists of a num-ber of pooled contracts issued by different insurance companies. GICs also may be undiversified, representing an investment in only one or two insurance companies. If you are invested in such a plan, you should be certain that the plan limits its investments to only the highest-quality issuers. In recent years, some partici-pants have found that their plan sponsors reached for extra yield by reducing contract quality, only to lose their supposedly guar-anteed principal when the insurance company ran into financial difficulties.

Municipal Bonds

In discussing long-term bonds, the emphasis thus far has been on taxable government and corporate bonds, which are most suitable for participants in tax-deferred plans and for investors in moderate to low income tax brackets. If you want to supplement your retirement savings by investing in taxable accounts, and especially if you are in one of the higher tax brackets, you may find that tax-exempt municipal bonds offer higher returns after taking into account the advantage of the tax exemption. Municipal bonds are issued by state and local governments to finance their day-to-day operations or to invest in new facilities, and the interest income paid on these bonds is free from federal income taxes (and may be exempt from state and local taxes as well).

Reflecting their tax-free status, municipal bonds generally provide lower yields than taxable government or corporate bonds of comparable maturity and quality. A straightforward calcula-tion can help you to determine whether a tax-exempt bond offers a higher after-tax yield than a taxable alternative. Put simply, the after-tax yield of a taxable bond may be calculated by multiply-ing the bond's yield by one minus your tax rate. For example, if you are taxed at a 31% marginal rate, a corporate bond with a taxable yield of 8.0% would provide an after-tax yield of 5.5% (.08 × [1 − .31]). In this case, all else being equal (i.e., quality and maturity), if a municipal bond alternative yields less than

5.5%, you should probably purchase the taxable corporate bond; if a comparable municipal bond yields more than 5.5%, you would likely choose it over the taxable alternative.

Mortgage-Backed Securities

Mortgage-backed securities are a very popular taxable fixed-income security, and include "Ginnie Maes" (GNMAs), "Fannie Maes" (FNMAs), and "Freddie Macs" (FHLMCs). Each of these instruments is backed by pools of residential mortgages, which "pass through" to the investor a proportionate share of the monthly interest and principal payments. Yields on GNMAs tend to be somewhat higher than the yields on other government securities, and credit quality is the highest available because the timely payment of interest and principal is guaranteed by an agency of the US government.

Mortgage-backed securities generally come with designated maturities of 30 years. But their effective maturities are actually much shorter, making them more comparable (at least as far as maturity is concerned) to intermediate-term bonds than long-term bonds. The reasons that mortgage-backed maturities are relatively short are twofold: (1) a gradually increasing amount of principal is returned along with each monthly payment, and (2) homeowners have the option to prepay their entire mortgages at any time, a risk not incurred by other types of bonds.

Homeowners typically elect to prepay their mortgages when interest rates decline, allowing them to secure a new mortgage at the lower prevailing interest rate. When this refinancing occurs, the unpaid portion of the existing mortgage is passed through to investors, who must reinvest the proceeds at the lower prevailing rates. This *prepayment risk* means that the prices of mortgage-backed securities do not move in lock-step with the prices of other types of bonds. Indeed, the responsiveness of mortgage-backed securities to changes in interest rates is much less predictable than for other government and corporate bonds. Nevertheless, because of their higher yields relative to other government securities, mortgage-backed securities may be appropriate for a portion of the bond component of your portfolio.

Small Capitalization Stocks

Common stocks can be subdivided along three levels of market capitalization. (A company's capitalization refers to the value of

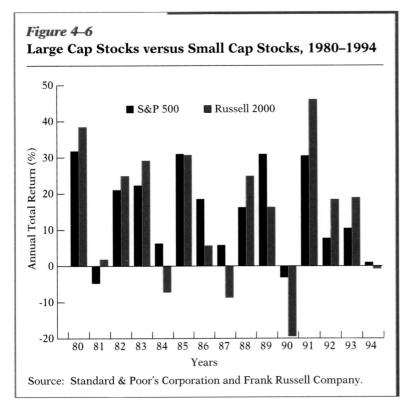

Figure 4–6
Large Cap Stocks versus Small Cap Stocks, 1980–1994

Source: Standard & Poor's Corporation and Frank Russell Company.

the company as determined by its total shares outstanding multiplied by its market price.) The large cap stock universe might include the stocks of all companies with market values in excess of $10 *billion,* while the small cap universe might include the stocks of companies with market values below $500 *million.* Mid cap stocks would fall somewhere in between.

Over time, small capitalization stocks have performed quite differently from the large capitalization stocks that compose the Standard & Poor's 500 Stock Index. For instance, Figure 4–6 shows the disparity in annual returns from 1980 to 1994 for the Standard & Poor's 500 Index and the Russell 2000 Index, a good proxy for small companies. On balance, the period shown favored large cap stocks over small cap stocks.

Despite their lagging performance over this relatively brief period, the record shows that over very long time periods the returns of small cap stocks have exceeded the returns of their larger counterparts. During the period from 1926 to 1994, the average annual rate of return for small cap stocks was +12.2%, compared to +10.2% for large cap stocks. Before you decide, based on this comparison, that small cap stocks should compose a major portion of your investment portfolio, you should know that the returns of small cap stocks have been even more volatile than the returns of large cap stocks. Indeed, since 1926 there have been protracted periods—most recently from 1983 to 1990—when small cap stocks have lagged far behind the broad stock market. In light of their higher potential return and commensurately higher volatility risk, small cap stocks may be appropriate for a portion of your common stock commitment.

Growth Stocks and Value Stocks

Both large cap and small cap stocks can be subdivided into two major groupings: growth stocks and value stocks. Growth stocks are generally defined as having higher-than-average earnings growth rates and lower dividend yields. Because of the perceived value of their future earnings, growth stocks tend to sell at higher price-earnings ratios (i.e., the price of a stock divided by its 12-month earnings) and higher price-book ratios (i.e., the price of a stock divided by its book value, as determined from its balance sheet). Value stocks, on the other hand, are characterized by much lower price-earnings and price-book ratios, and much higher dividend yields.

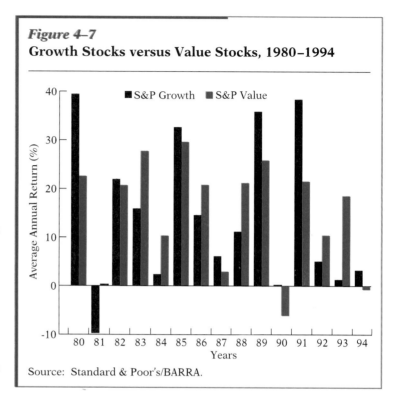

Figure 4–7
Growth Stocks versus Value Stocks, 1980–1994

Source: Standard & Poor's/BARRA.

Figure 4–7 shows the total returns since 1980 for growth and value stocks, as measured by the Standard & Poor's/BARRA Growth and Value Indexes. You can see that the relative performance of growth and value stocks has vacillated from year to year. Over time, the likelihood is that the average returns of the two indexes should be fairly similar. For the full period from December 31, 1979, to December 31, 1994, the results were: growth stocks +13.8% and value stocks +14.8%.

Despite the fact that the long-term returns of growth and value stocks are likely to converge, growth stocks may be more appealing to investors holding taxable accounts, since a greater proportion of the total return from growth stocks is derived from capital appreciation, on which no tax is paid until gains are actually realized. And, even when capital gains are realized, they will be taxed at the maximum capital gains rate—presently 28%—rather than the prevailing income tax rate.

In comparing the volatility of growth stocks versus value stocks, growth stocks tend to be somewhat more volatile and

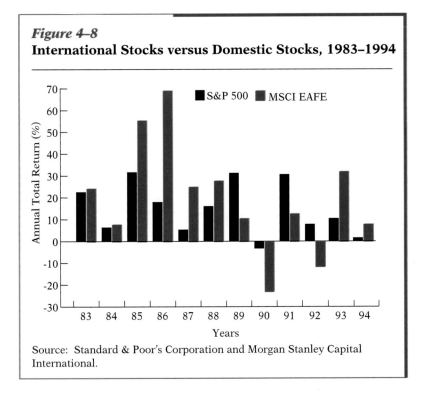

Figure 4-8
International Stocks versus Domestic Stocks, 1983–1994

Source: Standard & Poor's Corporation and Morgan Stanley Capital International.

therefore may be more suitable for younger or more aggressive investors. Value stocks, because of their higher income component, may appeal to investors holding tax-deferred retirement accounts, as well as older or more conservative investors who desire a higher income component.

International Stocks

In 1960, US stocks represented two-thirds of the value of all stocks outstanding worldwide, with stocks issued by foreign companies composing the remaining one-third. By the end of 1994, that distribution of market cap had been reversed: two-thirds of the world's total stock market value is now composed of companies that lie outside of the United States, with the remaining one-third composed of companies that lie within the United States.

As shown in Figure 4–8, the returns of the major stock markets of the world do not always move in tandem with the returns on US stocks; thus, international stocks offer US investors the opportunity to further diversify their portfolios. This divergence in returns is due to a number of factors, including, most importantly, regional economic and political conditions and varying levels of interest rates among countries. Given that there are many successful companies situated outside of US confines and that the economies of many emerging countries may be growing faster than the economy of the United States, the returns on international stocks should be fully competitive with, and in many cases greater than, the returns on US stocks.

As you would expect, investing in international stocks entails some incremental risks that you should be familiar with. Foremost among these is "currency risk." To understand how currency risk affects your foreign investments, suppose that you buy Japanese stocks and the value of the US dollar subsequently rises 10% against the value of the Japanese yen. In this case, even if the value of the stocks you hold remains unchanged, your holdings will show a decline of −10% when converted into US dollars.

Another risk to consider with foreign investments is "sovereign risk." While the trend over the past generation has been to open up national borders to allow for the free flow of capital and investment among different countries, future trade disputes, political unrest, or even war could disrupt international markets and imperil the value of your overseas investments. Sovereign risk is particularly relevant if you are considering an investment in any of the smaller emerging markets.

Final Thoughts

The overwhelming message of this chapter is that the only certainty about investing in the financial markets is that there is uncertainty. Stock prices may fluctuate widely, challenging your fortitude to "stay the course"; long-term interest rates may rise, causing sudden losses in your bond holdings; or interest rates may fall, threatening the stability of your income. What is more, inflation may accelerate, eroding the value of your total investment portfolio and reducing the purchasing power of any fixed-income payments. In all, it is enough to make you wonder, "Why bother?"

Fortunately, investors who are saving for retirement, and who presumably have a long-term investment horizon, can establish a balanced investment portfolio—including stocks, bonds, and short-term reserves—that will allow them to "take in stride" whatever the financial markets have to offer. In the final analysis, in spite of the short-term risks associated with investing in the stock market, the solid long-term returns of stocks—especially when inflation is taken into account—relative to those of other investment alternatives suggest that stocks should represent a fairly heavy component of your retirement portfolio.

To be sure, the appropriate allocation of your monies among the three asset classes will depend on your personal retirement objectives and risk tolerance. But before you approach this critical asset allocation decision, you should first consider how mutual funds might fit into your retirement portfolio. Chapter 5 provides a broad overview of mutual funds, and demarcates them by asset class and by risk level. Once you have a fundamental understanding of the types of mutual funds available, you may then move on to the selection of individual funds and the establishment of your investment portfolio.

Investing through Mutual Funds

The remarkable growth of mutual fund assets over the past decade suggests that mutual funds are becoming the investor's preferred medium for participating in the financial markets. Indeed, as shown in Figure 5–1, since 1975 the total assets of mutual funds have expanded from $40 *billion* to more than $2 *trillion*—an annual growth rate of 22%—and the number of funds has increased from 400 to over 5,000. Mutual funds have also become a popular investment vehicle for retirement investors, and they are now widely used in employer-sponsored retirement programs (e.g., 401(k) and 403(b) plans), profit-sharing plans, and individual retirement accounts (IRAs).

The primary message of this chapter is that, as you move from accumulating assets in your working years to spending these assets in your retirement years, mutual funds represent an ideal means to meet your investment savings objectives. This chapter is intended primarily as a primer on mutual funds, emphasizing both the advantages and the disadvantages of fund investing, and then providing an overview of the different types of mutual funds that are available to investors. As a result, much of the information will be very familiar to long-term

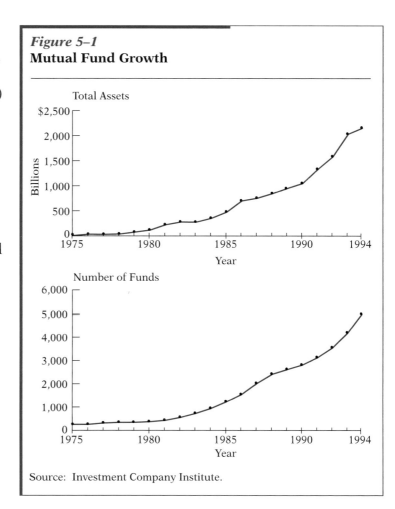

Figure 5–1
Mutual Fund Growth

Source: Investment Company Institute.

mutual fund investors, who may wish merely to quickly review this material and then move on to Chapter 6. Investors who are not particularly experienced with mutual funds should benefit considerably from a careful reading of this chapter.

What Is a Mutual Fund?

The simple premise of the mutual fund concept is that a group of people may invest more efficiently and with lower risk than any of the individuals in the group could invest on their own.

The idea of the mutual fund is that investors contribute to a collective pool of assets—the fund—and receive in return a proportionate ownership interest in the fund. In turn, the mutual fund (more formally known as an open-end investment company) invests the assets in a manner—known as the fund's investment objective—that is set forth in the fund's prospectus. For example, a fund's prospectus may cite as an objective "to provide long-term capital growth" or "to provide a current level of income that is exempt from federal taxes." Whatever the case, a fund's investment objective guides the investment adviser in managing the portfolio.

Mutual funds allow investors to sell their existing shares or purchase new shares on every business day. This "open-end" feature means that mutual funds provide daily liquidity to convert the investment into cash. In this regard, open-end mutual funds are clearly distinguished from closed-end funds (or closed-end investment companies). Closed-end funds also pool money from a group of investors; however, unlike their open-end cousins, closed-end funds issue a fixed number of shares at an initial offering. When the initial offering is over, investors may neither purchase additional shares nor sell their existing shares through the fund itself. Rather, investors must buy and sell shares in the stock market.

Mutual fund shares can be purchased primarily through two channels: (1) directly from the fund's sponsor, or (2) through an intermediary such as a broker, financial planner, or bank. Funds that are sold through intermediaries generally charge some form of sales commission, or "sales load," which reduces dollar for dollar the ultimate return to the investor. On the other hand, funds that sell their shares directly to the investor, without the use of an intermediary, typically do not assess a sales load. These funds are designated as "no-load" funds.

The share price of a mutual fund fluctuates daily depending on the total change in value of the securities that it holds. (Money market funds, of course, seek to maintain a constant net asset value of one dollar per share, although there is no guarantee that they will meet this objective.) Each business day a mutual fund determines the value of all of the securities in its portfolio based on their prices at the end of that day, deducts any accrued expenses, and divides this aggregate value by the current number of shares outstanding to determine the value of each single share in the fund. This figure is known as the fund's daily net asset value (NAV). The net asset values of mutual funds are published daily in most major newspapers.

Mutual funds are regulated by federal and state agencies—the most powerful being the United States Securities and Exchange Commission—and are required to provide full disclosure about their investment policies, objectives, and risks, as well as complete information about any fees, commissions, and operating expenses. This disclosure is included in the fund's prospectus, which must be provided to prospective investors either before or at the time they purchase fund shares. The Investment Company Act of 1940, the primary federal law regulating mutual funds, also contains numerous provisions designed to ensure that mutual funds are operated in the interests of shareholders rather than the interests of the fund sponsor.

The Advantages of Mutual Funds

It is difficult to articulate succinctly the precise reasons for the remarkable success, particularly during the past decade, of mutual funds. Nonetheless, four time-honored principles seem to lie at the heart of the mutual fund explosion.

Diversification   Investing in a mutual fund provides immediate diversification, even for an investor of relatively modest means. The reason, as noted earlier, is that your money is pooled along with the investments of tens of thousands of other investors, whose contributions in the aggregate enable the fund to invest in a wide array of companies. For instance, if you invest, say, $3,000 in a stock fund, you might effectively own 100 or more different stocks. It could take hundreds of thousands of dollars for you to achieve this same level of diversification purchasing individual stocks. In a long-term investment program, portfolio diversification is critical since it reduces, but does not eliminate, the volatility risk of investing in individual securities.

Professional Management   The investment activities of a mutual fund are overseen by a professional investment manager, who charges the fund a fee for his services. The job of the investment manager is to establish a portfolio that is consistent with the fund's investment objectives, as set forth in the fund's prospectus. Since most investors have neither the time nor the expertise to manage their personal investments on a day-to-day basis, the ongoing professional management available through mutual funds represents a valuable service. (Later in this chapter, you will learn of an alternative to "active" mutual fund management that has proved extremely effective in providing competitive long-term relative returns.)

Liquidity   Shares in a mutual fund may be sold literally at the drop of a hat. That is, a fund is required to redeem shares on each business day at its net asset value. While the same level of liquidity is often available for individual securities, you may redeem your shares in a mutual fund at no cost to you, provided that you are invested in a no-load fund.

Convenience   Mutual funds offer a variety of services that greatly facilitate investor activities. For instance, you may purchase fund shares by mail or by phone, and from any number of independent sources including brokers, banks, and insurance agents. Arrangements can be made for regular purchases of mutual fund shares through automatic deductions from your paycheck or bank account. Alternatively, you may deduct shares automatically from your fund account and have the proceeds credited to your bank account. At your option, dividends and capital gains distributions can be automatically reinvested in additional shares of the fund.

Just as you can conveniently buy and sell fund shares, your existing mutual fund shares also can be exchanged easily from one fund to another within the same fund complex, often at no cost to you. Mutual funds also provide extensive recordkeeping services to help you keep track of these transactions as well as any reinvested dividends and capital gains. On a daily basis, you can monitor and evaluate your fund's performance through newspapers, investment magazines, and independent fund rating services. You will also receive regular shareholder reports on your fund's performance along with a discussion of its investment activities. At year-end, mutual funds will provide important tax-reporting information to help you complete your tax return, including, in many cases, the average cost basis of any shares you may have sold during the year.

The Disadvantages of Mutual Fund Investing

In fairness, there are some disadvantages associated with investing in mutual funds that you should consider before investing your money.

No "Guarantees"   Unlike bank accounts, mutual funds, including money market funds, are neither insured nor guaranteed by an agency of the US government. While mutual funds are regulated by the US Securities and Exchange Commission and by state securities regulators, this oversight is aimed at assuring full disclosure of all of the pertinent information required by an investor to make an informed investment decision. Securities regulators can help to protect you from fraudulent activity, but they cannot protect you from investment risk.

Manager Risk   Gaining access to professional investment managers is an important advantage of mutual fund investing. However, the evidence suggests that few professional managers consistently exceed the results that could be achieved simply by owning an index fund, which mirrors the performance of the broad market. There are, to be sure, some notable exceptions, but identifying these "star" performers in advance is extremely difficult—if not impossible. (Even the managers who achieve returns that exceed those of the markets in which they invest often fall short after their expenses and transaction costs are taken into account.) There is also no guarantee that a particular fund manager will remain with a given fund after you have made your investment. Alternatively, the excellent performance that attracted you to a particular fund may actually have been achieved by a former manager. In either case, it is up to the investor to ascertain that a fund's record can be attributed to current management.

The Diversification "Penalty"   The diversification of mutual funds means that the returns of the best-performing mutual funds will rarely approach the returns of the best-performing individual stocks. Of course, the diversification of mutual funds also helps you to avoid the substantial losses that are incurred by the worst-performing individual stocks. Nonetheless, while diversification reduces the volatility risk of investing in any single security, it will not eliminate the market risk associated with an overall decline in the financial markets.

Potentially High Costs   In many cases, a combination of sales commissions and high operating expenses offsets the low-cost benefits of mutual fund ownership. Funds that are sold through brokers and other financial intermediaries usually incur sales commissions of one kind or another, sometimes in the form of front-end loads (typically in the 4% to 6% range) and sometimes in the form of contingent deferred sales loads (CDSLs). In the latter case, an initial sales load of, say, 6% is eliminated, only to be replaced with an annual charge of 1% and a redemption fee that begins at 5% and declines by one percentage point each year the shares are held. The redemption fee may be eliminated in the sixth year, but by that time the investor will have paid cumulative annual sales expenses totaling 6%, the same as if a 6% front-end load had been levied. In recent years, many funds also have adopted annual 12b–1 fees ranging from 0.25% to 1.00% of average net assets. This fee is typically paid directly to the fund's sponsor to help offset the costs of marketing the fund's shares.

In addition to these sales-related charges, *all* mutual funds incur annual expenses such as investment advisory fees and operating costs. These expenses are expressed as a percentage of a fund's average net assets. The ratio of fund expenses to average net assets may range from as low as 0.2% to as high as 3% or more. In combination, sales commissions, 12b–1 fees, and fund operating expenses reduce the *gross* returns to mutual fund shareholders. To state what may be obvious, funds with extremely high costs will have difficulty achieving competitive *net* (after expenses) returns over time. You should carefully investigate the total expenses of a fund before you invest, and avoid buying a fund that charges exorbitant fees and expenses.

Types of Mutual Funds

There are mutual funds that invest in virtually every type of security that is avail- (continued on pg. 67)

The mutual fund industry provides an almost overwhelming number of investment options. Some of these funds maintain well-diversified portfolios and provide relatively predictable performance, making them suitable investments for the core portion of your retirement portfolio. Other funds maintain highly specialized portfolios, and their volatility makes them suitable for only the most adventurous investor. This section provides an overview of the major types of mutual funds offered within each of the three financial asset classes. Figure 5–2 illustrates the allocation of mutual fund assets among the major market sectors.

Money Market Funds

These funds seek to provide a stable net asset value of $1.00 per share, while providing a current level of dividend income. As a result, the investment return of money market funds is composed solely of reinvested daily dividends. You should keep in mind that, while all money market funds expect to maintain a steady net asset value of $1.00 per share, there is no assurance that they will be able to do so. Remember also that an investment in a money market fund is neither insured nor guaranteed by the US government.

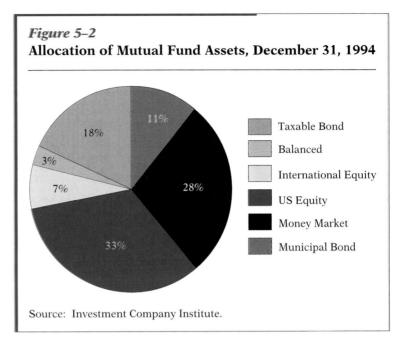

Figure 5–2
Allocation of Mutual Fund Assets, December 31, 1994

- Taxable Bond
- Balanced
- International Equity
- US Equity
- Money Market
- Municipal Bond

Source: Investment Company Institute.

Money market funds purchase short-term loans ranging in maturity from one day to one year; however, the *average* maturity of a money market fund's holdings in total may not exceed 90 days. Because of this very short average maturity, money market funds' exposure to interest rate risk is effectively nil. Nonetheless, you will recall from Chapter 4 that low interest rate risk goes hand-in-hand with high income risk. In other words, while price volatility is not a factor for money market funds, their dividends may decline dramatically over a short period of time.

The investment holdings of money market funds are generally of exceptionally high quality. Indeed, the SEC requires that all taxable money market funds invest at least 95% of their assets in securities of the highest grade, as rated by a major credit rating agency such as Moody's Investors Services or Standard & Poor's Corporation. Even with these stringent quality guidelines for money market funds, they can still be divided along three quality tiers:

US Treasury Funds   These funds invest principally in direct US Treasury obligations. As a result, all or a portion of the income from these funds may be exempt from state income taxes.

able in the financial markets. Many of these funds will be appropriate for only the most sophisticated investors; others, such as money market funds, will meet the requirements of even the most conservative-minded investors.

US Government Funds   These funds invest in obligations of the US Treasury as well as agencies of the US government.

General Funds   These funds invest principally in the short-term debt of large, high-quality corporations and banks.

Another separate category of money market fund—the municipal money market fund—invests in the obligations of state and local government agencies and pays income that is exempt from federal, and sometimes state and local, income taxes.

Taxable Bond Funds

As a general matter, all bond funds seek to provide a high level of current income. Indeed, over the long term, virtually all of the total return of bond funds comes in the form of reinvested interest income, with a much smaller portion resulting from capital growth. This capital component is primarily a function of interest rates. The reason, as noted in Chapter 4, is that bond prices—and therefore bond fund prices—fluctuate in response to changes in the general level of interest rates.

The key determinant of a bond fund's sensitivity to interest rate changes is its average weighted maturity, which takes into account the maturity level of each individual bond held by the fund. The longer a bond fund's average maturity, the greater the fluctuation in its net asset value in response to a change in interest rates. In return for accepting this interest rate risk, bond fund investors generally earn a higher income yield for each step out in length of maturity. So, bond funds may be particularly suited for investors who depend upon interest income to meet their monthly living expenses. Figure 5–3 illus-

Figure 5–3
**Average Taxable Bond Fund Yields and Maturities
December 31, 1994**

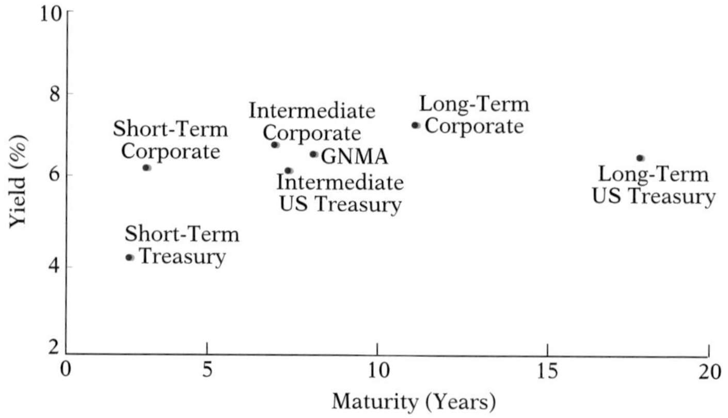

Source: Lipper Analytical Services, Inc.

trates the relationship between yield and maturity for various types of bond funds.

Bond funds may be divided into three major average maturity segments:

1. Short-term—average maturity of one to five years.
2. Intermediate-term—average maturity of 5 to 10 years.
3. Long-term—average maturity of 10 to 30 years.

In addition to these three maturity levels, bond funds also vary by investment objective. There are four primary investment categories. A fifth category of bond fund, the high-yield bond fund, will be discussed separately later in this chapter.

US Government Bond Funds   These funds invest in securities issued by the United States Treasury or agencies of the US government. (Funds that invest exclusively in US Treasury obligations are known as US Treasury bond funds.) Because these securities are obligations of the US government, they are considered to be of unparalleled credit quality. Even government bond funds, however, are subject to interest rate risk such that their net asset values will fluctuate commensurate with their maturity levels. Some US government funds may vary their maturity levels depending on the investment adviser's outlook for interest rates; other funds confine their investments to a particular maturity level.

Mortgage-Backed Securities Funds   These funds invest in mortgage-backed securities that represent interests in pools of residential mortgages. The most popular mortgage-backed securities fund is the GNMA fund, which holds mortgage "pools" that are backed by the Government National Mortgage Association (which in turn is backed by the full faith and credit of the US government). Mortgage pools represent individual residential mortgages that have been purchased and "packaged" by a government agency before being resold to investors as a single security. Each month, the holder of the mortgage pool—in this case the fund—receives an interest income payment as well as a portion of the principal from each underlying mortgage.

As is the case with other bond funds, mortgage-backed funds are subject to interest rate risk. But these funds are also subject to prepayment risk. That is, when interest rates decline, the total returns of mortgage-backed funds may lag behind those of other bond funds, since many homeowners will refinance their mortgages at the new lower rates and pay off their old mortgages. As a result of this incremental risk, the yields on mortgage-backed funds tend to be higher than those of funds that invest solely in US Treasury or government securities.

Investment-Grade Corporate Bond Funds   These funds invest principally in the debt obligations of US corporations. Corporate borrowers range from blue-chip (i.e., large and established) companies with investment-grade credit ratings to financially distressed companies with speculative-grade credit ratings. Investment-grade corporate bond funds generally limit their investments to issues rated Baa or higher by Moody's Investors Services and BBB by Standard & Poor's Corporation. Despite the relatively low credit risk of investment-grade corporate bond funds, they do not match the quality level of US government bond funds. As a result, corporate bond funds generally pay higher yields than US government bond funds.

Municipal (Tax-Exempt) Bond Funds

Municipal bond funds invest in the obligations of state and local government agencies. The interest income from municipal bond funds is generally exempt from federal income taxes (although any capital gains would be subject to taxation). Investors who are taxed at one of the higher marginal rates generally will benefit by investing in a municipal bond fund rather than a taxable bond fund. If you buy a bond fund that limits its investments to the state in which you reside, you may earn income that is exempt from state and local income taxes as well.

Like their taxable counterparts, tax-exempt bond funds are available in a range of maturity levels, including short-term, intermediate-term, and long-term. Most municipal bond funds purchase only investment-grade issues; some go one step further in credit quality, emphasizing municipal bonds that are insured by private insurance companies. At the extreme, a few municipal bond funds specialize in high-yield or lower-quality municipal bonds.

Common Stock Funds

Nearly all common stock funds seek to provide long-term growth of capital as an investment objective; more conservative stock funds may include dividend income as a secondary consideration. Table 5–1 provides an overview of the components of total return for the major common stock fund categories. In general, the higher the proportion of a fund's return that is derived from income, the less volatile its performance will be from one year to the next.

Equity Income Funds   These funds seek to provide a high level of current income and income growth by investing in the stocks of well-established companies that pay substantial dividends. In addition to common stocks, equity income funds often hold other income-oriented securities such as long-term corporate bonds, preferred stocks, and convertible bonds. While income is their primary objective, these funds also seek to provide a reasonable level of long-term capital growth. Given their relatively low price volatility (compared to other stock funds), high dividend yields, and potential for moderate long-term capital growth, equity income funds may serve well as a core holding in your retirement portfolio.

Growth and Income (Value) Funds   These funds seek to provide a balance between current dividend income and long-term growth of capital and income. The portfolios of growth and income funds vary tremendously from one fund to the next, but most are well diversified and emphasize the stocks of large and medium-sized companies that have demonstrated sustainable dividend income. Growth and income funds are often called "value" funds, since they tend to emphasize companies with below-average price-earnings ratios (i.e., the price of a stock divided by its annual earnings) and above-average dividend yields. In general, growth and income funds can be considered a middle ground between equity income funds and growth funds.

Table 5–1
**Components of Total Return
(10-year period ending December 31, 1994)**

Fund Type	Income Return	Capital Return	Total Return	Income as a Percentage of Total Return
Equity income	+5.4%	+5.2%	+10.6%	51%
Growth and income	+3.2	+9.0	+12.2	26
Growth	+1.8	+10.3	+12.1	15
Small company	+0.8	+12.3	+13.1	6

Note: This period reflects a time when stocks achieved returns well above their historical average. These results should not be considered indicative of possible future returns.

Source: Lipper Analytical Services, Inc.

Growth Funds   In contrast to equity income funds, growth funds seek to provide capital growth as a dominant objective. These funds typically invest in a mix of established and emerging companies with good prospects for sustainable long-term earnings growth. Current dividend income is usually considered incidental; thus, the dividend yield on the average growth fund is quite low relative to other stock fund offerings. The price volatility of the average growth fund is usually higher than that of equity income and value funds.

Small Company Funds   These funds seek to provide long-term capital growth by investing in the stocks of smaller, emerging companies. Rather than pay dividends, many of these companies retain their earnings and continue to invest in the company's growth. The stocks of smaller companies typically trade "over the counter" (i.e., not on one of the major stock exchanges) and tend not to be monitored as closely by Wall Street analysts as the stocks of major US corporations. Given this diminished level of scrutiny, the investment managers of small company funds hope to discover companies whose future growth potential is not yet reflected in their stock prices. The incremental risks in this type of strategy may be substantial, since these companies tend to be more susceptible to business setbacks and market disappointments. As a result, the price volatility of small company funds has been among the highest of all stock funds.

International Stock Funds   These funds invest in the stocks of companies that operate beyond the confines of the United States. Funds that hold exclusively non-US stocks are known as international funds, while those that invest in both US and non-US stocks are known as global or world funds. There are also subcategories of international stock funds that invest exclusively in companies from a particular region of the world, such as Europe or the Pacific Basin, or from a single foreign country, such as Japan.

The risks incurred by these funds vary widely depending on their individual investment policies. Some funds emphasize country allocations rather than individual stock selection, hoping to capitalize on those countries that will enjoy the highest future economic growth. Other funds employ a more fundamental investment approach, focusing on the most promising companies regardless of the countries in which they operate. Whatever their investment objectives, international stock funds enable US investors to participate in the stock markets around the world. As you can see in Figure 5–4, the US equity markets comprise just one-third of the total value of all of the world's equity markets.

In addition to the usual risks of stock investing, international funds also entail both political risk and currency risk. As noted in Chapter 4, if the value of the US dollar strengthens relative to foreign currencies, the return to US investors in international stocks will be reduced. Conversely, if the dollar weakens relative to foreign currencies, the return to US investors will be enhanced. This currency effect adds yet another layer of volatility to the returns of international stock funds. Before investing in these funds, you should carefully evaluate whether you are prepared to assume this extra risk. In all, international stock funds may be appropriate for a modest portion of your overall retirement portfolio.

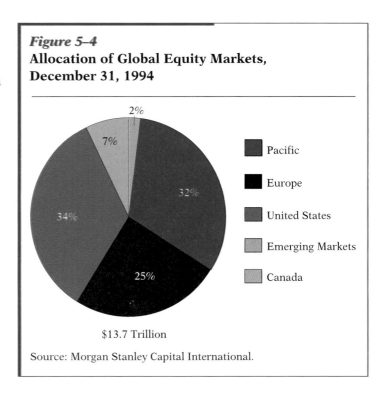

Figure 5–4
Allocation of Global Equity Markets, December 31, 1994

- Pacific
- Europe
- United States
- Emerging Markets
- Canada

$13.7 Trillion

Source: Morgan Stanley Capital International.

Balanced Funds

Balanced funds offer some of the characteristics of stock funds and some of bond funds in a single portfolio. These funds may be divided into two broad categories: traditional and asset allocation. A third category of balanced fund, the *life cycle* fund, is just beginning to emerge. All three of these types of balanced funds share some of the same portfolio characteristics and investment objectives, but the manner in which each achieves its objectives is unique.

Traditional Balanced Funds   These funds seek to provide a combination of growth, income, and conservation of capital. The average balanced fund typically invests about 50% to 60% of its assets in higher-yielding stocks, with the remainder invested in bonds and short-term reserves. Traditional balanced funds are considered to be a relatively conservative, "middle-of-the-road" investment option. Their net asset values will fluctuate along with the movements of the financial markets, but they tend to be less volatile than a portfolio composed entirely of stocks. Like growth and income funds, a balanced fund may be an excellent fund selection if you are just beginning to build your retirement portfolio.

Asset Allocation Funds   These funds are similar to the traditional balanced funds in that they invest in a mix of stocks, bonds, and short-term reserves. But the similarity ends there. Unlike the traditional balanced funds, asset allocation funds retain the flexibility to substantially alter their allocation among the three asset classes depending on the fund manager's outlook for the relative performance of the different financial markets.

Even among asset allocation funds investment policies vary widely, with some funds permitted to hold up to 100% of their assets in stocks, while others may have a much lower limit. In essence, all asset allocation funds engage in market timing to some degree, an endeavor that has rarely proved successful in the fallible world of investing. As a result, holding a particular asset allocation fund may entail much more risk than holding a particular traditional balanced fund. In any event, you should carefully evaluate the investment policies of these funds before you invest.

Life-Cycle Funds   In the past two years, the life-cycle fund has begun to emerge in the mutual fund industry, and the concept appears poised for even greater acceptance in the years ahead. A life-cycle fund typically consists of a series of distinct investment portfolios, each of which offers an investment profile that is specifically targeted to meet the objectives of an investor at a particular stage in life. While most life-cycle funds follow the traditional mutual fund approach of holding individual securities, some life-cycle funds actually hold shares of other mutual funds. This strategy provides the investor with a single fund that offers the same broad diversification as would be achieved by purchasing several individual mutual funds.

Using the life-cycle approach to investing, an investor saving for retirement might favor a fund that maintains an asset mix emphasizing capital growth. However, once this investor reaches retirement age, she may wish to switch her assets to a fund that maintains an asset mix emphasizing income. For investors who want a simplified investment program in a single investment portfolio, the life-cycle approach to investing may have considerable appeal.

Specialty Funds

In addition to the mainstream categories of mutual funds described above, there are two additional types of "equity-oriented" funds that are more specialized—and therefore more risky—but which nonetheless may be suitable for investors who understand and accept the incremental risks.

High-Yield Corporate Bond Funds   More commonly known as junk bond funds, these funds invest in the debt of corporations that carry below-investment-grade credit ratings (Ba or lower by Moody's Investors Services and BB or lower by Standard & Poor's Corporation). Many of these companies are simply too small or have too limited a history to earn an investment-grade rating. Others may be "fallen angels"—blue-chip companies that have experienced weakness in their financial condition. A tremendous volume of high-yield bond issuance occurred during the 1980s in connection with corporate mergers and restructurings, and the bonds of these highly leveraged companies were considered to be quite speculative.

Investors in high-yield bond funds are attracted by the higher yields that these funds promise compared to government and investment-grade corporate bond funds. But, as suggested by their speculative credit ratings, there is substantial risk that these companies will be unable to meet their semiannual interest payments or pay back principal upon maturity. The result is that the stated yields of high-yield bond funds may never actually be realized by the investor.

Like all bond funds, high-yield bond funds are also exposed to interest rate risk. However, the price volatility of high-yield bond funds tends to more closely resemble the volatility of a stock fund than that of a bond fund. If you are considering an investment in a high-yield bond fund, you should know that there are dramatic variations in the credit quality of these funds, and you would be wise to compare the average quality of each prospective fund prior to investing. Because of the substantial risks involved, a high-yield bond fund should represent only a modest portion (if any) of your portfolio holdings.

Sector Funds   These funds invest in the stocks of a single industry, such as energy, financial services, health care, utilities, gold, and the like. Sector funds offer investors a convenient means of participating in a particular industry that they expect to prosper, while still maintaining a reasonable level of diversification within that industry. These funds are much less risky than buying the stock of a single company, but much more risky than owning a portfolio of stocks that is diversified across a wide spectrum of industry sectors.

Final Thoughts

There are compelling advantages to using mutual funds to implement your retirement investment program. To be sure, there are also some disadvantages relative to holding individual securities, but these pale in comparison to the substantial benefits of diversification, professional management, liquidity, and convenience.

In a sense, however, mutual funds have become victims of their own success. With more than 5,000 funds to choose from, sorting through the myriad of fund prospectuses and promotions can make the selection of mutual funds a daunting endeavor. Even after you have narrowed your fund selection to a particular investment objective, such as growth funds, you will find enormous diversity in the investment *policies* of funds with purportedly identical investment *objectives*. For instance, most funds employ an "active" investment approach, using a professional investment manager; other funds employ an "index" strategy, seeking to match the performance and risk characteristics of a particular segment of the financial markets—without the use of an investment adviser. Some funds emphasize technical factors, hoping to identify trends from the past that will recur in the future; other funds emphasize fundamental valuation measures, such as price-earnings ratios, dividend yields, and the like.

Fortunately, you need not allow the challenge of selecting particular mutual funds to distract you from your retirement program. Indeed, over the long run, the success of your retirement investment program will depend much more on how you allocate your assets among stocks, bonds, and short-term reserves than which particular fund investments you choose. In Chapter 6, you will learn how to devise an allocation program that is suited to your personal investment objectives and risk tolerance. You also will be presented with some simple methods for narrowing down your fund selections to a more manageable universe.

Personalizing Your Investment Program

Ome of the great myths of investing is the so-called Wall Street guru who can consistently select the next "hot" investment opportunity that has somehow been overlooked by every other investor. The reality of investing is that finding the next great investment opportunity is an elusive endeavor. Indeed, buying the latest hot stocks or high-flying mutual funds is a perilous game, one that may well end badly for the investor.

What is it, then, that separates the successful investor from the unsuccessful investor? It comes as a surprise to many people that investment success has much more to do with how you allocate your assets among stocks, bonds, and short-term reserves, than the specific investments that you choose within each asset class. So, this chapter outlines a framework for developing an investment portfolio customized to reflect your personal investment objectives, financial resources, and risk tolerance. Personalizing your retirement investment program in this manner entails four steps:

(1) choosing an initial portfolio allocation based on your position in the life cycle;

(2) refining this allocation based on your personal risk assessment;

(3) selecting an investment management philosophy; and

(4) establishing the primary fund categories from which to select your investments.

The chapter concludes with four case studies, each illustrating how to construct a personalized investment program.

The Asset Allocation Decision

The most critical step in developing a retirement investment program is to choose an asset allocation that is right for you. Your allocation is the balance you maintain in your investment program among the three primary financial asset classes: stocks, bonds, and short-term reserves.

As noted at the outset, the manner in which you allocate your assets will be a critical determinant of your long-term performance. How critical? Studies conducted on the performance of corporate pension plans suggest that as much as 90% of your investment return will be explained by asset allocation, and only 10% by your choice of individual investments. Ironically, many people approach investing as if exactly the opposite were true. They spend very little time on the asset allocation decision, instead devoting most of their energies toward trying to discern meaningful differences among particular mutual funds. Savvy investors, on the other hand, initially put aside considerations of which individual mutual funds to own, and instead focus on their portfolio allocation. As you consider the appropriate allocation for your own portfolio, you should take into account four critical factors: (1) your investment objectives; (2) your investment horizon; (3) your risk tolerance; and (4) your financial resources.

Your Investment Objective

If you are saving for retirement, your primary objective should be to accumulate sufficient assets during your working years to maintain your standard of living during your retirement years. This gradual shift from accumulating assets to spending assets, as illustrated in Figure 6–1, is known as the investment "life cycle." In investment terms, your objective during the accumulation years is to achieve growth in your capital; your emphasis during the distribution years of retirement shifts to income generation, plus a modest level of capital growth to protect against inflation. Along with your primary long-term retirement objectives, you should have a secondary objective as well: short-term liquidity. Most financial planners recommend that, in addition to your long-term retirement savings, you should maintain an emergency fund in a nonretirement account equal to three to six months' worth of living expenses during your working years, and six months' to one year's worth of living expenses during your retirement years. (This reserve is distinct from any short-term reserves that you may elect to hold in your retirement portfolio.)

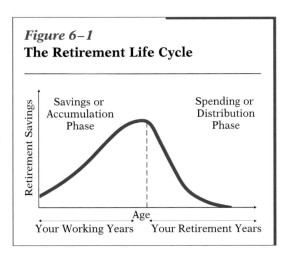

Figure 6–1
The Retirement Life Cycle

Your Investment Horizon

Your investment horizon can be measured on the scale of a human life span. On average, most individuals who reach the traditional retirement age of 65 will live into their 80s. Thus, when you begin to save for retirement in your 20s or 30s, you should anticipate an investment span of 50 to 60 years. Even after you reach your 40s and 50s, you still have an investment horizon of three to four decades.

As you age, your investment horizon obviously diminishes, so that by the time you reach your 80s it may extend 10 years or less. But if you plan to leave a portion of your retirement savings to your heirs, your investment horizon will extend well beyond your own life span. In contemplating your likely investment horizon, an important factor to consider is your own family history. If members of your family have lived into their 90s and you (and your spouse) are in good health, you probably should plan on your investment horizon extending as long as age 100.

Your Personal Risk Tolerance

Your asset allocation decision will also be influenced by your attitude toward investment risk. Since perceptions of risk vary from one investor to the next, two individuals with essentially identical personal profiles—the same income level, the same financial goals, the same Social Security benefits, and the same level of savings—may adopt quite different asset allocations.

Unfortunately, getting a feel for your level of risk tolerance is not a "cut and dried" issue. There is no risk scale to indicate whether you are a conservative, moderate, or aggressive investor. Nor are there set rules that link a specific asset allocation to your psychological attitude toward risk. That is, for some investors, a conservative investment posture may involve investing one-half of their savings in stocks; for others, a conservative posture may entail avoiding stocks altogether.

Assessing risk tolerance, then, tends to be more of an art than a science. Over the years, various questionnaires have been developed to assist investors in gauging their attitudes toward risk, but the fact remains that only you can provide a definitive answer to the question: What level of risk am I willing to assume? When all is said and done, it takes some knowledge of the workings of the financial markets to even begin to responsibly address this question.

Your Personal Financial Resources

Your financial situation will be the final factor that influences your asset allocation decision. If you feel that your financial situation is tenuous—for example, your company has been experiencing lay-offs—you may want to reduce your investment risk. On the other hand, if your finances are on sound footing, you may be able to assume a higher level of investment risk. When evaluating your financial situation, you should consider factors such as the stability of your job and career, current income relative to your income needs, your level of emergency savings, and additional income sources that will be available to you during your retirement.

Asset Allocation Recommendations

For retirement investors, the asset allocation decision begins with their position in the life cycle. In general, the earlier you are in the life cycle, the more aggressive your portfolio allocation should be.

As noted at the outset of this chapter, before you begin accumulating even one dollar in your long-term retirement program you should establish a short-term emergency reserve equal to at least three to six months' worth of living expenses. This emergency fund should be invested in some form of cash reserves, such as a money market fund or a bank certificate of deposit (CD), or perhaps a short-term bond fund. These monies are meant to be immediately accessible, and therefore should not be invested in a tax-deferred retirement plan where they may be subject to premature withdrawal penalties.

Once your emergency reserve is in place, you can then turn your attention toward determining the appropriate asset allocation for your long-term retirement program. For these assets, your initial portfolio allocation should be based on your position in the retirement life cycle, which encompasses four stages: (1) the accumulation years; (2) the transition years; (3) the early retirement years; and (4) the late retirement years.

Although your position in the life-cycle will dictate your initial asset allocation, your risk tolerance will play a decisive role in making your final allocation decision. As noted earlier, risk tolerance cannot be easily quantified, but you can gauge your sensitivity to risk by examining the historical record of investment losses on each of the four life-cycle portfolios. Looking at investment losses is a useful starting point since it captures the potential downside risk of each portfolio. That is, it measures the amount you might lose in any single year based on the suggested asset allocation. (Of course, it goes without saying that these risk measures are merely a reflection of history, and there is no guarantee that your portfolio will exhibit a similar level of volatility in the future.)

The downside risk of each life-cycle portfolio is measured in three ways. First, the frequency of annual losses over the period since 1926 is reviewed. Second, the magnitude of these yearly losses on average is examined. Third, the performance of the portfolio during the bear market of 1973–74—the worst bear market since the Great Crash of 1929—is considered. In the light of your reaction to the downside risks of each life-cycle portfolio, you may wish to reduce or increase your risk exposure by adjusting your allocation to common stocks, as suggested by the appropriate life cycle portfolio.

Before you move to the four life-cycle portfolios, keep in mind that these guidelines assume that: (1) you work most of your adult life; (2) your retirement assets are derived primarily from your personal savings (as opposed to a lump-sum inheritance); (3) you are saving on a regular basis; and (4) you retire sometime in your early 60s. If you have an interrupted working career, expect to receive a sizable inheritance, or plan to retire at a substantially younger (or older) age, you will need to modify these guidelines. In this case, you can make appropriate adjustments on your own or seek additional advice from a financial planner or adviser.

Accumulation Years (Age 20–49)

In your early and middle working years, when your investment horizon extends 40 years or more, your primary investment objective should be to accumulate capital for your retirement. At this point in your life, common stocks should be your dominant investment option, for two reasons: (1) stocks have provided the highest long-term total returns of any major asset class, and (2) while stocks also have had the highest volatility level of any asset class, the passage of time has a dampening effect on their short-term fluctuations. Although a 100% stock portfolio may be appropriate for accumulation investors in the earliest stages of the investment life cycle, few investors possess the necessary fortitude to commit all of their savings to stocks. For most investors, it is probably wise to maintain a modest investment in bonds as well. The recommended allocation during the accumulation years is 80% stocks/ 20% bonds.

How would this asset allocation have performed in the past? To calculate an historical return, the Standard & Poor's 500 Composite Stock Price Index can be used as a proxy for the returns on common stocks, and the long-term US government bond can be used as a proxy for the returns on bonds. Of course, while historical returns are useful in assessing the past

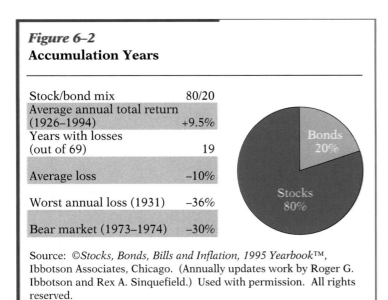

Figure 6–2
Accumulation Years

Stock/bond mix	80/20
Average annual total return (1926–1994)	+9.5%
Years with losses (out of 69)	19
Average loss	–10%
Worst annual loss (1931)	–36%
Bear market (1973–1974)	–30%

Source: ©*Stocks, Bonds, Bills and Inflation, 1995 Yearbook*™, Ibbotson Associates, Chicago. (Annually updates work by Roger G. Ibbotson and Rex A. Sinquefield.) Used with permission. All rights reserved.

performance of particular investments, they do not represent the returns that will be achieved in the future. Financial markets are unpredictable, and all that can really be said about the future is that investment returns will fluctuate.

In any event, using these two benchmarks, the total return for the 80%/20% stock/bond allocation would have averaged +9.5% annually from 1926–1994 (before taxes and any investment expenses). But this long-term *average* performance figure conceals more than it reveals in terms of the actual risks to the investor. For instance, if you held an 80/20 stock/bond mix during this period, you would have experienced a loss in 19 of the 69 calendar years. That equates to a loss in one out of every four years. The losses in these years would have amounted to about –10% on average. In other words, during these 19 "down" years, your savings would have been an average of 10% lower at the end of the year than at the beginning. In 1931, during the Great Depression (the worst single year on record for stocks), an 80/20 stock/bond portfolio would have declined a staggering –36%. During the 1973–1974 bear market, an 80/20 portfolio mix would have declined –30% over the two-year period. Figure 6–2 presents a profile of the accumulation years portfolio.

Transition Years (Age 50–59)

With a decade or so to go before retirement, your objectives are twofold. You'll want to continue accumulating assets for retirement, but you'll also want to preserve the capital you have accumulated so far. While stocks should continue to be your primary investment vehicle, it may be time to realize some of your stock market gains and gradually move to a more conservative investment stance. Your recommended asset allocation should approximate 60% common stocks/40% bonds.

Using the performance benchmarks described earlier, this allocation would have provided an average annual total return since 1926 of +8.5%. While this annual return is one percentage point lower than the return for the 80/20 stock/bond portfolio, the risk profile reflects a more conservative posture. The 60/40 mix would have resulted in 16 years with losses, averaging −8% annually during these years. The worst single year (1931) would have seen a decline of −28%, and the two-year bear market of 1973–1974 would have resulted in a drop of −22%. Figure 6–3 presents the profile of the transition years portfolio.

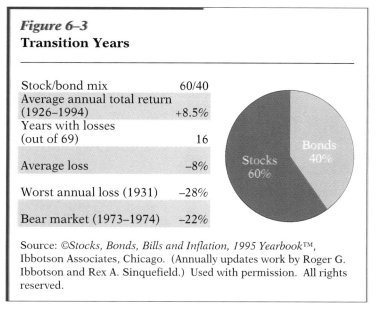

Figure 6–3
Transition Years

Stock/bond mix	60/40
Average annual total return (1926–1994)	+8.5%
Years with losses (out of 69)	16
Average loss	−8%
Worst annual loss (1931)	−28%
Bear market (1973–1974)	−22%

Source: ©*Stocks, Bonds, Bills and Inflation, 1995 Yearbook*™, Ibbotson Associates, Chicago. (Annually updates work by Roger G. Ibbotson and Rex A. Sinquefield.) Used with permission. All rights reserved.

Early Retirement Years (Age 60–74)

During retirement, you will begin to spend the capital that you have accumulated. At the same time, your investment horizon may still extend—given current life expectancies—20 or 30 years. So, some growth in savings is needed to protect your assets against the ravages of inflation. In this case, it seems appropriate to reduce your common stock commitment while moving some of your assets into shorter-term reserves. Your recommended asset allocation would be 40% stocks/40% bonds/20% short-term reserves.

To determine how the early retirement portfolio would have performed in the past, the 90-day US Treasury bill is used as a benchmark for short-term reserves. The 40/40/20 mix would have provided an average annual return of +7.3% going all the way back to 1926. Reflecting its more conservative asset allocation, this portfolio would have achieved an annual return well below those of the two prior recommended portfolios. But even this conservative allocation would have entailed 15 years with a loss, although the magnitude of the average loss (−5% annually) and the worst case scenario (−19% in 1931) are muted. This allocation also would have fared considerably better during the 1973–1974 bear market, declining −12% over the two years.

While the +7.3% return of the early retirement portfolio assumes that short-term reserves are held in a Treasury bill equivalent (such as a money market fund or a bank CD), you need not

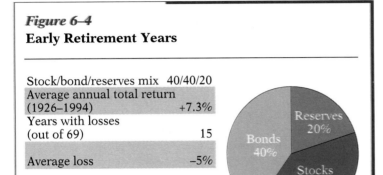

Figure 6–4
Early Retirement Years

Stock/bond/reserves mix	40/40/20
Average annual total return (1926–1994)	+7.3%
Years with losses (out of 69)	15
Average loss	–5%
Worst annual loss (1931)	–19%
Bear market (1973–1974)	–12%

Source: ©*Stocks, Bonds, Bills and Inflation, 1995 Yearbook*™, Ibbotson Associates, Chicago. (Annually updates work by Roger G. Ibbotson and Rex A. Sinquefield.) Used with permission. All rights reserved.

limit yourself to these investments. One alternative would be to substitute a short-term bond fund for a money market fund. While this substitution would barely alter your risk profile, it would nicely enhance your annual total return. Indeed, the returns on short-term bond funds have averaged about two percentage points higher than prime money market funds over the past 10 years. In any event, Figure 6–4 presents the profile of the early retirement years portfolio.

Late Retirement Years (Age 75+)

After age 75, for most people maximizing spendable income becomes the critical factor. However, stocks should still be included in your portfolio to diversify your holdings and protect your portfolio against inflation. This strategy involves shifting a portion of your stock holdings into bonds to arrive at a recommended allocation of 20% stocks/60% bonds/20% short-term reserves.

This conservative posture would have resulted in an average annual return of +6.0% from 1926–1994, more than 30% below the +9.5% return earned by an 80/20 stock/bond portfolio over the same period. (You may recall that an "all-Treasury-bill" portfolio would have earned but +3.7% annually.) Nonetheless, at this stage in the life cycle you can ill afford to incur dramatic fluctuations in the value of your total portfolio. The late retirement years portfolio would have experienced losses in 12 years, but these losses would have averaged but –3% annually. What is more, the worst annual loss would have been –12%, compared to –36% for the 80/20 portfolio. Finally, during the 1973–1974 bear market, this portfolio would have declined just –3%. Figure 6–5 presents the profile for the late retirement investor.

The clear message of each of these sample portfolios is that as you move through the investment life cycle, common stocks should play a significant role in your asset allocation when you are younger, while bonds should take on greater importance in your later years. As you move into the final stages of your life cycle, short-term reserves should also be added to your portfolio. It is interesting to note that in each case the portfolio returns are comfortably ahead of the +3% average rate of inflation during the 1926–1994 period.

Of course, as you would expect, the higher the allocation to stocks, the higher the average portfolio return has been. In that regard, as you review the respective total returns for each portfolio, do not underestimate the impact of seemingly marginal differences in annual return. For example, assuming annual investments of $2,000, the difference between, say, a +9% return and a +10% return over a 30-year period would mean the difference between a final accumulated value of $297,000 versus $362,000. This difference suggests that even investors who are in the later years of retirement might continue to allocate a fairly sizable portion of their retirement assets to common stocks—provided they can tolerate the incremental volatility.

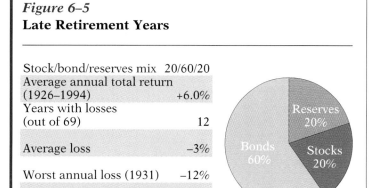

Figure 6–5
Late Retirement Years

Stock/bond/reserves mix	20/60/20
Average annual total return (1926–1994)	+6.0%
Years with losses (out of 69)	12
Average loss	–3%
Worst annual loss (1931)	–12%
Bear market (1973–1974)	–3%

Source: ©*Stocks, Bonds, Bills and Inflation, 1995 Yearbook™*, Ibbotson Associates, Chicago. (Annually updates work by Roger G. Ibbotson and Rex A. Sinquefield.) Used with permission. All rights reserved.

Fine-Tuning Your Portfolio Allocation

Now that you have four working models to use as your baseline, how can you use this information to choose an asset allocation that is right for you? First, you select an asset allocation based on your position in the life cycle. Then, you review the historical record on investment losses and determine if you are comfortable with the potential risks, taking into account your investment objectives and your financial resources. If the recommended allocation entails risks beyond the level that you are prepared to incur, you should adopt a more conservative approach, perhaps reducing the recommended stock allocation by 10 percentage points. By the same token, if you are willing to assume greater risk than the recommended portfolio, you may wish to choose a more aggressive allocation.

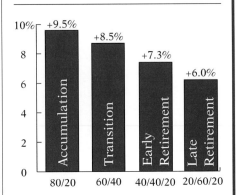

For example, suppose you are in your early 30s and are just beginning your retirement savings program. The life-cycle framework suggests an 80/20 mix of stocks and bonds. After reviewing the risks incurred by such a portfolio in the past, you feel comfortable with the recommended portfolio allocation, even though such a portfolio declined −36% in 1931 during the Great Depression, and −30% during the bear market of 1973–1974. In fact, you may be prepared to assume even greater risks. Since you expect to be saving for retirement for many years, the record of short-term losses may not concern you given the superior long-term results of the 80/20 portfolio. You may also work for a fast-growing company where your future earnings seem quite secure. Based on all of these factors, you decide to invest 100% of your portfolio in common stocks.

As another example, suppose you are in your 60s and are about to retire. The life cycle allocation suggests a 40/40/20 mix of stocks, bonds, and short-term reserves. While you want to earn the highest possible return that you can, you are very concerned with potential investment losses. According to the historical record, the recommended life cycle portfolio lost −12% during the 1973–1974 bear market. Over this two-year period, a $100,000 retirement portfolio would have fallen to $88,000. From your perspective, it simply may not be worth the anxiety associated with this level of risk. As a result, you might decide to adopt a less aggressive stance by holding 30% in stocks and 50% in bonds, with the remainder in short-term reserves. There will still be annual losses with this more conservative allocation, but they are likely to be smaller and less recurrent.

Both of these examples reinforce an important point about risk. There is no guarantee with any of these recommended asset allocations that you will be protected from investment losses. As illustrated in each portfolio profile, investment losses can be expected to occur with some frequency—historically about once every four to six years—whatever asset allocation you choose. With more aggressive portfolios, the losses are likely to be larger and more frequent; with more conservative portfolios, the losses are likely to be smaller and less frequent. In either case, the successful investor must recognize that these losses will occur, and accept them as part and parcel of investing.

Once you arrive at an appropriate asset allocation, the next decision you face in personalizing your investment program concerns investment management strategy. Mutual funds traditionally have been managed using an "active" investment approach. In the case of stock funds, active management simply means that portfolio managers select investments based on an evaluation of the factors that they believe have predictive value. More recently, investors have also been offered an alternative investment approach—indexing—which involves matching the performance and risk characteristics of a particular segment of the financial markets.

Whether you prefer active or passive management, you also must determine the segments of the financial markets in which to focus your investment strategy. Most investors will favor either growth funds or value funds for the core portion of their retirement portfolio. This section reviews some management style issues and suggests ways to determine the best fund mix to meet your long-term objectives.

Considering Management Styles

The first steps in personalizing your investment program are to determine an asset allocation based on your position in the life cycle and then to refine that allocation based on your risk tolerance. Then you are ready to consider the types of mutual fund investments that will compose your portfolio.

Index versus Active Strategies

Indexing, or "passive" management, is an investment management approach based entirely on quantitative methods. An index fund manager generally holds all of the securities that are included in a particular stock or bond market index, in the same proportion as they are represented in the index. (Index funds that track very broad markets may hold a representative sample of the securities in their benchmark indexes.) By comparison, traditional active fund managers select investments based on analytical research, judgment, and experience.

All active fund managers endeavor to outperform a broad-based market index, and, perhaps more importantly, the portfolios of other fund managers. From the perspective of active fund managers, the stock and bond markets are inefficient, and it is therefore possible to find undervalued securities that will provide higher returns than the broad market averages.

It may be obvious that all of these fund managers simply cannot be right. Indeed, all investors, in the aggregate, can perform no better than the market itself. Thus, for every investor who beats the market index by a given amount, there is another investor who must underperform the index by a like amount. The catch, as it were, is that all investors in the aggregate must match the return of the market *before expenses*. Therefore, when fund expenses and sales loads are taken into account, not to mention the costs of portfolio transactions, all investors actually must underperform the market index, which incurs no such costs. Given the drag that these costs represent on a fund's performance, it is easy to see the difficulty that active fund managers face in trying to beat the stock market with any consistency.

Index investors believe that the financial markets are relatively efficient, at least in the long run. They observe that all professional investment managers constantly seek to gain a competitive edge over other managers. However, once a manager discovers an "inefficiency" that results in superior performance, the market gradually adjusts to the inefficiency and eliminates any advantage that may have existed before. Thus, while a particular money manager may beat the market average over a short period of time, it is extremely difficult to sustain a long-term performance advantage.

Of course, there are a handful of "star" managers (e.g., Warren Buffet, John Neff, and Peter Lynch) who have beaten the market over very long periods. And there will surely be others who will do so in the future. But it is impossible to know in advance who this next generation of top-performing investment managers will be. More often than not, today's top-rated funds will "regress to the mean" (become average) over the long term. You have to decide if it is worthwhile risking below-average performance for the slim chance of selecting one of the few truly gifted (or lucky) investment managers.

As noted earlier, the case for selecting an index fund is compelling due to indexing's inherent cost advantage. Because index funds employ no high-cost advisers, they have minimal operating expenses and very low brokerage transaction costs (since they buy and sell securities infrequently). A typical low-cost index fund might incur expenses of as little as 0.20% annually. In contrast, the average actively managed stock mutual fund incurs operating and advisory expenses totaling 1.30%, as well as transaction costs that may total another 1% annually. This expense differential of 2.1% annually makes it extremely difficult for active fund managers to beat an index fund. In fact, academic studies have shown that only about two out of every five equity mutual funds have beaten the stock market average over time. The odds drop to one out of every five when fund sales charges are taken into account.

This index advantage can mean an enormous difference in performance over time. For example, as shown in Figure 6–7, over the past 20 years the Wilshire 5000 Index, an index that tracks the performance of all US common stocks, outperformed about two-thirds of all actively managed stock funds in 8 years and failed to outperform at least one-third only once (in 1982). The same general trend can be observed in a comparison of bond fund returns versus the returns of the Lehman Aggregate Bond Index, a broad index of investment-grade US bonds. While indexing can never promise the highest returns in any given year, by being consistently above average the index builds a formidable long-term record compared to the average active fund manager.

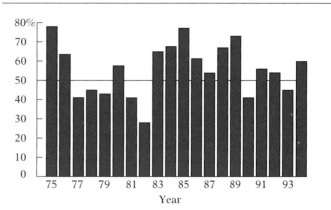

Figure 6–7

Percent of General Equity Funds Outperformed by the Wilshire 5000 Index, 1975–1994

Note: The returns of the Wilshire 5000 Index have been reduced by 0.2% per year to reflect fund costs.

Source: Wilshire Associates.

Given the natural competitive spirit of wanting to beat the market, many first-time investors seem to favor traditional active management. On the other hand, more-experienced investors, who presumably understand the difficulty of identifying in advance those fund managers who will provide superior investment returns over the long run, tend to choose an index fund for at least a portion of their total investment portfolio. Implicitly, large corporate and government pension plans also seem to recognize the fallibility of active investment management, as it is estimated that they have committed more than $400 billion in assets to index strategies.

This statistic is revealing since individual retirement investors share some important characteristics with large pension funds. Specifically, both are setting aside money that will not be needed for many years, and thus have long-term investment horizons. Both are making regular contributions to an investment program—irrespective of prevailing market conditions—and so need "all-weather" investment vehicles that are not tied to short-term investment management trends. Both want to minimize the costs of investing. And, finally, both have difficulty identifying investment managers who can deliver consistently competitive investment returns over time.

When it comes down to making the active fund versus index fund decision, most investors seem to favor one of three strategies, as outlined below.

All-Active Strategy   You may elect to use active management for your entire retirement portfolio. In taking an all-active approach, you incur the risk that a fund may underperform the market average, but you also have the opportunity to earn above-average returns. In any event, you should be prepared to spend considerable time learning about the many types of active funds that are available and examining their long-term records, expenses, management styles, and the like.

All-Index Strategy   In adopting an all-index approach, you expect to be rewarded with above-average returns over time because of indexing's sustainable low-cost advantage. However, you forfeit the opportunity to own one of the very best-performing mutual funds.

A "Core" Strategy   With a core strategy, employed by many large pension funds, a major component of your investment portfolio is indexed, with the remainder invested in actively managed funds. For example, you might invest one-half of your retirement savings in index funds and the rest in actively managed stock and bond funds that you believe have the potential to outperform the market over time. The main consideration here is what percentage of your savings to invest in indexed versus active accounts.

Mutual Fund Choices

Once you have determined how your portfolio will be allocated among index funds and active funds, you must then determine how your portfolio will be allocated among the various fund categories described in Chapter 5. The foundation of your retirement portfolio should consist of a diversified equity fund investing in US common stocks, and a diversified bond fund investing in investment-grade US bonds. If you are pursuing an index strategy, you should consider for your stock component a fund that tracks the performance of the Standard & Poor's 500 Index or the Wilshire 5000 Index. Both of these indexes provide broad exposure to the US stock market. If you are using actively managed funds, you should start with a broadly diversified "value" fund or "growth" fund.

As noted in Chapter 5, value and growth are broad terms for describing types of stock funds. Both value funds and growth funds seek to provide above-market total returns from investing in stocks; the styles differ in their emphasis on dividends versus capital growth in generating those total returns. Value funds emphasize stocks with above-average dividend yields and tend to appeal to more conservative, income-oriented investors. Value funds may make more sense in a tax-deferred account than a taxable account, since the high income component of value funds escapes current taxation. (While value funds are distinct from equity income funds, investors of a more conservative bent may want to substitute an equity income fund based on its lower volatility and higher dividend yield.)

Growth funds, on the other hand, emphasize capital growth over dividend income. They invest in companies with greater potential for sustainable long-term earnings growth and tend to appeal to more aggressive investors. Because of their lower income component, growth funds are particularly appropriate for high tax bracket investors with assets outside of a tax-deferred investment program. Table 6–1 summarizes the characteristics of growth funds, value funds, and a broad market index fund.

Not all stock funds can be easily categorized as having a value or growth objective. What is more, the terminology used to describe stock funds is not uniform across the mutual fund industry. A selection of funds identified as value funds may actually include equity income funds or even growth funds; growth funds are sometimes classified as growth and income funds or capital appreciation funds. Nonetheless, the growth and value distinction can be helpful in classifying the array of stock mutual funds that are offered in the marketplace, and it will allow you to make useful comparisons when selecting an actively managed stock fund for your retirement portfolio.

For the bond portion of your retirement portfolio, your fund choices are somewhat simpler. If you are pursuing an index

Table 6–1
Value Funds versus Growth Funds

Fund Characteristics	Value Funds	Growth Funds	Market Index Fund
Dividend income	Higher	Lower	Average
Capital growth	Lower	Higher	Average
Volatility risk	Lower	Higher	Average

strategy, the appropriate choice is likely to be a bond market index fund that tracks the entire bond market. A total bond market index fund will be invested largely in high-quality government securities and will maintain an intermediate-term average maturity. Depending on your risk profile, you may wish to invest in a discrete segment of the bond market, say, long-term bonds. In this case, you might select a bond index fund that matches the performance and risk characteristics of long-term bonds.

If you are using actively managed bond funds, you need to choose first between government and corporate bond funds, which differ in terms of credit quality and thus current yield. As is the case with index funds, your next decision relates to the average maturity of the fund—whether short-term, intermediate-term, or long-term. As noted in Chapter 4, this decision will determine your portfolio's level of exposure to interest rate (principal) risk and income risk. Finally, if you are in a high tax bracket and you are investing in a taxable account, you probably should consider municipal bond funds (instead of taxable bond funds) for your bond allocation.

Refining Your Fund Choices

It is possible to construct a diversified retirement investment program using only the basic types of mutual funds identified thus far. For the index investor, all that is needed are two broad-based index funds: one for stocks and one for bonds. For the investor interested in actively managed funds, a value or growth stock fund and a corporate or government bond fund will suffice. And for the investor pursuing a "core" strategy combining index and active management, four funds (two active, two index) would be the maximum number needed to establish a balanced retirement program.

Some investors, however, will want to augment their basic fund holdings with some of the other types of mutual funds described in Chapter 5. These funds generally will add an additional element of risk to your portfolio, but they may actually reduce the overall risk level of your portfolio through added diversification. Their inclusion may also offer the possibility of enhanced returns over the long run. For example, the stocks of small US companies have provided higher long-term returns than large blue-chip stocks. If you are willing to assume the added risk of including a small company stock fund in your portfolio, you should probably invest only a limited portion, say, 20%, of your retirement savings.

Similar refinements may be made to your bond fund holdings. Risk-tolerant investors might consider a high-yield or junk bond fund. In each case, remember that these additions to your investment program should be made "at the margin" since they inject an added risk dimension into your portfolio. As a general rule, your investment in any combination of these fund categories probably should not exceed 20% to 30% of your total retirement savings. Table 6–2 provides an overview of the major "supplemental" fund options.

Table 6–2
Refining Your Fund Choices

Investment Class	Type of Fund
Stocks	International fund Small company stock fund Sector fund
Bonds	High-yield bond fund

Some Implementation Issues

After the framework of your retirement portfolio is complete, you still need to consider several factors that will impact the long-term return on your portfolio.

Timing Your Investments

Even if you find it to be relatively easy to select an initial asset allocation for your retirement program, when it comes time to actually invest your monies, you may hesitate because of fears about short-term market fluctuations. You may ask yourself questions such as these: Are stocks at an all-time high? Are bonds "too expensive" relative to other investment alternatives? Is now the right time to invest? Surely there is nothing more disheartening than embarking on a long-term investment program only to have your initial investment fall in value because of a sudden market correction.

In dealing with this problem, some investors attempt to implement a "market timing" strategy. They wait to invest until stock or bond prices seem to be at an appropriate level relative to various historical measures (such as the ratio of stock prices to corporate earnings), or until some Wall Street expert declares stocks or bonds a "good deal." Then, these market timers rush to make substantial stock or bond investments "at one fell swoop." When prices reach what they regard as high valuation levels, as measured by historical benchmarks or expert opinion, these same investors rush to sell their investments, again at one fell swoop. As soon as the prices of stocks and bonds return to reasonable levels, the cycle begins again.

While this strategy sounds ideal in theory, in truth it is a "fool's errand." Few investors, even those with years of experience and access to the best analytical tools, can predict with any degree of accuracy the vagaries of the stock and bond markets. Professional and amateur investors alike frequently are led astray by the emotions of the financial markets. They may jump on the proverbial bandwagon and buy stocks just after a sustained rally, or, as happened in the bond and stock markets in 1987, they may panic when prices fall and sell at a loss.

What makes market timing even more difficult to execute successfully is that stock and bond market rallies tend to occur in brief spurts. So, market timers run the substantial risk of being "out of the market" during these precipitate market gains. The actual risk of being out of the market is startlingly high. Indeed, one study indicated that during the period from December 31, 1981, to August 25, 1987, stocks returned an average of +26.3% annually. But if you were out of the market on the 10 days when the largest price advances occurred, you would have earned an annual return of but +18.3%. Missing the 40 largest daily gains during this same period would have reduced your return by an unbelievable 84%, to +4.3% annually. Table 6–3 summarizes the results of this study.

One highly effective strategy to avoid the temptation of market timing is known as dollar-cost averaging. Simply put, dollar-cost averaging is a disciplined program of making systematic investments in the stock and bond markets, irrespective of current market conditions. You commit to investing a particular dollar amount on a set schedule, usually monthly, and then adhere to the program through good markets and bad markets alike. A dollar-cost averaging program can be set up through an employer savings plan, such as a 401(k) or 403(b) plan, or through electronic transfers from your checking account into a mutual fund investment program. You can also do it the old-fashioned way:

Table 6–3
The Cost of Being "Out of the Market" (1982–1987)

Investment Period	Average Annual Return	Percent of Return Missed
Entire 1,276 trading days*	26.3%	0.0%
Less the 10 biggest gain days	18.3	30.4
Less the 20 biggest gain days	13.1	50.2
Less the 30 biggest gain days	8.5	67.7
Less the 40 biggest gain days	4.3	83.7

*Period ending August 25, 1987.
Source: University of Michigan, *Bull Market of 1982–1987.*

the first bill you pay each month can be a check deposited to your fund account.

Over the long run, dollar-cost averaging helps market fluctuations work for you, rather than against you. That is, when prices decline, you buy more fund shares with each subsequent investment. When prices rise, you automatically buy fewer fund shares. For example, say you invest $250 every month. If your fund is selling at $10.00 per share in the first month, your $250 investment buys 25 shares. If the price declines to $8.50 per share in the second month, the same $250 investment buys 29 shares. Because you buy more shares when prices are lower and fewer shares when prices are higher, the average cost of your total accumulated shares will be below the average market price for all of the shares over the period you are investing. Table 6–4 illustrates a simple example of how dollar-cost averaging might work in a fluctuating market.

Dollar-cost averaging is an eminently sensible way to build your retirement portfolio. You should recognize, however, that dollar-cost averaging cannot assure a profit or protect you against a loss in declining markets. Nonetheless, a commitment to dollar-cost averaging reduces the odds of investing a large sum at a market high. It also eliminates the emotional factor from your savings program. As a long-term strategy, then, dollar-cost averaging is especially suited to retirement investing.

Table 6–4
Dollar-Cost Averaging

Month	Contribution	Price per Share	Number of Shares Purchased
1	$250	$10.00	25.000
2	$250	$8.50	29.412
3	$250	$11.00	22.727
4	$250	$10.80	23.148
Total shares purchased			100.287
Total investment			$1,000
Average price per share			$10.08
Average cost per share			$9.97

Portfolio Rebalancing

Rebalancing your portfolio is another discipline that you should consider as you personalize your retirement investment program. Rebalancing simply means periodically bringing your asset allocation back to its original target mix. For example, suppose you have selected a 60/40 stock/bond mix for your asset allocation. Following a strong period of stock performance, you find that you now have 75% of your savings in stock funds and 25% in bond funds. You have to decide whether you want to let your profits run, as it were, or return to your more conservative original asset allocation.

The most important reason for rebalancing is to maintain a consistent portfolio allocation. Your initial asset allocation is determined, in part, by the level of risk that you are willing to accept and the potential rewards that such a portfolio might offer. When your stock holdings rise above your original allocation, your risk exposure increases beyond the level that you determined at the outset. Conversely, if your stock holdings fall below their target level, your future earnings may be diminished. The same is true of the types of funds you use in your investment program. If you initially invested 10% of your portfolio in an international stock fund, you may wish to maintain the percentage at 10% in order to control your risk exposure. You may also want to keep the holding from falling much below 10%.

Another reason for rebalancing annually is that, as you age, it is important to revisit your retirement strategy. The strategy that you adopted as a 30-year-old may no longer be suitable once you have reached age 50. An annual rebalancing represents a good opportunity to review your risk profile and determine whether your initial investment strategy still matches your current needs. While an annual rebalancing should suffice, some investors adjust their portfolios quarterly, or even monthly. However, in the long run it is unlikely that such a level of precision will alter the long-term return of your portfolio to a measurable degree.

Before you do any rebalancing, be sure to take into account the impact of taxes and any transaction costs that you may incur, such as fund purchase or redemption fees. Of course, taxes are not a concern if you are rebalancing a portfolio that is invested in a tax-deferred retirement plan. But if your investments are held in taxable investment accounts, you will want to avoid selling appreciated investments in order to minimize capital gains taxes. As an alternative to selling shares in a particular fund to achieve your new allocation, you might consider rebalancing your portfolio by directing additional contributions to the lagging investment until you attain your desired mix. (Of course, while minimizing capital gains taxes is important, at some point you may have to sell an investment that no longer fits your investment strategy or has an especially poor track record.)

When all is said and done, rebalancing is an essential discipline that should be incorporated into your retirement investment program. Without rebalancing, your asset allocation will fluctuate along with the financial markets, and your portfolio risk profile could rise substantially. Through regular monitoring of your portfolio's asset allocation and fund mix, you can ensure that you maintain an investment portfolio that is suited to your personal objectives and needs.

Final Thoughts

At this point, you should have an understanding of the four steps involved in establishing your retirement investment program:

1. An initial portfolio allocation of stocks, bonds, and short-term reserves based on your position in the investment life cycle.
2. Any portfolio adjustments to reflect your investment objectives, risk tolerance, and financial resources.
3. A decision on the role of active versus passive management.
4. A decision on the types of mutual funds that will comprise your portfolio.

As you begin to apply these four steps to your own circumstances, the "Retirement Investment Program Overview" on the following page should serve as a helpful reference. You may also be interested in reviewing the four case studies that conclude this chapter. Each case study reflects a hypothetical investor in one of the four stages of the retirement life cycle and offers some counsel on how these investors might approach the establishment of their own retirement portfolios. You may be interested in reviewing all four case studies, or you might focus exclusively on the one that relates specifically to your position in the life cycle.

Once you have reviewed the case studies and completed the Strategy Checklist, the next step in implementing your retirement program is to gather and analyze information from mutual fund companies and other sources, and then begin the process of selecting individual mutual fund options. This challenge is discussed in Chapter 7.

Retirement Investment Program Overview

Here is a checklist you can complete to summarize your retirement investing strategy.

1. Initial Asset Allocation

Based on your position in the life cycle, identify your target asset allocation among stocks, bonds, and short-term reserves.

❏ 80/20/0 ❏ 60/40/0 ❏ 40/40/20 ❏ 20/60/20

2. Risk Assessment

After considering the potential risks and rewards of the suggested life-cycle allocation, my financial resources, and my investment objectives:

❏ I am comfortable with the risk profile of the suggested portfolio.
 •Allocation unchanged
❏ I can incur a higher risk profile than the suggested portfolio.
 •Increase stock allocation
❏ I am not comfortable with the risk profile of the suggested portfolio.
 •Decrease stock allocation

3. Active versus Index Management

❏ All-active. 100% of savings invested in actively managed stock and bond funds.
❏ All-index. 100% of savings invested in stock and bond index funds.
❏ "Core" strategy. Combination of actively managed and index funds.

Percent of index assets:	Total ____%	Stock ____%	Bond ____%
Percent of active assets:	Total ____%	Stock ____%	Bond ____%

4. Fund Choices

Identify the types of funds you plan to use in your investment strategy:

❏ Core stock funds.
 ❏ Value stock fund ____%   ❏ Growth stock fund ____%
 ❏ Market index ____%   ❏ Equity income fund ____%
❏ Core bond funds.
 Identify both fund type and average maturity:
 Type: ❏ Government ____%   ❏ Corporate ____%   ❏ Municipal ____%
 Average maturity: ❏ Short-term ____%   ❏ Intermediate-term ____%
  ❏ Long-term ____%
❏ Other funds (should be limited to no more than 20% to 30% of your total portfolio).
 ❏ International stock fund ____%   ❏ Sector fund ____%
 ❏ Small company stock fund ____%   ❏ High-yield bond fund ____%
 ❏ International bond fund ____%

Four Case Studies

The following four case studies encompass all of the aspects of personalizing an investment program.

Case Study 1: Anne DeVries

Anne, age 28, works as an account manager for a communications firm and is just beginning to participate in her employer's 401(k) savings plan. Though relatively new to investing, Anne realizes the importance of accepting investment risk in order to reach her long-term retirement goals. Her employer's 401(k) plan offers several investment options, including four actively managed stock funds, one stock index fund, one bond index fund, and a guaranteed investment contract (GIC). Having reviewed the framework in this chapter, Anne is wondering exactly how she should allocate her retirement savings.

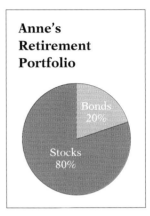

Anne's Retirement Portfolio

Step 1: Initial Asset Allocation   According to the life-cycle framework, Anne is in the accumulation years of her retirement program, with a long-term investment horizon. Her suggested allocation is 80% stocks and 20% bonds.

Step 2: Risk Assessment   After reviewing the historical information on potential investment losses and considering her investment objectives and financial resources, Anne feels confident with the 80/20 stock/bond mix. She feels that although her savings may experience short-term losses along the way, stocks are likely to offer higher returns than bonds and short-term reserves over the long run. (Of course, if she were uncomfortable with the potential risk, she might reduce her percentage commitment to stocks.)

Step 3: Index versus Active   The idea of indexing appeals to Anne because it means that her savings will perform in lock-step with the financial markets. She doesn't mind the volatility so much, as long as she is doing about as well as the market itself.

Step 4: Fund Choices   For her company savings plan, Anne decides to allocate 80% of her savings to a Standard & Poor's 500 Index fund and 20% to a long-term bond index fund.

Anne's contributions to her employer's retirement plan will be made through payroll deductions, one of the best ways to dollar-cost average. As for rebalancing, Anne's plan is to review her portfolio once a year and to adjust it as needed to maintain her original 80/20 allocation. Because she is investing through a tax-deferred plan, Anne can make these asset shifts without any tax impact.

Case Study 2: Leon Palandjian

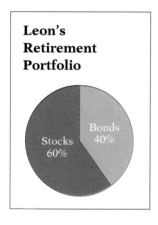

Leon's Retirement Portfolio

Stocks 60%
Bonds 40%

Leon, who has just turned 53, works at an engineering consulting firm. His company offers a defined contribution plan where he makes all of his own investment decisions. His savings are currently invested in two stock funds and a money market fund. He has also just received a small inheritance. Because of the increase in the stock market over the past decade, stocks currently comprise 85% of his total retirement savings. Now that he is approaching retirement, Leon is wondering what changes he needs to make to his employer's retirement program and what to do about his inheritance.

Step 1: Initial Asset Allocation   According to the life-cycle framework, Leon is in his transition years and should commit 60% of his savings to stocks and 40% to bonds.

Step 2: Risk Assessment   After his experience with investing in his employer's plan, Leon feels comfortable with the 60/40 stock/bond mix. Since his current allocation (85% of savings in stocks) is well above the recommended allocation, he wants to make some portfolio changes to ensure that the percentage of assets in stocks is reduced to a lower, less risky level.

Step 3: Index versus Active   Leon traditionally has used actively managed stock and bond funds.

Step 4: Fund Choices   Leon's retirement plan savings are currently invested in aggressive stock fund options; however, he feels that it may be time to move to more conservative stock funds that pay higher dividends. He has decided to move into an equity income fund and a value fund. For his inherited money, Leon plans to take an all-in-one approach by investing in a balanced fund that combines stocks and bonds in a single investment. He will look for a balanced fund that maintains a mix of stocks and bonds close to his target 60/40 allocation.

Within his employer's retirement plan, Leon must reduce his stock holdings from 85% of his portfolio to 60%, while at the same time moving money to more conservative stock fund options. To accomplish these objectives, he plans to shift savings in the aggressive stock funds to more conservative stock funds and to bonds. Leon feels that the move from aggressive stock funds to conservative stock funds can be made quickly without worrying about the timing of the switch. But when moving money from his stock funds into bond funds, Leon will proceed more slowly, making the shift over a period of months. Leon also plans to adjust his current plan contributions to reflect a 60/40 allocation.

As for his inheritance, Leon plans to invest the money immediately in a balanced fund. While there is some risk involved in investing his inheritance in one lump sum, Leon is willing to assume this risk since the inheritance represents only a small portion of his total investment savings.

Case Study 3: James Flynn

James, age 62, recently notified his employer of his intention to retire in several months. He is excited about the prospect of retirement and is planning an active life of traveling and community affairs. At the same time, James does have some concerns about his financial security—in particular, he is worried about how his retirement savings should be invested for the next 25 or more years. Social Security will provide the foundation of James' retirement program and will pay many of his fixed expenses, but he will need to supplement his Social Security benefits with his retirement savings.

James' Retirement Portfolio

James has three sources of savings for retirement: a lump-sum payment from his employer's pension plan (James has the option of taking the pension as a lump sum or as a fixed monthly payment); monies in his employer's 401(k) savings plan; and personal mutual fund investments.

Step 1: Initial Asset Allocation   According to the life-cycle framework, James is in the early years of retirement investing, so he should commit 40% of his long-term savings to stocks and 40% to bonds, with the remaining 20% in short-term reserves.

Step 2: Risk Assessment   After reviewing the risk profile of the suggested allocation, James is somewhat leery of the potential investment risks he is assuming. So, he decides to lower his stock commitment to 30% and boost his bond commitment to 50%, leaving 20% in short-term reserves.

Step 3: Index versus Active   James' approach to investment management is to utilize a core strategy. He plans to index one-half of his savings in order to assure some degree of relative predictability in his investment performance. At the same time, he believes he will have more time to spend reviewing potential investments, and therefore he intends to use actively managed funds for the remainder of his savings.

Step 4: Fund Choices   For the indexed component of his savings, James will use a Standard & Poor's 500 Index fund and an intermediate-term and a long-term bond index fund. For his non-indexed component, James' stock fund choices will center on more conservative, yield-oriented value funds. On the bond side, his preference is for corporate bond funds (because of their somewhat higher yields), with a combination of intermediate- and long-term average maturity funds to boost current income. The corporate bond funds will be used for his tax-deferred monies. James plans to use tax-free municipal bond funds for his personal bond investments because he will be in a high tax bracket during retirement.

James' lump sum from his employer's pension plan is eligible to be rolled over into an IRA. He intends to invest the money in a money market fund within the IRA and gradually dollar-cost average into stock funds and bond funds. Because he worries about financial market fluctuations, James plans to take three to five years to shift all of the assets. He will use an automatic exchange program offered by his mutual fund provider that automatically transfers money each month from his money market fund account to his stock and bond fund accounts.

James' 401(k) savings are also eligible to be rolled over into an IRA. Because his 401(k) monies are already invested in stock funds and bond funds (in roughly a 40/60 mix), James will invest them immediately without being overly concerned with short-term market risk. Finally, his personal mutual fund accounts are currently invested in growth-oriented stock funds. Although James knows he should take a more conservative investment stance, he doesn't want to sell all of these investments at once because of the capital gains tax he will have to pay. Instead, he will sell some of his stock funds over a period of years to lower his stock market exposure, moving the proceeds into tax-exempt bond funds.

Case Study 4: Cynthia Jackson

Cynthia has just reached her 76th birthday and is beginning a much-delayed review of her retirement portfolio. Her portfolio consists of IRA monies that originally came from an employer retirement plan and a personal mutual fund portfolio consisting of high-yielding stock funds, government bond funds, a money market fund, and a bank savings account. Currently, about 40% of Cynthia's long-term savings are in stock funds and 60% in bond funds. Her general concern is whether her overall portfolio is "on course."

Cynthia's Retirement Portfolio

Cynthia began taking required minimum distributions (see Chapter 10) from her IRA at age $70\frac{1}{2}$. The distributions have been deposited in her money market account, and, as a result, the balance in her money market fund has grown substantially. Cynthia is wondering whether these monies could be more effectively deployed.

Step 1: Initial Asset Allocation   According to the life-cycle framework, Cynthia has just entered the late retirement phase of retirement investing and so should commit 20% of her portfolio to stocks, 60% to bonds, and 20% to short-term reserves.

Step 2: Risk Assessment   After reviewing the historical data on investment losses and considering her personal finances, Cynthia feels comfortable with the recommended asset mix and the level of risk it implies. In fact, she would prefer to hold as much as 30% of her portfolio in stock funds. As for her short-term savings, she calculates that they now total nearly 30% of her total retirement portfolio.

Step 3: Index versus Active   Cynthia has always utilized actively managed funds in her retirement portfolio. Her approach has been to emphasize established mutual funds with below-average risk and investment holdings that she understands. She has read recently about indexing, and she thinks it might be worth experimenting with the concept for a portion of her bond investments.

Step 4: Fund Choices   Cynthia feels comfortable with her current stock and bond fund selections. Her only change would be the addition of a bond index fund.

To bring her current asset allocation (30/40/30 mix of stocks, bonds, and short-term reserves) into line with her target allocation (30/50/20), Cynthia plans to take the extra 10% in her money market fund and invest it in a bond index fund. That will bring her current asset allocation closer to the target she has set for herself.

Selecting Mutual Funds

I n Chapter 6, you saw that the starting point for building a successful investment portfolio is to conceive a personalized investment program by determining (1) how you will allocate your portfolio among stock funds, bond funds, and short-term reserves; (2) the extent to which you will emphasize actively managed mutual funds or index funds, or some combination of the two; and (3) a preliminary selection of fund types, such as growth funds or value funds, that may be suitable for inclusion in your retirement portfolio. Although personalizing your investment program in this manner will sharply curtail the number of individual funds to choose from, at some point you will have to select specific funds for your portfolio from among a huge group of fund options. How do you even begin to make well-reasoned choices?

The guidelines in this chapter address this fund selection issue by illustrating how to gather fund information, interpret past investment performance, and understand the impact of costs and taxes on your portfolio returns. By using these guidelines, you should find that the task of selecting funds is manageable, if not the model of simplicity.

Gathering Mutual Fund Information

With the rising popularity of mutual funds as an investment vehicle, information and analysis about mutual funds has become extensive. Perhaps the most widely available independent sources of fund information are the annual fund reviews published by *Business Week, Forbes, Money,* and other financial magazines. Each of these annual reviews provides broad coverage for a wide variety of funds and includes information on each fund's investment objectives, performance (both short-term and long-term), costs, investment managers, and account services. Pertinent articles on fund investing, asset allocation, and other topical issues typically accompany these annual fund issues.

Newspapers are also useful sources of information on mutual fund investing, and many large metropolitan newspapers have strengthened their fund coverage in recent years. For investors

Valuable information on investing in mutual funds is widely available, yet it can be daunting to sift through this material and arrive at an appropriate investment choice.

who want to monitor their funds' daily net asset values, *The Wall Street Journal* and most larger newspapers report fund prices in their business sections. *The Wall Street Journal* also offers daily updated performance data and fund rankings, a quarterly review of fund performance, and periodic articles on investing for novice and experienced investors. *Barron's,* the financial newsweekly, targets a more sophisticated investment audience, but it too covers topics of interest to fund investors of all stripes.

As the fund industry has grown, so too have the number of independent rating services that evaluate funds and fund performance. *Morningstar Mutual Funds* is particularly strong in this area. On a single page, its individual fund reports reflect an astounding amount of data about a fund, including long-term performance results, portfolio holdings, investment manager and tenure, expenses, portfolio turnover rates, potential tax liability, and similar information. Each summary fund page also includes a brief commentary by a *Morningstar* analyst. *Morningstar*'s comprehensive service can be purchased directly by investors and also may be available through your local public library. Other good sources of fund information include *Lipper Analytical Services, Inc.,* and *CDA/Wiesenberger Investment Companies Service.* Table 7–1 provides the address and phone number for the three major publications for mutual fund performance evaluation; Table 7–2 provides the address and phone number for three agencies that serve as valuable information resources for mutual fund investors.

Notwithstanding the valuable independent information available on mutual funds, for most investors the fund companies themselves will be the primary sources of fund information. The most important documents you will receive are the fund prospectus and the annual shareholder report, both of which will alert you to important facts about the fund that won't necessarily be disclosed in advertisements, in marketing literature, or by brokers and financial advisers. You should take advantage of the full disclosure requirements of the Securities and Exchange Commission and always review these documents carefully to determine if a fund is suitable for your investment program. Investors may also find a company's marketing and educational literature useful, but it goes without saying that such information generally should be viewed with a more skeptical eye.

Reading a Mutual Fund Prospectus

The mutual fund prospectus, like many legal documents, can be cumbersome to read, even for experienced investors. Part of the

---

Table 7–1
Mutual Fund Performance Services

Morningstar Mutual Funds
225 West Wacker Drive
Chicago, IL 60606
1-800-876-5005

Lipper Analytical Services
74 Trinity Place
New York, NY 10006
(212) 393-1300

CDA/Wiesenberger Investment Companies Service
1355 Piccard Dr.
Rockville, MD 20850
(301) 975-9600

problem is that much of the critical information is written in legalese, and you are left to sort out the "hidden" meaning. Fund sponsors contribute to this problem by not prioritizing the importance of information within the prospectus. For example, the prospectus for an aggressive stock fund may offer only a brief description of the fund's investment policies and risks. Ironically, the same prospectus might also include an in-depth discussion of how the fund's excess cash is invested each night. It is easy for novice investors to spend too much time on the unimportant details, while overlooking the more pertinent discussions of investment policies and risks.

The following section provides a framework for quickly reviewing a fund's prospectus. Remember that if you have any questions when reading a prospectus, you should not hesitate to call the fund's investor information department for additional details.

Investment Objective   Does the fund seek capital growth? Current income? Stability of principal? A combination of both? The prospectus should have a clear statement of the fund's basic investment objective. For money market funds and bond funds, investment objectives are usually clearly stated; for stock funds, objectives tend to be vaguely written at best and outright misleading at worst.

Investment Policies   The prospectus should describe the types of securities that the fund expects to hold. Most prospectuses list minimum or maximum percentage limitations for certain types of securities. For example, the fund's policies may require the manager to invest at least 80% of the fund's assets in US Treasury bonds. Alternatively, the fund's investment policies may limit international holdings to 25% of total assets. The fund's investment policies should also describe the extent to which the fund is permitted to purchase more speculative investments, such as derivatives, or to employ "hedging strategies" to manage the portfolio risk exposure.

Investment Risks   This section describes the risks engendered by the fund's investment objectives and policies. In most cases, the section on investment risk tends to be written in very general terms. Nonetheless, you should review this section carefully. If you don't understand the nature of the risks being discussed, ask questions before investing in the fund. If you still do not understand all of the risks, find another fund!

Table 7–2

Mutual Fund Information Sources

American Association of Individual Investors
625 N. Michigan Ave., Suite 1900
Chicago, IL 60611
(312) 280-0170

Investment Company Institute
1401 H Street N.W.
Suite 1200
Washington, DC 20005
(202) 326-5800

The Mutual Fund Education Alliance
The Association of No-Load Funds
1900 Erie St.,
Suite 120
Kansas City, MO 64116
(816) 471-1454

The risk disclosure in a prospectus should relate specifically to the types of securities being held by the fund. For instance, money market funds should focus on the quality of their portfolio holdings. Bond funds should emphasize the level of risk exposure in three primary areas: interest rate risk, credit risk, and income risk. Stock funds should compare the fund's expected volatility with that of the overall stock market. Stock funds that use terms such as *speculative, unseasoned,* or *above-average risk* are providing an obvious warning to conservative investors. International funds should give a full accounting of currency and political risks, as well as volatility risk.

Fund Costs   You should always know what it will cost you to invest in a particular fund. Since costs vary substantially from one fund to the next, it is important to understand all of the expenses you will incur. Fortunately, cost comparisons among funds are facilitated by the fee table found at the front of every mutual fund prospectus. Mutual funds costs are such a critical consideration in your fund selection analysis that they are addressed in a separate section near the end of this chapter.

Ten-Year Financial Table   Located near the front of every mutual fund prospectus is the 10-year financial table. The table covers the fund's "per share" financial results over the past decade, or, for funds that have been in existence for shorter periods, the life of the fund. The information in this table may be confusing for first-time investors since it is presented on a fiscal year basis, which is used for legal, tax, and accounting purposes, rather than a calendar year basis. It is important to remember this fiscal year convention when comparing the performance results of different funds.

The financial table incorporates several useful pieces of information. First, total returns are shown on a year-by-year basis. (Performance data may appear elsewhere in the prospectus, as well as in the fund's annual report to shareholders and in sales and marketing literature.) To gain a sense of the volatility of the fund's share price, take note of the annual changes in the fund's total return and in its year-end net asset values. If income is a primary concern, note the fund's yearly dividend payments. They will indicate how much income the fund has distributed in the past and whether that income has fluctuated or relatively stable over time.

The 10-year table also lists the fund's yearly expense ratio, which will indicate whether costs have declined as the fund has grown in size. If you are investing through an ordinary taxable account, check on the size and frequency of taxable dividends and especially capital gains distributions. (For information on capital gains, see page 124.) You should also note the level of accumulated unrealized capital gains that may be realized—and become taxable to you—in the future. The fund's portfolio turnover rate will tell you whether the fund buys and sells securities frequently or whether it takes a longer-term approach to investment management.

Investment Manager Since there is some evidence that successful funds tend to exhibit continuity of fund management, you should know the name, qualifications, and tenure of the fund's portfolio manager. A recent study by *CDA/Wiesenberger Investment Companies Service* found that changes in investment advisers can have a big impact on a fund's performance. The study found that funds with above-average past performance that changed investment advisers were much more likely to experience below-average returns than funds with above-average performance in which managers stayed put. On the other hand, funds with below-average performance tended to improve their results following a change in fund management. In any event, you should know whether a fund's record was achieved by the present management.

Shareholder Services The prospectus will explain how to buy and sell fund shares and will highlight related services such as checkwriting, whether there are free exchanges permitted to other funds within the fund family, the policy on telephone exchange privileges, the availability of automatic investment programs, and any minimum investment requirements.

Reading an Annual or Semiannual Report

Every mutual fund must provide its investors with an annual and semiannual performance update. Like the prospectus, however, the fund report also tends to suffer from an excess of legal and accounting jargon. So, you must read selectively to find information that is relevant and useful. Fund reports are also issued on a fiscal year basis; thus, performance comparisons with other funds must be drawn carefully.

One of the most useful pieces of information in the fund report is a listing of the fund's portfolio holdings. The holdings should help to clarify the fund's investment policies as stated in the prospectus. For instance, the portfolio holdings will tell you whether a US Treasury bond fund holds all Treasury securities or invests a portion of its assets in non-Treasury securities. The holdings will indicate whether a stock fund invests in blue-chip stocks whose names you easily recognize, or whether it emphasizes riskier medium- and small-sized emerging companies. You may also find out about any "surprise" holdings that you were not aware of (e.g., international stocks in a US stock fund or junk bonds in an investment-grade bond fund).

A related concern that may be addressed by looking at the portfolio holdings is the degree of portfolio concentration, which is typically measured by the percentage of fund assets invested in the top 10 securities. A concentrated fund may have 50% or more of its assets invested in its top 10 holdings. A more conservative fund offering may limit its top 10 holdings to no more than 30% of assets. Sometimes the fund report will provide this statistic; other times you will have to calculate the percentage on your own.

Although not required to do so, some funds will provide other important statistics, such as a breakdown of credit quality in a bond fund, industry concentration in a stock fund, or recent significant purchases or sales of securities. This information will reinforce and clarify the policies presented in the fund's prospectus.

To encourage fund companies to provide better information on investment performance, the Securities and Exchange Commission recently mandated that funds compare their 10-year performance record with a relevant broad-based market index, and illustrate the comparison using a 10-year line graph. This chart may appear in the fund's annual report or prospectus and must be accompanied by a message from the investment adviser explaining the fund's results.

You should make a point of reviewing this commentary from the fund sponsor and/or portfolio manager. This forum should be the ideal opportunity for the fund sponsor to offer a candid assessment of the fund's performance and investment strategy. Unfortunately, more often than not these reports contain little more than puffery. Ideally any message from the fund sponsor should address at least the following issues:

- How has the fund performed? Both short-term and long-term performance should be explained.
- How does the fund's performance record compare when measured against funds with similar investment policies? When compared to the broad market averages? The report should include long-term performance results for the fund, a group of competitors, and an appropriate market index.

- What factors explain the fund's performance? If a fund has performed well, the report should address the extent to which the returns reflect the skill of the adviser and the extent to which they simply reflect strong performance from the markets in which the fund invests. By the same token, if a fund has not performed well, the factors contributing to the shortfall should be documented.

A thorough fund report will address—at the minimum—all of these questions. If the commentary does not candidly discuss these issues, you should turn to independent sources for insight into the fund's performance.

Understanding Investment Performance

Ask investors for the one feature that they look for most in a mutual fund, and the response will be almost unanimous: investment performance. Investors want their mutual funds to "do well" in the future, and in pursuit of that goal, they look for funds that have "done well" in the past. If only it were so easy to identify future superior fund performance.

Unfortunately, many investors make two common mistakes in their pursuit of top-performing mutual funds. The first is a tendency to misinterpret historical performance data. Unless you review a fund's performance record carefully, it is easy to draw the wrong conclusions. The second is relying on superior past performance as a predictor of superior future performance. Surprisingly, numerous studies have indicated that superior past performance does not necessarily equate to superior future performance. Indeed, picking last year's winners rarely produces next year's winners, nor does picking a top performer over the past decade guarantee a top performer in the ensuing decade. In all, there is an overwhelming tendency for the performance of mutual funds to "regress to the mean." That is, the more extreme a fund's performance is relative to other funds over a given period, the more likely it is that the fund's performance will move closer to the average over the next period. Before selecting any fund for your portfolio, you should understand the implications of past performance and the linkage, if any, to future performance.

The convenience, professional management, and service offerings of a mutual fund are fine as far as they go, but for most investors the crux of the investment decision is performance.

Evaluating Past Investment Performance

Fund performance results appear regularly in fund advertisements, marketing literature, newspapers, magazines, and independent rating services. Thus, the opportunities for misrepresentation of these returns are significant. Without a doubt, it takes a certain level of skill and skepticism to get at the true meaning of past performance. Consider the following examples.

- "Earn 10% on your savings today," advised a headline in a financial magazine during a period when money market funds were earning only 3%. The 10% return seems enticing, until you read the fine print: the headline refers to the funds' returns during the past year, when more than one-half of their returns came from capital gains, which are unlikely to recur in the future.
- An advertisement for a stock fund states, "Up over 200% in the past 15 years." While that figure seems astounding at first blush, it is the equivalent of only 8% per year. Over the same period, an investor in a stock market index fund would have earned 700%, or 15% per year.
- A headline reports, "Top funds are up over 40% this year," a great disappointment to an investor whose own mutual fund has increased only a fraction of that amount. This particular investor, however, owns a conservative income fund, while the headline refers to high-risk small company funds.
- "Invest abroad for higher returns," suggests one international fund, buttressing its case with a table emphasizing recent returns. Unmentioned in the advertisement is that most of the fund's recent returns came from currency gains rather than the superior performance of foreign stock markets.

These examples offer ample evidence of how perplexing the performance claims of mutual funds can be. The following points should help you to sift through the hype and get to the reality of fund performance.

Understand the Components of Total Return   Mutual funds report their investment performance in terms of total return, which reflects the reinvestment of all income plus any capital appreciation. To get a better understanding of a fund's performance, you should determine how much of its total return came in the form of income and how much came in the form of capital growth. A fund's income return tends to be fairly stable from one year to the next, while capital growth is more spasmodic and unpredictable. By analyzing these two components of total return, you will have a clearer sense of whether a fund's past performance is likely to be repeated in the future.

In the first example above, it is true that some investors "earned 10%" on their savings by investing in bond mutual funds. But once you learn that one-half of the funds' returns came from an increase in bond prices (resulting from a sharp decline in interest rates), you would know that it is unlikely that the high capital component would be repeated in the coming year. You would also realize that you simply cannot compare the 10% returns on bond funds with the 3% yields being offered at the same time by money market funds and bank CDs.

Don't Be Misled by Cumulative Returns   Another source of confusion for investors is the reporting of fund returns on a cumulative basis, rather than on an average annual basis. The stock fund that advertises a "200% return" for a 15-year period is using large numbers to appeal to investors' emotions. The reality—an 8% average annual return—is far less likely to catch the eye of a prospective investor. It is almost always best to use average annual returns in your fund performance comparisons.

Even as you compare average annual returns, never underestimate the dramatic impact of compounding over long periods. A $10,000 investment earning 12% annually over a decade will grow to $31,060. Another investment earning 11% annually will grow to $28,400. In other words, a 1% difference in annual return may seem modest, but as you extend the investment horizon the difference becomes dramatic. In this case, the disparity in returns would amount to a 9% difference in the final value of your investment (i.e., $31,060 vs. $28,400).

Time Periods Matter   The time period over which performance is reported matters in several ways. First, all performance results are "period dependent." In order to make a judgment about a fund's performance, you need to understand the underlying financial and economic environment of the measurement period. For example, the 1980s was an exceptional decade for stocks and bonds, a fact reflected in the inordinately high returns on financial assets during that period.

Time periods also are a critical consideration when comparing the track records of two funds. Even a seemingly inconsequential difference in the measurement period of two funds can alter the relative comparison. For instance, if you compared the performance of one stock fund for the year ended October 31, 1987, with the performance of another stock fund for the year ended September 30, 1987, the latter fund's record would exclude the crash in the stock market that occurred on October 19, 1987.

Needless to say, the first fund would be at a distinct disadvantage in a head-to-head performance comparison. To encourage consistent performance comparisons, the Securities and Exchange Commission requires that all fund marketing literature and advertisements report one-, five-, and 10-year total returns as of the most recent calendar quarter.

One final point about time periods: the longer the period covered by the performance data, the more reliable your interpretation of the fund's record will be. While comparing returns over a one-year period will be of little value in differentiating the relative merits of two funds, comparing returns over a decade—especially year-by-year returns, which indicate how a fund's performance varied over time—is a telling piece of information.

Consider Sales Charges and Taxes   When evaluating past performance, don't forget to consider the impact of any sales charges and taxes. Reported fund returns rarely take into account the impact of any sales commissions on the fund's performance. For a fund that charges a sales load of 5%, a one-year return of, say, +10% would drop to +5%—a 50% performance reduction. Over a period of five years, a +10% average annual return would decline to +9% annually—still a 10% reduction to the investor.

Performance results also ignore the impact of taxes on your return. If you are investing through a taxable account, you should investigate how the investment policies of a fund (e.g., the rate of portfolio turnover) may impact your after-tax return.

Compare "Apples with Apples"   Evaluations of fund performance are only relevant when you compare funds with similar investment objectives and policies. You cannot fairly compare the return on a money market fund with the return on a stock fund. The risk and return characteristics of the underlying investments are too dissimilar.

Even when comparing two funds within the same asset class, you need to be diligent in your analysis. For example, while both value funds and growth funds invest in common stocks, each often provides disparate returns over different time periods. When value funds prosper, growth funds often languish, and vice versa. You will have better results with your fund selections if you compare "value with value" and "growth with growth." In this regard, a fund's portfolio holdings may be a useful reference. If one value fund holds only US stocks, whereas another holds a significant portion of its assets in international stocks and junk bonds, you probably should not be comparing the two funds' records head to head.

Compare a Fund with an Unmanaged Index   It is revealing to compare a fund with a market index, not only on a performance basis, but on a risk basis as well. By observing the extent to which a fund falls short of (or exceeds) a stock or bond market index, you can gauge how effective the fund's investment manager has been in adding value over a market index rate of return. (Remember that the performance of an unmanaged index does not include the "real world" costs of investing, and therefore represents tough competition for all cost-burdened mutual funds.)

The recommendation to compare apples with apples also applies when comparing a fund to a market index. A broadbased US stock fund should be compared with a broad US stock market index, such as the Standard & Poor's 500 Composite Stock Price Index or the Wilshire 5000 Index. A small company stock fund, on the other hand, would be more appropriately matched with an index of small company stocks, such as the Russell 2000 Index. As shown in Table 7–3, indexes exist to cover virtually every sector of the stock and bond markets.

Table 7–3
The Major Market Indexes

Common Stocks

Standard & Poor's 500 Composite Stock Price Index—Tracks 500 large-capitalization stocks representing about 70% of the value of all US stocks.

Wilshire 4500 Index—Tracks the portion of the US stock market not included in the Standard & Poor's 500 Stock Index.

Wilshire 5000 Index—Tracks the entire US stock market.

Russell 2000 Index—Tracks small company stocks.

Morgan Stanley Europe, Australia, and Far East (EAFE) Index—Tracks the world's major non-US stock markets.

Morgan Stanley Europe Index—Sub-index of the EAFE that tracks European stocks.

Morgan Stanley Pacific Index—Sub-index of the EAFE that tracks Pacific Rim stocks.

S&P/BARRA Growth Index—Sub-index of the S&P 500 Stock Index that tracks stocks with "higher than average" ratios of market price to book.

S&P/BARRA Value Index—Sub-index of the S&P 500 Stock Index that tracks stocks with "lower than average" ratios of market price to book.

Bonds

Lehman Brothers Government Bond Index—Tracks US government agency and Treasury bonds.

Lehman Brothers Corporate Bond Index—Tracks fixed-rate, nonconvertible, investment-grade corporate bonds.

Lehman Brothers Mortgage-Backed Securities Index—Tracks fixed-rate securities of the Government National Mortgage Association (GNMA), the Federal National Mortgage Association (FNMA), and Federal National Loan Mortgage Corporation (FHLMC).

Lehman Brothers Aggregate Bond Index—Tracks some 5,000 investment-grade fixed income securities, weighted by the market value of each security.

Investment Fundamentals Many investors don't fully understand the fundamentals of investing and therefore may have unrealistic expectations about a fund's future performance. For instance, money market funds represent a low-risk haven for emergency reserves and should not be expected to match the performance of more volatile bond funds. In the same context, bond funds should not be expected to generate sustainable capital growth over the long run. While the steady decline in interest rates that began in the mid-1980s has resulted in substantial capital returns for bond funds, inexperienced investors may view these yield driven price gains as a sustainable component of the investment returns on bond funds. When interest rates reverse their protracted decline, these investors may be severely disappointed.

With respect to stock funds, do not be lulled into believing that the +15% annual returns earned on stocks over the past decade are "the norm." In fact, these returns are well above the +10% historical average. On a related note, many investors have a tendency to buy "styles" of mutual funds—say, small company funds—*after* these funds have enjoyed a long period of excellent returns. These investors may not have the long-term perspective to recall the numerous periods when these same funds were distinctly poor performers. In the same vein, some international investors seem surprised when currency risk reduces their returns, even though such risk goes hand-in-hand with international investing.

Once you understand how to analyze a fund's past performance record, you have to decide how much weight to give fund performance in the selection process. As noted earlier, even if the long-term record of the fund you are considering compares favorably with similar funds, and even if the fund has outpaced a relevant broad-based market index, there is still no necessary linkage between the fund's past performance and its future performance.

Does the Past Prologue the Future?

Numerous research studies have indicated that a stock fund's superior past performance is rarely repeated in the future. Obviously, there will always be some funds that are "top performers"; the problem lies in identifying these funds in advance. As an illustration of this dilemma, consider the record of the *Forbes* Honor Roll. Each year, *Forbes* magazine prepares a list of the top-performing stock funds—the Honor Roll—as part of its annual mutual fund issue. Among the factors that *Forbes* considers in selecting funds for the Honor Roll are total return over at least 10 years, performance in "up" and "down" markets, and continuity of portfolio management. In essence, the Honor Roll funds are the "star" performers that, based on their long-term records, should provide investors with above-average returns in the future.

Unfortunately, as shown in Figure 7–1, when you examine the performance of the Honor Roll funds, the expectation exceeds the reality by a wide margin. Indeed, if you had invested equal amounts in each of the funds included in the *Forbes* Honor Roll since its inception in 1974, making any subsequent changes as the list was updated each year, you would have earned an annual rate of return of +10.7%, taking into account any applicable sales commissions. While this return is satisfactory in an absolute sense, it fell short of the +11.8% annual return achieved by the average equity mutual fund, and finished well behind—nearly two percentage points annually—the +12.3% return earned by the market as a whole.

Figure 7–1
The *Forbes* Honor Roll (1974–1994)

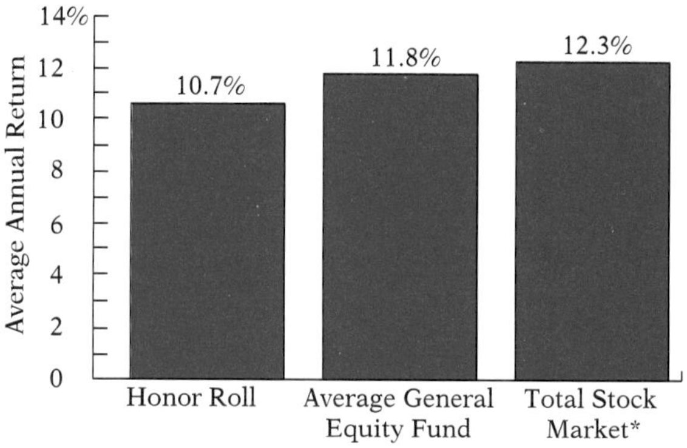

*Wilshire 5000 Index (adjusted for annual expenses of 0.20%)

Source: The Vanguard Group.

As this example illustrates, it is one thing to identify funds that have provided superior returns in the past; it is quite another matter to use this information to predict the top-performing funds of tomorrow. Even a method such as that employed by the *Forbes* Honor Roll, using sensible criteria based on past performance, proves unreliable as a predictor of superior future performance.

Given the limited predictive value of past performance, how can you use fund performance to aid in the selection of particular mutual funds? Here are some guidelines:

Look for Demonstrated Investment Skill   Despite the limited value of past fund performance in identifying the best future fund performers, it still makes sense to select funds that have demonstrated a reasonable level of investment competence in the past. As a general rule, you should probably limit your selections to funds that have ranked—over an extended period—at least in the top half of all funds in their category.

Relative predictability of returns is also a good barometer. When a fund's returns seem erratic compared to the returns of other funds with similar investment objectives, it could be evidence of an undisciplined investment approach.

Avoid the Very Worst Performers   While superior past performance may not lead to superior future performance, there is evidence that funds with poor relative performance records tend to remain at the bottom of the fund performance rankings. One of the reasons may be that the worst-performing funds also tend to have the highest costs, which of course represent an ongoing "drag" on performance.

Consider Costs   The one undisputed fact of investment performance is this: costs represent a certain reduction in investment returns. In the case of money market funds, costs are virtually the sole determinant of relative investment performance. With few exceptions, if you want to be assured of owning a top-performing money market fund, choose the fund with the lowest costs. (Since all index funds will presumably be able to match the performance of their respective indexes before costs are taken into account, the top-performing index funds will also invariably be of the low-cost variety.)

In the case of actively managed bond funds, there is some limited opportunity for an investment manager to add value above the market averages. More often than not, however, the relative performance of bond funds is determined by their stated investment policies (the quality level and average maturity of the portfolio holdings) and costs. While costs are not the sole determinant of relative performance among bond funds with similar investment policies, fund expenses are so influential in the long run that higher-cost bond funds generally should be avoided.

In the case of actively managed stock funds, the relationship between costs and performance is tenuous. The difficulty with stock funds is that the flexibility of their investment policies allows funds with identical investment objectives to incur substantially different levels of risk. While a stock fund with a 2% expense ratio and a 5% front-end load is at a considerable disadvantage relative to a similar low-cost, no-load fund offering, the high-cost fund may endeavor to close this "cost gap" by incurring more "risk." Nonetheless, all other factors held equal, it seems sensible to choose a no-load fund over a load fund and a low-cost fund over a high-cost fund.

When making your final fund selections, three simple rules should help: (1) never pay a sales charge; (2) avoid the highest-cost funds, period; and (3) view with considerable skepticism all funds with above-average costs.

Ignore Short-Term Performance   If the long-term track record of a fund has dubious predictive value, a fund's short-term performance results are virtually meaningless as a guide to selecting mutual funds. Short-term returns typically are driven by short-lived market conditions: a sudden resurgence of value stocks versus growth stocks, a brief rally for small company stocks, short-term currency fluctuations in international markets, or an unexpected rise or fall in interest rates in the bond market. Quite often, the top-performing funds over shorter time periods are invested in narrow segments of the stock market enjoying a sudden surge in popularity. Buying mutual funds on the basis of transitory market movements is one of the biggest mistakes an investor can make.

Set Realistic Performance Expectations   In the final analysis, it is important to set realistic expectations for the future results of your mutual fund holdings. Given the hyperbolic performance claims touted by many mutual fund sponsors, investors may find it difficult to comprehend the enormous challenge of providing superior investment performance over the long run. A stock fund that consistently beats the market average by 1% annually—after taking into account all costs—is exceptional. Yet inexperienced investors often expect their funds to exceed market averages by 5% or more each year. That kind of performance record is rare—if indeed it ever occurs.

In this age of heightened consumer awareness, all investors should know what they are paying to invest in a particular mutual fund. Costs vary widely among mutual funds, and you can reap substantial savings by eschewing high-cost funds and investing in low-cost equivalents. Because costs represent a certain reduction in your total return, the higher a fund's costs the less likely the fund is to provide above-average performance over time.

Mutual Fund Costs

It is interesting the number of people who will clip a $.50 coupon from the newspaper, yet never give a thought to the fees that they will pay over a lifetime of investing.

Fund investors incur costs in three ways: (1) through sales commissions; (2) through expenses incurred in the operation and management of the fund; and (3) through transaction costs paid by the fund when buying and selling securities.

Sales Commissions

In the early days of the mutual fund industry, all sales commissions were incurred at the time a fund purchase was made. As investors became more conscious of the negative impact of sales loads on their performance, other types of commissions emerged. The most common types of sales commissions are front-end loads, back-end loads, and 12b–1 fees.

Front-End Loads   This traditional sales commission is levied when you purchase fund shares, and typically ranges from 4% to 6%. So-called low-load funds are load funds that assess a reduced sales charge, generally in the area of 1% to 3%. Front-end loads are deducted from your initial investment.

Back-End Loads   These sales charges are incurred when you redeem your fund shares. Back-end loads may be assessed either as a percentage of the value of your redemption or as a flat fee. In many cases, the percentage that you pay for a back-end load decreases by, say, one percentage point for each year that you are invested in the fund, up to a total of six years. In the interim, you typically pay a 1% annual fee based on your average account balance. While the load may be eliminated in the seventh year, you will still have paid the equivalent of a 6% load over the six years. When a back-end load is assessed in this manner, it is called a contingent deferred sales load.

12b–1 Fees   These fees generally are used to pay for distribution-related expenses. Like fund operating expenses, they are assessed as a percentage of your average net assets, and must be included in the fund's stated expense ratio.

You should recognize that paying a sales commission, whatever the type, has no bearing on the quality of the investment management services you will receive from a fund. These commissions essentially are fees paid to a salesperson for directing assets to the fund. Nonetheless, some investors continue to harbor the notion that high fees and commissions equate to better investment management. If you need advice on selecting particular funds, it may be worth paying a commission to a financial adviser or broker. But the advice given must outweigh the costs of the advice.

Operating Expenses

These include both the advisory fee charged by the fund manager and the expenses incurred in the administration of the fund's daily operations. Operating expenses are expressed as a percentage of a fund's average net assets for the year. For most funds, this expense ratio will fall in a range of 0.25% to 2.50%, with some funds charging expenses outside these two extremes.

In general, the level of fund expenses is related to the investment objective of the fund. For example, advisory expenses typically will be higher for funds—such as small company stock funds—where extensive research is conducted in the selection of fund investments. In contrast, advisory expenses will generally be lower for funds that do not require as much investment research, such as money market funds. Surprisingly, even among funds with the same investment objectives, expenses often vary significantly.

Portfolio Transaction Costs

Transaction costs are incurred in conjunction with the buying and selling of securities and reflect brokerage commissions as well as the market impact of a transaction. These costs are not reflected in the expense ratio or sales commission reported by a fund. Instead, transaction costs are paid directly out of fund assets and have the effect of reducing the fund's investment return. The greater the volume of buying and selling by the fund, the greater the drag on the fund's investment return from brokerage commissions and other transaction costs. Thus, you should review a fund's rate of portfolio turnover for an indication of the potential impact of transaction costs on the fund's future returns.

The Fee Table

Mutual fund costs can be easily compared by referring to the fee table presented in the front of every mutual fund prospectus. This table breaks down all of the fees incurred by the fund, and it also presents the fund's total expense ratio. Cumulative expenses are expressed in terms of dollars paid on a hypothetical $1,000

Table 7–4
Mutual Fund Fee Table

	Fund A	Fund B	Fund C
Shareholder Transaction Expenses			
Sales load imposed on purchases	None	None	7.25%
Sales load imposed on reinvested dividends	None	None	7.25%
Redemption fees	None	None	None
Exchange fee	None	None	None
Annual Fund Operating Expenses			
Management expenses	0.13%	0.94%	0.70%
Investment advisory fees	0.20	—	—
Shareholder accounting costs	0.08	—	—
12b–1 fee	—	0.50	—
Distribution costs	0.02	—	—
Other expenses	0.03	0.46	0.25
Total Operating Expenses	0.46%	1.90%	0.95%

investment at the end of one-, three-, five-, and 10-year periods, assuming a +5% total investment return on the fund.

Table 7–4 illustrates a sample fee table showing all expenses and fees that shareholders of three hypothetical mutual funds would incur. The purpose of this table is to assist you in understanding the impact of costs and expenses on investment return. Table 7–5 illustrates the expenses that a shareholder would incur on a $1,000 investment in each of these funds over various time periods, assuming (1) a +5% annual rate of return, and (2) full account redemption at the end of each period.

It could take several chapters to provide an in-depth examination of the relationship between mutual funds and taxes. While you do not need to be a tax expert before you invest in mutual funds, you should be familiar with some basic tax rules so that you can avoid some of the tax pitfalls that fund investors encounter.

Although the next few pages should provide you with a good foundation for understanding tax implications in your investment portfolio, there are more comprehensive sources of tax information that you might consider. One valuable tax reference is Publication 564, *Mutual Fund Distributions*, available from the Internal Revenue Service. (The IRS may be reached toll-free at

Table 7–5
Mutual Fund Fee Table

	Fund A	Fund B	Fund C
1 year	$ 5	$ 19	$ 82
3 years	15	59	101
5 years	26	99	121
10 years	58	207	181

Mutual Funds and Taxes

Most investment managers ignore the tax impact of their investment decisions on fund shareholders. Indeed, over a typical decade it is likely that 100% of an equity mutual fund's capital growth will be subject to taxation.

1-800-TAX-FORM.) Large mutual fund companies also publish annual tax guides, and books on mutual funds often address tax issues as well. When in doubt about any tax issue, you should contact an accountant, lawyer, or other qualified tax professional for expert assistance.

From the outset, you should know that taxable fund accounts are governed by one set of tax rules and tax-deferred fund accounts by another. In fact, tax-deferred plans are governed by many sets of rules, which vary from one type of plan to the next. There is one set of rules for IRAs, another for employer "qualified" retirement plans, and still others for nonprofit 403(b) plans, 457 government plans, annuities, and so on. While Chapter 8 addresses many of the tax issues for these tax-deferred plans, the tax rules are complex and you may need expert assistance in dealing with them. In contrast, the rules governing taxable mutual fund accounts are fairly straightforward.

Reporting Your Fund's Taxable Income

Perhaps the easiest aspect of mutual fund taxation is reporting the taxable income distributed by your fund. Your taxable income will be reported to you on IRS Form 1099-DIV, issued in late January. You are responsible for reporting this income on your federal income tax return (and any state and local returns) by the appropriate filing deadline.

Taxable distributions on mutual funds come from two sources: (1) dividends, which represent income earned on the fund's underlying securities; and (2) net capital gains, which are realized by the fund on sales of securities that have appreciated in value. Capital gains that are designated as "short-term" are treated as ordinary dividend income for tax purposes. Long-term capital gains are currently taxed at a maximum rate of 28%. The procedures for reporting dividends and capital gains are described in the IRS instructions accompanying your tax return.

Calculating Your Gains or Losses

While reporting your fund's taxable distributions is relatively easy, determining your own capital gains or losses on sales of fund shares can be a frustrating experience. Whenever you sell shares of a fund, you are responsible for determining whether or not you realized a capital gain or a capital loss. To calculate your gain or loss, the Internal Revenue Service permits you to use one of four "cost basis" methods: (1) first-in, first-out (FIFO), (2) specific identification, (3) average cost single category, and (4) average cost double category. The four approaches are explained in IRS Publication 564.

Using one of these four methods, you must first calculate how much it cost you to acquire the fund shares that you sold. In tax terms, this is the "cost basis" of your investment. The cost basis is deducted from the proceeds you received from the sale of your fund shares. (The proceeds of the sale are reported to you on Tax Form 1099-B.) The net result is your capital gain or loss, and this figure must be reported on Schedule D of your federal income tax return as well as your state and local tax returns.

In response to investor demand for assistance in calculating capital gains and losses (and in response to pending Congressional legislation), many mutual fund companies have begun to offer "tax cost" services. These services calculate your gains and losses for you, typically using the "average cost single" method. You may save substantial time using these tax services, or they may help to lower your accountant's fees. In any event, before you invest in a fund, check and see if the fund sponsor offers such a service.

Tax-Exempt Funds

For taxpayers in the highest tax brackets, the potentially higher after-tax yields of municipal money market funds and municipal bond funds may make them appropriate alternatives to taxable funds. Municipal funds typically pay lower pre-tax yields than taxable funds, but their "tax-adjusted" yields should be superior for high tax bracket investors.

Interest income from municipal bond funds is generally exempt from federal income taxes. In addition, if a fund invests primarily in the debt obligations of the state in which you reside, the fund's dividend income will be exempt from state and local taxes as well. Some municipal bond funds also generate "tax preference items," which may affect high-income taxpayers who are subject to the federal Alternative Minimum Tax (AMT). You should note that, while dividend income from municipal funds escapes federal taxation, capital gains distributions do not. They are fully taxable at the federal level and may be subject to state and local taxes as well.

One final tax exemption worth noting applies to funds that invest in US Treasury securities. All income that is derived from US Treasury obligations is exempt from state and local taxes in every state. The rules governing the tax exemption vary somewhat from state to state, so check with your state tax authority for details. Of course, federal income taxes will still apply to US Treasury income, but in states with high income tax rates (such as California, up to 11%; New York, up to 7.59%; and Massachusetts, 12% tax rate on investment income) the tax exemption on Treasury income may be quite lucrative.

In addition to *tax-exempt* funds, a new type of mutual fund—the *tax-managed* fund—is now available. These funds employ specific strategies to minimize an investor's tax liability, such as holding stocks that provide low income yields, holding portfolio turnover to very low levels, and offsetting realized gains with realized losses. There is also a tax-managed balanced fund, which holds only municipal bonds for its fixed-income portion.

Avoid the Year-End "Tax Trap"

At the end of each year, funds must distribute to investors all of the net capital gains that they have realized during the year. If you are a taxable investor purchasing a fund just prior to these year-end distributions, you may find yourself facing a substantial tax liability. To avoid this potential tax consequence, it may be prudent to delay your investment until after any large year-end distributions.

For example, suppose you invest $10,000 in a fund at $10 per share and receive 1,000 shares. The day after you invest, the fund declares a $2 per share capital gains distribution. You must now report $2,000 in taxable income for the year ($2 per share capital gain times 1,000 shares), even though you were invested in the fund for just one day. (Of course, if you are investing through a tax-deferred retirement plan, this issue would not be relevant.)

Be "Tax Smart"

Some of the tax consequences of your investment strategy were addressed in Chapter 6, but it is worth reviewing two points:

1. If you are investing through a taxable investment account, emphasize low-yielding growth funds rather than high-yielding value funds. In this manner, you will minimize your current taxable dividend income.

2. As you change your portfolio allocation over time, try to minimize the extent of capital gains realization from the rebalancing. It's always more tax-effective to adjust your asset allocation by adding new contributions to a lagging investment, rather than selling an appreciated investment.

Selecting a Financial Adviser

If you are convinced that you simply do not have the ability to establish a retirement investment program on your own, then you might consider using the services of a financial adviser.

A financial planner or adviser may be invaluable in helping you to sift through the many aspects of retirement planning, from setting your portfolio allocation to selecting specific portfolio investments. Your attorney or accountant should be able to refer you to a financial planner with expertise in retirement issues. Or you can call any of several national professional organizations for the names of members who are financial planning practitioners in your community.

Since financial planners are not covered by any uniform state or federal regulations, their qualifications and business practices vary considerably. Top-flight financial planners are highly trained, with knowledge of accounting, tax and estate laws, pension planning, and investment management. They will also have certification from one or more professional organizations in the financial planning field. You should be wary of individuals who hold themselves out as financial planners but do not have appropriate training or certification. The wide variety of professional certifications for financial planners can lead to confusion for those who are not familiar with the planning profession. Here is a summary of the relevant certifications:

Certified Financial Planner (CFP). This designation is awarded by the International Board of Standards and Practices for Certified Financial Planners in Denver, Colorado.

Chartered Financial Consultant (ChFC). Planners with the ChFC designation usually are also insurance agents or have an insurance industry background. The ChFC is awarded by The American College in Bryn Mawr, Pennsylvania.

Chartered Financial Analyst (CFA). The CFA designation is awarded by the Association for Investment Management and Research in Charlottesville, Virginia. Financial planners who are CFAs often have a background as stock market analysts and professional money managers.

Personal Financial Specialist (PFS). This designation is awarded by the American Institute of Certified Public Accountants in New York City to CPAs who meet certain qualifications. Financial planners with the PFS designation often have a background as tax specialists.

Fees versus Commissions

Financial planners are compensated in two basic ways: through fees or commissions. Fee-only planners often charge by the assignment. For example, they may have a minimum charge for preparing a comprehensive financial plan, with an escalating scale of higher fees for clients with substantial wealth or complex financial circumstances. They also may offer financial consultation on an hourly basis or charge for investment advice with a flat fee based on the dollar value of your investment portfolio.

Commission-only financial planners expect you to purchase insurance or investment products from them, compensating them for their services through commissions on the sale of those products. Some planners charge a combination of fees and commissions, in some cases agreeing to reduce or offset their fees by the amount of any commissions they earn from you. Before you hire a financial planner, you should understand how the planner will be compensated. Ask for full written disclosure of all fees and commissions, and for information about incentives, bonuses, or anything else of value that the planner is eligible to receive if a client buys a particular product. Do not hire a financial planner who is reluctant to provide full disclosure of all compensation in advance.

After checking a prospective financial planner's references, professional credentials, and compensation, be sure that you are personally comfortable with the planner you want to hire. Can he or she explain complex tax or investment issues in simple words that you can understand? Do you feel you are talking to a professional adviser, and not a salesperson? A good financial planner will approach your assignment by looking at the whole of your personal life, financial circumstances, and investment goals, and provide objective advice based on your particular needs.

Final Thoughts

This chapter concludes Part Two, "Make Your Retirement Investments Work for You." As a summary to this section, here is a final checklist of some "Do's" and "Don'ts" of investing.

The "Do's" of Fund Investing

- **Do establish your investment strategy.**   Asset allocation, not the selection of mutual funds, is the most critical retirement investment decision you will make. Among the factors you should consider in arriving at your portfolio allocation include these: your position in the life cycle, your investment objective, your risk tolerance, and your financial situation.

- **Do consider index funds.**   In designing your investment program, consider establishing your "core" portfolio holdings in stock and bond index funds. Given their low costs, relative performance predictability, and broad diversification, index funds represent an ideal foundation on which to build your retirement portfolio.

- **Do consider balanced funds.**   All it takes to get started with your retirement program is a balanced mutual fund (60% stocks, 40% bonds). With this simple strategy, you can obtain a high level of diversification in a single portfolio.

- **Do be skeptical of past performance.**   Future performance cannot be predicted based on past performance, although funds that have been consistently poor performers over extended periods do tend to repeat their sub-par performance. Also, when you look at a fund's performance record, evaluate it in the context of the performance of other funds with the same investment objectives and policies, as well as in the context of the overall financial markets.

- **Do pay attention to costs.**   Over the long run, costs will have a dramatic impact on your investment return. For money market funds and index funds, low costs should be virtually your only consideration in selecting a fund. For bond funds, costs will be a critical concern, but other factors may also impact your selections. For stock funds, the cost argument is not as compelling, but costs should nonetheless be a strong consideration. All other factors held equal, choose a low-cost fund over a high-cost fund.

- **Do dollar-cost average.**   Dollar-cost averaging is a disciplined investment approach that every investor should use for a long-term investment program. With dollar-cost averaging, you make regular investment contributions regardless of market movements, mitigating some of the risks of investing.

The "Don'ts" of Fund Investing

- **Don't invest in "hot" funds.**   One of the worst ways you can begin your investment program is by simply picking the top-performing funds over the last month, quarter, or year. Many of these funds earned spectacular returns because of temporary market movements or because they invest in narrow segments of the stock market. These "hot" investments usually will "cool" soon enough and will be replaced by another round of short-term stars.

- **Don't pay a sales commission.**   You should never pay a sales commission to buy a mutual fund unless you receive a level of advice and guidance from the salesperson sufficient to offset the commission. Remember that paying a sales load does not mean that you have invested in a better-performing fund. On the contrary, the load will make it harder for the fund to match the return of a similar no-load fund. In short, if you don't require the services of a salesperson or adviser, don't pay a sales commission.

- **Don't accept cold calls.**   If a sales pitch sounds too good to be true, it probably is. Your decision to purchase a mutual fund should be preceded by thoughtful consideration on your part.

At the end of the day, when you think about all of the investment advice that is offered by financial experts, the news media, and all would-be prognosticators, perhaps the best advice is this: Choose an investment strategy that you are comfortable with, invest small amounts on a regular basis, stay with your strategy through market rallies and declines alike, and then retire and enjoy the results of your investment program.

BUILD A COMPLETE RETIREMENT PROGRAM

Getting the Most from Retirement Savings Plans

To encourage retirement savings, the federal tax code provides for several types of tax-favored retirement plans. Each of these plans permits some form of tax deferral on investment earnings until the assets are withdrawn from the plan or paid out as benefits. In many cases, contributions to these retirement plans may be fully or partially tax deductible as well.

This chapter provides an overview of the different types of tax-favored retirement plans. It begins by reviewing the traditional employer-sponsored plans—the defined benefit plan and the defined contribution plan—as well as other popular variations, such as 401(k)s, Keoghs, SEPs, and 403(b) plans. The chapter also addresses the following questions:

- If you are a participant in an employer-sponsored plan, what should you do to maximize your retirement plan benefits?
- If you are a sole proprietor or business owner, what types of retirement plans should you consider for yourself and your employees?

The chapter concludes with a review of two "personal" retirement programs: the individual retirement account (which still holds considerable advantages for many investors) and the variable annuity.

Traditional Employer-Sponsored Retirement Plans

Roughly one-half of all US workers are covered by an employer-sponsored retirement plan. If you work for a relatively large corporation, the chances are you currently participate in such a plan. If you're not covered by an employer plan, the burden of your retirement benefits will be derived principally from Social Security and your personal savings. Employer-sponsored retirement plans generally can be divided into two broad categories: the defined benefit plan and the defined contribution plan.

Most US workers look to their employers to provide a pension that will furnish a significant portion of their retirement income.

The Defined Benefit Plan

The defined benefit plan represents the traditional form of retirement plan offered by large and mid-sized corporations. These plans typically promise a retirement benefit or pension based on two factors: (1) your salary prior to retirement, and (2) your total years of service. For example, you might be covered by a defined benefit plan that promises you an annual pension equal to 1.5% of your average annual salary over your final five years of employment multiplied by your total years of service. Under this type of formula, if you retired with 30 years of service, you would receive a pension equal to 45% of your final five-year average annual pay.

Under a defined benefit plan, the employer makes contributions to the plan to pay for the expected costs of the promised pension benefits (as determined by an actuary). As a result, the employer bears virtually all of the risk associated with the plan's investments. That is, if the defined benefit plan's investments lose money or don't earn enough to meet future pension liabilities, the employer must make additional contributions to ensure that the plan can meet its employee benefit obligations.

The Internal Revenue Code sets a limit on the amount of annual pension benefits that can be provided to you under a qualified defined benefit plan. That limit, adjusted annually for inflation, is $120,000 for 1995 (or 100% of your average annual pay during your three highest consecutive salary years, if less). In most cases, pension benefits are guaranteed up to a certain monthly limit ($2,574 in 1995) by the Pension Benefit Guaranty Corporation, an agency of the federal government.

For More Information

- **Your Guaranteed Pension** and **Your Pension: Things You Should Know About Your Pension Plan**
  Write for either booklet in care of:
  Pension Benefit Guaranty Corporation
  2020 K Street N.W.
  Washington, DC 20006
- **What You Should Know About the Pension Law**
  Write for it in care of:
  Pension and Welfare Benefits Administration
  US Department of Labor, Room South 2524
  200 Constitution Avenue N.W.

The Defined Contribution Plan

Defined contribution plans are generally simpler, more flexible, and less costly to administer than defined benefit plans. For these reasons, defined contribution plans are being adopted in significantly greater numbers than defined benefit plans. Nearly all large employers sponsor a defined contribution plan as a supplemental retirement savings plan to their defined benefit plan (the "core" retirement plan). Many mid-sized to smaller employers sponsor one or more defined contribution plans to provide both core retirement and supplemental savings benefits to their employees.

A defined contribution plan is an "individual account" plan, which means that a separate account is established in your name to record the plan contributions on your behalf and the associated investment gains and losses. Unlike a defined benefit plan, a defined contribution plan does *not* promise or guarantee you a particular level of pension benefits at retirement. Rather, your final benefits will depend on the total contributions made to the plan on your behalf and on the rate of return earned by those contributions.

The Internal Revenue Code sets a limit on the annual contributions that can be made on your behalf to a defined contribution plan. That limit is the lesser of $30,000 or 25% of your current-year pay. Beginning in 1996, this $30,000 limit may be adjusted annually for inflation. Unlike a defined benefit plan, the defined contribution plan offers no guarantee by the federal government of your pension benefits.

Many defined contribution plans permit you to select the particular investments for the contributions made to the plan on your behalf. In managing your defined contribution plan assets, you are typically allowed to choose from among several investment options. Under this type of "participant-directed" plan, *you* bear the responsibility if your selected investments do not provide adequate returns to meet your retirement needs.

There are several different types of defined contribution plans. Some of the more common forms include the following.

Profit-Sharing Plan   This is the most flexible type of defined contribution plan from the employer's standpoint, since it generally allows the employer to determine how much—if any—is contributed to the plan each year. In most cases, annual profit-sharing plan contributions are allocated to employees in proportion to their current-year compensation.

Money Purchase Plan   This plan is less flexible than the profit-sharing plan but allows for potentially larger contributions. Unlike a profit-sharing plan, a money purchase plan requires that the employer commit to contributing a fixed amount or a fixed percentage of compensation every year (say, 15% of pay) on behalf of each participating employee.

Thrift or Savings Plan   This is a plan where employees are permitted to contribute to the plan with the employer agreeing to match all or a fraction of their contributions. For example, a thrift plan might provide that for every dollar an employee contributes to the plan the employer will contribute 50 cents on the employee's behalf.

Employee Stock Ownership Plan (ESOP)   This is a special type of plan that is generally designed to invest in the stock of the sponsoring employer. In addition to fostering employee ownership, an ESOP offers special tax advantages and favorable financing opportunities for the employer.

The 401(k) Revolution

In recent years, a new variation of profit-sharing/thrift plan, the 401(k) plan, has come to dominate the world of defined contribution plans. 401(k) refers to a section of the Internal Revenue Code, added in 1978, which authorizes this type of employer-sponsored plan. Although only a few 401(k) plans appeared in the late 1970s and early 1980s, thousands of employers soon rushed to offer what quickly became an extremely popular employee benefit. Nearly all large employers currently offer 401(k)s, and increasing numbers of smaller employers are providing them as well. In just a little more than a decade, the assets in 401(k) plans have grown to where they now represent the lion's share of the financial assets of many households.

While there are different types of 401(k)s, the following features are commonly found in most companies' plans.

Pretax Contributions   The vast majority of 401(k)s are salary reduction plans that permit you to make regular pretax contributions to the plan through convenient payroll deductions. Under this type of arrangement, your 401(k) pretax contributions are deducted from your current-year pay for federal and state (with the exception of Pennsylvania) income tax purposes. For example, if you earn $50,000 and make $5,000 of pretax contributions to your 401(k), your taxable salary is reduced to $45,000. If you pay federal and state income taxes at a combined 40% rate, you receive an immediate income tax savings of up to $2,000. The Internal Revenue Code limits the level of pretax contributions you may make each year to a 401(k) plan to an indexed dollar amount (which is $9,240 for 1995).

Employer Matching Contributions   Many 401(k) plans provide for matching contributions by the employer. In fact, nearly all large companies match some portion of each employee's pretax contributions, and one out of every four matches contributions dollar for dollar up to specified levels. Matching contributions are a powerful incentive for employees at all income levels to participate in a 401(k) to the maximum extent possible.

Plan Loans and Hardship Withdrawals   Many 401(k) plans allow you to borrow money from your plan account (which you must repay, with interest). In addition, most plans permit you to make hardship withdrawals from your account to cover certain contingencies, such as medical expenses, the purchase of a principal residence, or college tuition.

It's easy to see how this special package of benefits—pretax contributions resulting in current-year tax savings, employer matching contributions, and access to savings through plan loans and withdrawals—has made 401(k)s so popular with employers and employees alike.

Other Types of Retirement Plans

Here is a brief summary of several other types of employer-sponsored retirement plans.

Keogh Plans   Keogh plans are simply qualified defined benefit or defined contribution plans that cover self-employed individuals, such as sole proprietors or partners. Today, the rules for Keogh plans are essentially the same as those governing the qualified plans of large corporations. (Keogh plans are discussed in greater detail later in this chapter.)

403(b) Plans   A 403(b) plan, also known as a tax-sheltered annuity (TSA), is a special type of retirement plan for employees of public schools and other tax-exempt organizations, such as colleges, universities, hospitals, and churches. A 403(b) plan can work like a 401(k) plan by allowing employees to make pretax salary reduction contributions (the current 403(b) limit on pretax contributions is $9,500 per year). A 403(b) can also provide for employer contributions. However, the law permits only two types of funding arrangements for 403(b) plans: (1) annuity contracts with insurance companies, and (2) custodial accounts invested in mutual funds (often called 403(b)(7) accounts). If your employer is an eligible school or nonprofit organization, you may be permitted to arrange for an individual 403(b) plan directly through an insurance company or mutual fund.

Simplified Employee Pension (SEP)   As its name implies, a SEP is a simple retirement plan designed primarily for smaller businesses. A SEP permits employers to make tax-deductible contributions directly to the individual retirement accounts (IRAs) established for their employees. A more complicated variation of the SEP, called the Salary Reduction Simplified Employee Pension (SARSEP), permits employees to make pretax salary reduction contributions, much like a 401(k) or 403(b) plan. (SEPs and SARSEPs are discussed in greater detail later in this chapter.)

Nonqualified Deferred Compensation Plans   Many employers offer nonqualified deferred compensation plans that do not meet the Internal Revenue Code's rigorous requirements for qualified retirement plans. In most cases, these nonqualified plans, sometimes referred to as excess benefit plans or supplemental executive retirement plans (SERPs), are established for highly paid employees to make up for the tax code's limitations on contributions and benefits under qualified plans. The major risk associated with nonqualified plans is the lack of protection from the employee's perspective. That is, in many cases, nonqualified plans are not funded with monies to cover future benefits. What is more, even in cases where nonqualified plans are funded, the monies are generally not protected from the creditors of the company in the event of bankruptcy.

Maximizing Retirement Plan Benefits

If you are covered by an employer-sponsored retirement plan, there are some simple methods to maximize your benefits under the plan.

After reading about all of the different employer-sponsored retirement plan options, you may be concerned that you are not taking full advantage of the opportunities available to you. You also may be wondering whether your employer's plan will provide you with sufficient income to meet your retirement needs. This section offers some suggestions to help you address these two issues.

Learn about All Relevant Provisions and Options of Your Employer's Plan

The first step in maximizing your retirement plan benefits is to learn all that you can about your employer's plan. Whether your employer sponsors a defined benefit plan or a defined contribution plan, you are entitled to receive the following information about the plan.

Summary Plan Description   This is a particularly important document that explains the fundamental features of your employer's plan, including eligibility requirements, contribution formulas, vesting schedules, benefit calculations, and distribution options. You should receive a copy of the summary plan description within 90 days of becoming a participant in the plan. You should also receive copies of any updated versions of the summary plan description.

Individual Benefit Statement   The law does not require that you be provided with personal statements showing your benefits under the plan. However, it is common practice for many plans, especially 401(k) plans, to send participants periodic statements showing their current account balances or accrued benefits. If individual benefit statements are not automatically sent to you, you are permitted to request such a statement once each year from the plan administrator. At a minimum, your individual benefit statement should list your total accrued benefits under the plan and your vested and nonvested portions. Make sure that you retain copies of your individual benefit statements.

Summary Annual Report   This report describes the plan's aggregate financial status over the past year. This report is particularly meaningful if you are a participant in a defined benefit plan since it shows the overall funding status of the plan.

Survivor Benefits Explanation   This notice describes the survivor benefits available to spouses under certain types of pension plans. If your plan has such a provision, this explanation must be provided to you between the ages of 32 and 35.

Once you have gathered all of this information, you should be able to determine the following about your plan.

Participation   On what date did you become—or will you become—eligible to participate in the plan? Your employer's plan may require you to reach age 21 and to complete one year of service before you are eligible to participate. (Plans that provide for immediate 100% vesting may require up to two years of service.)

Contributions   If your employer's plan is a defined contribution plan, what types of contributions are permitted or required to be made to the plan by you? By your employer? What's your current account balance under the plan for each contribution type?

Benefits   If your employer's plan is a defined benefit plan, what is the formula for calculating the pension you will receive upon normal retirement? Is there a reduced early retirement benefit? What is your current accrued benefit under the plan?

Vesting   When do you become vested under the plan? Becoming vested under a retirement plan simply means that you have been credited with enough years of service to ensure that you receive your plan benefits even if you leave your job prior to retirement. Employees who are 100% (or fully) vested will be entitled to the full value of their accumulated benefits. Those who are 40% vested will receive 40% of their accumulated benefits, and so on.

By law, your employer's plan must provide you with 100% vesting after no more than seven years of service. Common vesting schedules in employer-sponsored plans include (1) five-year "cliff vesting" (i.e., 0% vesting for the first five years of service and 100% vesting after the fifth year of service), and (2) three- to seven-year "graded vesting" (i.e., 20% vesting after three years of service, with an additional 20% vesting per year of service thereafter, until you reach 100% vesting after seven years of service). Figure 8–1 shows how vesting might work under each alternative.

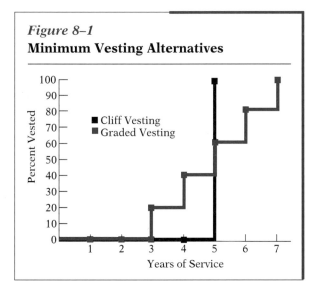

Figure 8–1
Minimum Vesting Alternatives

In-Service Withdrawals/Loans   Are you permitted to withdraw any of your benefits under the plan prior to retirement? Are you permitted to borrow amounts from the plan? Under what terms and conditions?

Distribution of Benefits   When will you be entitled to receive distributions of your benefits under the plan? In what form— annuity, lump-sum, installments?

If your plan is a *participant-directed* defined contribution plan, in which you are responsible for managing your investments, you should obtain from your plan administrator all relevant information concerning the plan's investment privileges and options. At a minimum, this information should include a description of each available investment option under the plan, its risk and reward characteristics, fees, expenses, and so on. If prospectuses are available for your plan's investment options, it would be worthwhile to obtain and review this information prior to making your investment selections.

Maximize All Contribution/Deferral Opportunities Available under Your Employer's Plan

If your employer's plan provides for employee pretax or after-tax contributions, it is generally to your advantage to contribute as much as you can to the plan (assuming the plan is appropriately invested). This is clearly the case with thrift or savings plans in which your employee contributions are matched by employer contributions. Even plans that do not offer employer matching are worthwhile since your contributions grow on a tax-deferred basis. And if your plan allows contributions to be made on a pretax basis (i.e., it is a 401(k), 403(b), or SARSEP), your contributions will reduce the amount of your income that is subject to current-year taxes. Over time, the combination of pretax contributions and tax-deferred earnings can produce significantly greater retirement savings than a conventional investment program.

For example, assume you pay federal and state taxes at a 40% rate and you save $3,000 each year in a taxable investment program. If you earn a +8% pretax total return over a 20-year period, the final value of your account (after reduction for taxes on investment earnings) would amount to about $102,000. Now assume that you save for retirement by making pretax contributions to a 401(k), 403(b), or SARSEP. Because of the current-year tax savings, you can effectively make annual pretax contributions of $5,000 at the same "cost" as a $3,000 after-tax annual investment. Assuming you earn the same +8% annual return, your tax-deferred account would total $247,000—a 142% increase—at the end of 20 years.

Of course, your tax-deferred account will be subject to taxation when you begin receiving withdrawals at retirement. But even taking this factor into account, your retirement savings will be substantially greater than through the taxable investment program. Indeed, even assuming a relatively "worst case" scenario, where you remain in the 40% tax "bracket" at retirement and elect to withdraw all your retirement savings in one year with no favorable tax treatment, your net after-tax savings of $148,000 would be $46,000 greater—a 45% increase—than through the conventional taxable investment program.

Take the Time to Invest Prudently and for the Long Term!

At first blush, this suggestion may not seem to be particularly enlightening. The important point, however, is to recognize how critical your investment decisions can be in determining your ultimate retirement savings under a participant-directed plan. In the preceding example, you invested $5,000 a year in a tax-deferred account earning a +8% annual return, resulting in a $247,000 balance after 20 years. If your investments were to earn +10% annually (about the average annual return on common stocks over the past 30 years) rather than +8%, your account would total $315,000 at the end of 20 years, a 28% increase. The message is clear: it pays to do your homework and make every effort to ensure that you have invested your retirement plan assets in an appropriate manner, with a focus on the long term.

Never Access Your Retirement Plan Savings Prior to Retirement unless an Emergency Arises

This is simply the flip side to the second suggestion that you contribute as much as you can to a tax-deferred retirement plan. There are several reasons why you want to defer withdrawing assets from your retirement plan until the latest date possible. The first is that the taxes and penalties for preretirement withdrawals can be draconian, particularly if you are already in a high tax bracket by virtue of your current-year wages. Indeed, taking into account the 10% penalty tax on withdrawals before age $59^{1/2}$ (discussed in Chapter 10), you could pay more than 50% federal and state taxes on a retirement plan withdrawal—even if it's a hardship withdrawal!

The second reason is that by withdrawing assets from your retirement plan, you are forfeiting the important benefit of generating future tax-deferred earnings on those assets. Therefore, the recommendation would be to put as much of your first investment dollars into retirement plans as soon as you can, and take out your last dollars as late as you can. (One possible exception to this recommendation would be in cases where you are actively seeking to avoid the 15% tax on "excess" distributions over $150,000, as discussed in Chapter 10.)

Determine the Extent to Which Your Employer Plan Will Provide Adequate Retirement Security

You should perform periodic projections to determine the extent to which your employer's plan, along with your Social

Security benefits and personal savings, will provide you with sufficient income for your retirement. As noted in Chapter 1, you will need about 70% to 80% of your current income to maintain your standard of living during retirement. To the extent that you expect to need additional retirement income, your options include (1) contributing more to your employer's plan, if possible; (2) reexamining your investment options (if your employer's plan is a participant-directed plan) to make sure that your investment selections are not too conservative; and (3) increasing your personal savings.

Delay Your Retirement and Increase Your Employer Plan Benefits

Under a defined benefit plan, your employer must continue to credit years of service for purposes of calculating your pension—up to the plan's maximum service limit—even if you work beyond the normal retirement age. For example, say you are 60 years old, have 20 years of service, and earn $75,000 a year. Your company's defined benefit pension plan provides a benefit of 1.25% of your average salary in the final three years of employment, times your number of years of service. If your company allows early retirement at age 60, your annual pension benefit at this point would be about $17,900 (assuming you had received 5% annual salary increases over your final three years of service). At the normal retirement age of 65 you would be entitled to an annual pension benefit of about $28,500, based on five additional years of service and a higher average final salary. If your company plan's service limit is 30 years, you could continue to build your annual pension benefit by working until age 70, at which point you would be entitled to an annual benefit of $43,700. You can see that working five years beyond your normal retirement age provides a 53% increase in your annual pension benefit.

Figure 8–2 illustrates the striking advantage of delaying your retirement, even for a relatively

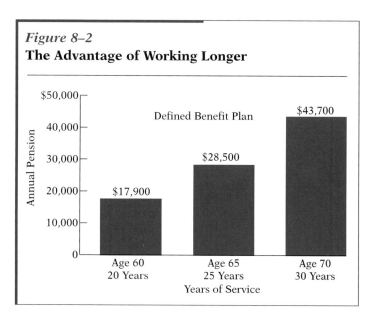

Figure 8–2

The Advantage of Working Longer

short period. As you consider the merits of your own pension benefits, you should keep in mind that some company plans allow for actuarial adjustments that may lower your benefit if you retire earlier or raise your benefit if you retire later.

A similar result can be achieved under a defined contribution plan. For example, suppose you are 40 years of age, your employer contributes 10% of your salary each year to a defined contribution plan, and your current salary of $28,000 increases by 5% each year that you are employed. Assuming a +8% annual return on your investments over 20 years (until age 60), your total account value will be $202,400. At your normal retirement age of 65, your account will be worth $349,000. And if you stay with your employer for an additional five years, until age 70, your account will be valued at $578,700. You can see in Figure 8–3 that, in this case, working 10 extra years increases your final account value almost threefold.

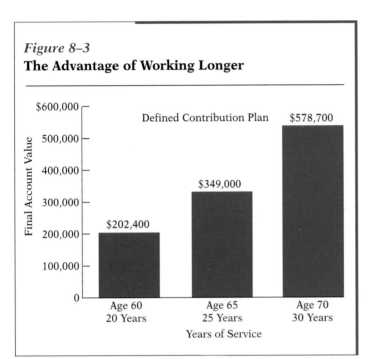

Figure 8–3
The Advantage of Working Longer

Retirement Plans for Sole Proprietors and Business Owners

If you are a sole proprietor or business owner, there are special types of retirement plans that you should consider for yourself and your employees.

This section provides a brief summary of some of the retirement plans commonly used by small businesses. Remember that in all cases these retirement plans offer two important tax benefits: (1) contributions by the employer (or self-employed individual) are deductible for federal income tax purposes, and (2) plan investment earnings grow on a tax-deferred basis. The plans differ, however, in terms of their complexity and their legal limits on contributions and benefits.

You should also recognize that under all of these tax-favored retirement plans, the law imposes a $150,000 limit on the amount of compensation you can take into account on behalf of any individual when calculating plan contributions. This $150,000 limit, which first became effective in 1994, is indexed for inflation in $10,000 increments. When applicable, this $150,000 compensation cap can limit the retirement plan contributions that would otherwise be made for higher-paid individuals. For example, if an individual with compensation of $300,000 is covered by a retirement plan providing for contributions equal to 10% of compensation, the annual contribution on behalf of the individual would be limited to $15,000 (10% of 150,000).

The SEP IRA—the No-Frills Alternative

Probably the best starting point for any review of small business retirement plans is the Simplified Employee Pension or SEP. Indeed, SEPs represent a particularly attractive alternative for many smaller companies and self-employed individuals who want a retirement plan with the substantial tax benefits available under qualified pension and profit-sharing plans (including Keoghs), without the burdens and headaches associated with administering these plans.

In a nutshell, a SEP permits employers to make deductible contributions directly to IRAs established for their employees. Using a SEP, you can make employer contributions to each employee's IRA for any year, up to the lesser of $30,000 or 15% of the employee's current-year compensation. For 1995, the maximum compensation that may be considered when making SEP contributions is $150,000. Therefore, the maximum SEP contribution that may be made on behalf of any employee for 1995 is effectively limited to $22,500 ($150,000 × 15%). In addition, employees can make their own deductible or nondeductible contributions to their IRAs each year, up to the lesser of $2,000 or 100% of compensation, resulting in total annual contributions to their IRAs of up to $24,500 (for 1995).

Employer contributions under a SEP are discretionary, meaning that the employer may choose to contribute different amounts in different years or may even elect to skip a contribution entirely. Generally, the only requirement is that the annual SEP contribution on behalf of each employee, including the owner-employee, must represent the same percentage of each employee's compensation (although it is possible to integrate a SEP with Social Security, as discussed later). SEPs may be established by sole proprietors and other self-employed persons, permitting them to make their own deductible "employer" contributions to their IRAs each year. In the case of self-employed individuals, annual SEP contributions are limited to the lesser of $30,000 or 13.04% of their net self-employment earnings (which are determined after the deduction allowed for one-half of their self-employment taxes). Due to the limit on compensation that may be considered when making plan contributions, $150,000 for 1995, the maximum SEP contribution that may be made on behalf of a self-employed individual will effectively be reduced below the $30,000 threshold.

SEPs offer several advantages over other retirement plan options, the most notable of which are these:

1. SEPs are inexpensive and easy to set up and administer. In most cases, a SEP can be established by signing a one-page form that authorizes the employer to make contributions directly to each employee's IRA. The money is held and administered on behalf of the employee according to the regular IRA rules governing distributions, withdrawals, and the like. (If you are self-employed, you simply make your own "employer" contributions directly to your IRA.)

2. SEPs are exempt from the annual reporting requirements of Keogh plans and other types of qualified retirement plans.

3. You can establish a SEP and make contributions to a SEP for any year up until you file your tax return, including any extensions. Most other retirement plans must be established by December 31, although contributions can be made until the tax filing deadline, again including any extensions.

Some of the disadvantages of SEPs include the following:

1. Employer contributions under a SEP are deposited directly into employees' IRAs. These contributions are immediately vested and withdrawable by employees at any time (subject to the 10% penalty on withdrawals prior to age 59$\frac{1}{2}$). Thus, SEPs do not permit employers to exercise the same degree of control over employees' retirement savings that they can under other types of qualified retirement plans (including Keogh plans).

2. A SEP generally must cover all employees—including part-time employees—over age 21 who have worked for the employer during any three of the past five years. It is possible to impose somewhat stricter coverage and eligibility requirements under other types of qualified retirement plans.

3. The annual contribution limit under a SEP for 1995 is, in effect, the lesser of $22,500 or 15% of compensation (or 13.04% of self-employment income). It is possible to

---

For More Information

You may order the following publications by calling the IRS Forms Distribution Center at 1-800-TAX-FORM:

- **Publication 560**
  Retirement Plans for the Self-Employed
- **Publication 571**
  Tax Sheltered Annuity Programs for Employees of Public Schools and Certain Tax-Exempt Organizations
- **Publication 575**
  Pension and Annuity Income
- **Publication 590 (IRAs)**
  Individual Retirement Arrangements

obtain higher contribution amounts—up to $30,000 per year—using other qualified retirement plans such as a money purchase plan.

4. All SEP distributions will be taxed as ordinary income. Thus, SEP monies are not eligible for the special five-year averaging taxation that applies to certain lump-sum distributions from qualified pension and profit-sharing plans. (Of course, this limitation does not affect you if you intend to receive your retirement plan distributions in installments over your retirement years, rather than in a lump sum.)

Adopting a SARSEP as a 401(k) Look-Alike

If you are a small employer (i.e., 25 or fewer employees) you may be interested in adopting a somewhat more complicated variation of the SEP, called the Salary Reduction Simplified Employee Pension Plan, or SARSEP. The primary benefit of a SARSEP is that it enables employees to make pretax salary reduction contributions to their IRAs each year in an amount up to the same indexed dollar limit that applies to 401(k) plans ($9,240 for 1995). For this reason, SARSEPs are generally viewed as a simple, low-cost alternative to a 401(k) plan. Moreover, it's possible to adopt both a SARSEP that allows your employees to make pretax contributions to their IRAs and a conventional SEP that allows you to make employer contributions to their IRAs. However, given the contribution limitations described earlier, the combined annual contribution to any employee's IRA for 1995 under both the SEP and SARSEP plans cannot exceed the lesser of $30,000 or 15% of the employee's compensation (or 13.04% of self-employment income).

There are several limitations associated with SARSEPs that have hindered their widespread adoption. These limitations include the following:

1. The SARSEP is available only if the employer has no more than 25 eligible employees and at least 50% of the eligible employees choose to make pretax contributions under the plan.
2. Employees' pretax contributions must satisfy strict nondiscrimination tests each year, which generally require that the amount of pretax contributions by any "highly compensated" employee, as a percentage of his or her total compensation, not exceed 1.25 times the average deferral percentage of all other eligible employees. It is this nondiscrimination requirement that adds considerable administrative complexity to the SARSEP.

3. Unlike a 401(k) plan, SARSEPs do not allow plan loans, nor can they accommodate matching employer contributions.

Increase Contributions and Benefits through Qualified Plans (including Keoghs)

There are several reasons why you may wish to consider a so-called qualified pension or profit-sharing plan as your retirement plan, in lieu of the simpler SEP or SARSEP arrangements. The first is that you may be permitted to make greater deductible contributions, and ultimately receive greater benefits, under a qualified plan. A second reason is that you may wish to exercise greater control over employees' retirement plan benefits by limiting their plan investments or their opportunities to make in-service withdrawals. A third reason is that you may be interested in imposing stricter coverage, eligibility, and vesting requirements for employees. Finally, there is the fact that, unlike a SEP or SARSEP, lump-sum distributions from a qualified plan may be eligible for favorable tax treatment.

Generally, a tax-qualified pension or profit-sharing plan may be adopted by any type of employer or self-employed individual, including any sole proprietor, partnership, or corporation. Historically, qualified pension and profit-sharing plans adopted by self-employed individuals have been referred to as Keogh plans. Over the years, however, changes in the tax code have eliminated most of the differences between self-employed retirement plans and corporate retirement plans. Today, the rules for self-employed plans are essentially the same as those governing the pension and profit-sharing plans used by large corporations.

The following is a brief summary of some of the popular types of tax-qualified pension and profit-sharing plans.

Defined Benefit Pension Plan   One type of qualified retirement plan you may wish to consider is the defined benefit pension plan. In many cases, this type of plan can generate the greatest level of deductible contributions and plan benefits. Indeed, as shown earlier, you could fund a defined benefit plan to provide an annual retirement benefit of up to $120,000 for 1995 (or 100% of your average annual pay for your three highest consecutive years, if less). However, a defined benefit plan is probably the most complicated and costly type of qualified retirement plan to establish and maintain. At a minimum, you will need the services of a professional actuary to fund and administer the plan.

Defined Contribution Pension and Profit-Sharing Plans As an alternative to the defined benefit pension plan, there are several types of qualified defined contribution plans that you should consider, including the following.

Conventional Profit-Sharing Plan This plan offers the most flexibility, since you may vary the amount you decide to contribute to the plan each year, perhaps contributing only in those years in which you have earnings and profits. Under a profit-sharing plan, the maximum annual contribution on behalf of an employee is limited to the lesser of $30,000 or 15% of compensation. For a self-employed individual, the limit is the lesser of $30,000 or 13.04% of the individual's net self-employment earnings (which are determined after the deduction allowed for one-half the individual's self-employment taxes). For 1995, the maximum compensation that may be considered when making plan contributions is $150,000. Thus, the maximum profit-sharing plan contribution on behalf of any plan participant is effectively limited to $22,500 for 1995. You will note that the rules for profit-sharing plan contributions are essentially the same as those for SEP contributions.

Money Purchase Pension Plan This plan is less flexible, since you are generally required to contribute a fixed percentage of each employee's compensation to the plan, regardless of your earnings or profits. However, a money purchase plan may allow for greater contributions, since the limit for employees is the lesser of $30,000 or 25% of compensation. For a self-employed individual, the limit is the lesser of $30,000 or 20% of the individual's net self-employment earnings (which are determined after the deduction for one-half of the individual's self-employment taxes).

Paired Profit-Sharing and Money Purchase Plans This popular arrangement involves adopting both a profit-sharing plan and a money purchase plan. With paired plans, you can retain some degree of flexibility through the profit-sharing plan, while maximizing your deductible contributions to both plans. For example, you could adopt a profit-sharing plan with discretionary employer contributions of up to 15% of compensation and a money purchase pension plan requiring employer contributions of 10% of compensation. Under this arrangement, you could decide for any year to reduce or skip your profit-sharing plan contribution, or you could decide to maximize your contributions to both plans up to the $30,000/25% of compensation (or 20% of net self-employment earnings) limits.

401(k) Plan As described earlier, 401(k) plans have become the savings plan of choice for most large and many mid-sized corporations. With a 401(k), you can permit your employees to make pretax salary reduction contributions to their individual plan accounts each year up to an indexed dollar amount ($9,240 for 1995). In addition, you can add popular plan features, such as employer matching contributions, plan loans, and hardship withdrawals. However, as you might expect, 401(k) plans can be burdensome and costly to administer. The plan accounting and recordkeeping necessary to satisfy the strict nondiscrimination tests that apply to 401(k)s and to implement certain plan features such as employee loans, can be particularly complicated.

Remember that there are drawbacks to tax-qualified plans, most having to do with the fact that these plans are generally more complicated and costly to administer than the simpler SEP and SARSEP arrangements. One notable administrative requirement for tax-qualified plans is that you must file "Form 5500" on an annual basis with the IRS. Under a SEP or SARSEP, once you make your contributions to employees' IRAs, your administrative responsibilities are essentially ended.

Some Final Considerations

For sole proprietors and business owners who are interested in adopting one or more of the retirement plans described above, here are two final points to consider.

Consider Integrating Your Plan with Social Security One option you have under most retirement plans (including SEPs) is to integrate the plan's contributions or benefits with Social Security. Under an integrated plan, you can provide different contribution or benefit rates for employee compensation below and above an appropriate integration level or dollar amount. For example, an integrated defined contribution plan could provide for 10% employer contributions on employee wages up to the Social Security taxable wage base (which is $61,200 for 1995) and 15.7% employer contributions on employee wages over the Social Security taxable wage base. This example shows how integrating a plan with Social Security can permit higher-paid employees to receive greater overall rates of contributions or benefits. However, it also makes the plan's administration more complicated, and you should probably consult an expert in this area if you wish to integrate your plan.

Consider Using a Prototype Retirement Plan   Many financial institutions, including mutual funds, banks, and brokerage firms, sponsor IRS-approved prototypes of the popular forms of retirement plans, including prototype SEPs, SARSEPs, profit-sharing plans, and money purchase plans. By adopting a prototype plan, you can save the expense of having a professional prepare your own individually designed plan, and you should receive assistance from the prototype plan sponsor with respect to your plan's administration. Of course, you'll want to make sure, first and foremost, that any prototype plan sponsor's investments are the appropriate ones for your retirement plan.

The Individual Retirement Account

Remember the IRA, the tax break for the little guy that appeared and then seemed to disappear sometime during the 1980s? Well, it's still here and it retains much of its usefulness as a tax-sheltered savings vehicle for retirement.

Like everything else touched by the tax laws, IRAs are more complicated today than when they first became part of the tax code in 1981. For a few years, up until 1986, IRAs were fairly straightforward: anyone with at least $2,000 of earned income could contribute up to $2,000 each year and take a tax deduction for the full amount of the contribution. Since the Tax Reform Act of 1986, the rules for IRAs have become somewhat more complex. Nonetheless, IRAs continue to provide substantial advantages for retirement investors.

1. If you and your spouse are not covered by an employer-sponsored retirement plan, including a 401(k) plan, each of you can make a $2,000 annual IRA contribution and receive a full tax deduction (provided you both have at least $2,000 in earned income). If your spouse does not have earned income, you may contribute a tax-deductible total of $2,250 to your and your spouse's IRA, with a maximum contribution of $2,000 in any one account.

2. If you have a company retirement plan at work but your adjusted gross income is less than $25,000 as a single person or $40,000 as a married couple, you and your spouse can each take a full $2,000 tax deduction for an equivalent IRA contribution.

3. If your income as a single person is between $25,000 and $35,000, or you are married and your combined income is between $40,000 and $50,000, you can still deduct a portion of your IRA contribution even if you are covered by an employer plan. For example, if you are single and

Table 8–1
The IRA Deduction

Adjusted Gross Income		Available IRA Deduction
Single	**Married**	
$25,000 and under	$40,000 and under	$2,000
26,000	41,000	1,800
27,000	42,000	1,600
28,000	43,000	1,400
29,000	44,000	1,200
30,000	45,000	1,000
31,000	46,000	800
32,000	47,000	600
33,000	48,000	400
34,000	49,000	200
35,000 and over	50,000 and over	0

Note: If you are not covered by an employer-sponsored retirement plan, you may take the full $2,000 IRA deduction *regardless* of the level of your adjusted gross income.

earning $30,000, up to $1,000 of your IRA contribution is tax deductible. A married couple earning $45,000 may also deduct $1,000. The available IRA deduction for various income levels is provided in Table 8–1.

4. If your income is above the dollar limits and you are covered by an employer plan, you can still make up to $2,000 each year in *nondeductible* contributions to an IRA.

Calculating Your IRA Deduction

The following example illustrates how you would calculate the portion of your IRA contribution that is tax deductible. Mr. and Mrs. Jones have adjusted gross income (AGI) of $43,000, and each is covered by an employer-sponsored pension plan. The threshold amount above which IRA deductions are reduced for couples filing jointly is $40,000. The deductible IRA contribution for Mr. and Mrs. Jones is $1,400, calculated as follows:

$$\frac{\$10,000 - (\text{AGI} - \text{Threshold amount})}{\$10,000} \times \$2,000 = \text{Tax deduction}$$

$$\frac{\$10,000 - (\$43,000 - \$40,000)}{\$10,000} \times \$2,000 = \text{Tax deduction}$$

$$\frac{\$7,000}{\$10,000} \times \$2,000 = \text{Tax deduction}$$

$$\$1,400 = \text{Tax deduction}$$

You should be aware of two significant drawbacks to making nondeductible contributions into an IRA. First, you will face an additional recordkeeping burden tracking the amount of any nondeductible contributions, which are not subject to taxation when withdrawn. That is, only the *earnings* on your nondeductible contributions are taxed. And if you need your money prior to age 59$\frac{1}{2}$, you will pay an additional 10% penalty on these earnings. Second, nondeductible contributions must be reported each year on IRS Form 8606 and should be attached to your tax return. For as long as you have money in an IRA, you should retain a copy of every Form 8606 that you file.

The Tax-Deferred Annuity

Annuities are life insurance policies with a twist. While life insurance protects your dependents in the event of your death, an annuity covers the risk that you will live longer than expected. An annuity pays you a fixed amount of money each year for the rest of your life, regardless of how long you live.

Annuities may be purchased with a lump sum or with a series of fixed or variable payments over time. There is no dollar limit on the amount of money you can invest. During the accumulation period, the money grows tax-deferred. At retirement, you will normally have the option of taking the money as a lump sum (and paying taxes on your earnings) or receiving a fixed monthly benefit for life. (See Chapter 10 for more on annuities.) The tax rules for early withdrawal are the same as for IRAs: you pay ordinary income taxes and a 10% penalty if you withdraw funds from an annuity before age 59$\frac{1}{2}$.

Many annuities offer attractive investment options. Fixed annuities, for instance, guarantee a particular rate of interest for a predetermined period of time. At the end of this period, the guaranteed rate is reset by the insurance company. Variable annuities permit you to allocate your money among a group of mutual funds. Transfers between funds are typically permitted without additional charge.

Of course, annuities have disadvantages as well. Most importantly, many annuities carry heavy sales commissions and high annual costs. Because of these higher costs, variable annuities are generally worthwhile only if you have fully utilized all other available tax-deferred retirement vehicles, such as IRAs and 401(k)s. At the minimum, you should expect to keep your annuity investment for 20 years, since it can easily take that long before the benefits of tax-deferral outweigh the added costs of the annuity.

Final Thoughts

This chapter addresses many of the technical issues related to retirement plans. To be sure that you are familiar with all of the details of the particular retirement programs that may be available to you, you should check with your employer and review the plan features described in this chapter.

In the final analysis, "getting the most from retirement savings plans" simply means taking advantage of every available investment program that allows pretax contributions and tax-deferred earnings. These types of programs should be selected for your first investment dollars and should be utilized to their full potential before any taxable investments are made. For instance, if your employer offers a 401(k) plan, generally you should fund the maximum amount in this plan before investing in any taxable account. The 401(k) should also be fully funded before contributing to an IRA, which may not allow pretax contributions and will not offer the flexibility of a 401(k).

The extent to which you take advantage of the retirement programs described in this chapter will importantly influence your retirement security. But you will face other financial issues in your retirement, many of them having to do with the Social Security system. Chapter 9 takes a look at the Social Security system and the types of benefits you can expect to receive. It also provides an overview of the actions that you can take to be assured of receiving all of the benefits to which you are entitled.

An Overview of Social Security and Medicare Benefits

S ince the enactment of Social Security in 1935 and Medicare in 1965, these social welfare programs have been the mainstay of many people's retirement programs. The basic goals of Social Security and Medicare are to provide retirees with a foundation for their retirement income and medical needs. Although Social Security was widely viewed in the United States as a revolutionary concept, it was not the first national social program of its kind. That distinction belongs to the old-age and disability pension plan introduced in Germany in 1889.

Unfortunately, the once finely tuned Social Security system has come under pressure, as the number of workers available to support the system's largely pay-as-you-go structure has declined. In 1983, a Presidential Commission was charged with the mission of overhauling the Social Security system to ensure that benefits would be available for future generations. The task force accomplished its mission by recalibrating the Social Security structure itself, making modifications to the normal retirement age and the level of allowable benefits.

This chapter reviews two "arms" of our national social insurance system: (1) monthly Social Security retirement benefits, and (2) Medicare coverage. The first section of the chapter discusses the implications of retiring either before or after the "normal" retirement age, as well as the impact to your pension benefits if you continue to work after you begin collecting Social Security benefits. This section also includes a worksheet to determine how much of your Social Security benefits, if any, may be taxable. The second section discusses the medical benefits available under the federal Medicare program, particularly some coverage limitations that you will have to prepare for as you plan for your retirement. The final section of this chapter provides a brief description of supplemental coverages that will be needed by most retired persons.

Social Security Pension Benefits

While the pension benefits of the Social Security system will represent an important component of your retirement income, these payments should nonetheless be viewed merely as a foundation upon which you will build your total retirement savings program.

The level of Social Security pension benefits that you ultimately receive will be greatly influenced by the employment decisions you make beginning at age 62 and continuing through age 70. It is during this stage of your life that you will decide whether to retire early and receive partial benefits, retire at the "normal" retirement age and receive full benefits, or delay retirement and receive augmented benefits. Alternatively, you might decide to retire and continue some reduced level of employment.

Normal Retirement Benefits

For anyone born before 1938, the normal retirement age for the purpose of receiving full Social Security benefits is 65. For anyone born in 1938 or later, the normal retirement age for receiving full pension benefits will be increased gradually (by two months per year) beginning in the year 2003, until the normal retirement age becomes 66 in the year 2009. Then, beginning in 2021, the normal retirement age again will be increased by two months a year until it reaches age 67 in the year 2027. Table 9–1 illustrates the gradual progression of the normal retirement age.

Table 9–1

Normal Retirement Age Increases

Year of Birth	Normal Retirement Age
1937 and earlier	Age 65
1938	65 and 2 months
1939	65 and 4 months
1940	65 and 6 months
1941	65 and 8 months
1942	65 and 10 months
1943–54	Age 66
1955	66 and 2 months
1956	66 and 4 months
1957	66 and 6 months
1958	66 and 8 months
1959	66 and 10 months
1960 and after	Age 67

Source: Reprinted with permission: 1995 William M. Mercer, Inc.

To be eligible for Social Security retirement benefits, you must have at least 40 quarters of coverage if you were born after 1928. (If you were born in 1928 or earlier, the number of quarters of coverage that you need is reduced, depending on your year of birth.) You gain one quarter of coverage each time that you earn an established minimum amount ($630 in 1995) and you and your employer pay the Federal Insurance Contributions Act (FICA) tax on these wages. You can earn up to a maximum of four quarters of coverage annually. For example, if you earned at least $2,520 ($630 × 4) during 1995, you would have been credited with four quarters of coverage.

Your monthly Social Security benefit is based on the year of your birth, your career average earnings covered by Social Security, and the age at which you begin benefits. Your noninsured spouse (at normal retirement age) receives a monthly benefit equal to one-half of the benefit you would receive if you retired at the normal retirement age. An insured spouse (i.e., one who has at least 40 quarters of coverage) is eligible for benefits individually. Alternatively, one eligible spouse may begin receiving benefits and, when the other spouse retires, switch to a spousal benefit if it is higher. The maximum monthly benefit for retirement at age 65 in 1995 is $1,199 for a worker and $1,798 for a worker and a spouse combined.

Early Retirement Benefits

Today, nearly one-half of working men and 60% of working women begin receiving Social Security benefits during the first year that they become eligible (age 62). Of course, if you retire early, your benefit will be reduced, as shown in Figure 9–1 for retirement in 1995. You can see that if you retire at age 62 (the earliest age at which you may retire and still receive a partial benefit), you will receive only 80% of your full Social Security benefit, with a slightly larger reduction (75% of full benefits) for your nonworking spouse.

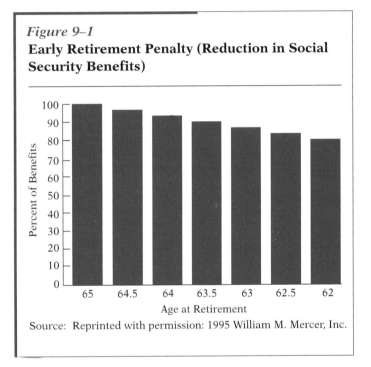

Figure 9–1

Early Retirement Penalty (Reduction in Social Security Benefits)

Source: Reprinted with permission: 1995 William M. Mercer, Inc.

   You should note that in 1983 the Presidential Commission changed the rules for early retirement. Beginning in the year 2000, benefits for early retirees will again be gradually reduced, reaching the 70% level (65% for a nonworking spouse) by the year 2022, when those born in 1960 attain age 62. If you are considering early retirement, you should know that receiving reduced retirement benefits before the normal retirement age results in a permanent reduction.

Late Retirement Benefits

If you delay your retirement beyond your normal retirement age, up to age 70, you can receive delayed-retirement credits (DRCs). For persons who are age 65 in 1995, the DRC rate provides a graduated annual increase in your benefits (but not your spousal benefits) of 4.5% for each year of delayed retirement up to age 70. The delayed retirement credit also raises the benefits paid to your surviving spouse.

As shown in Table 9–2, the credit per year of delayed retirement is being raised by 0.5% every other year until it reaches 8% for those born in 1943 or later. Accordingly, the delayed retirement credit will become a much more important inducement for workers to consider a delayed retirement. One caveat: the extra benefits you receive by delaying your retirement may not make up for the payments you lose by forgoing Social Security benefits at your normal retirement age.

Table 9–2

Increase for Each Year That Benefits Are Delayed beyond the Normal Retirement Age

Year of Birth	Delayed Retirement Credit
1929–30	4.50 %
1931–32	5.00
1933–34	5.50
1935–36	6.00
1937–38	6.50
1939–40	7.00
1941–42	7.50
1943 or later	8.00

Source: Reprinted with permission: 1995 William M. Mercer, Inc.

Working during Retirement

If you continue to work after your retirement, your Social Security benefits will be reduced (until age 70) if your earnings exceed the allowable limit. The allowable limit is raised each year based on the change in the average wage for all employees. If you are under age 65, you will begin to lose Social Security benefits once your earnings exceed $8,160 (for 1995). Specifically, for every two dollars you earn above the allowable amount, you lose one dollar in benefits, which is the equivalent of a 50% marginal income tax rate. For those age 65 to 69, the 1995 wage limitation is $11,280. In this age group, for every three dollars you earn above the allowable limit, you lose one dollar in benefits, the equivalent of a 33.3% marginal tax rate. However, when benefits are withheld, later benefits are increased (by either a smaller reduction for early retirement or more delayed-retirement credits). Beginning at age 70, your Social Security benefits will not be reduced whatever your earnings level. These rules apply to both wages and self-employment income.

If you work during the first year you receive Social Security benefits, you are eligible to use a special monthly test to determine if your benefits will be reduced. During this period, you will receive your benefit for any month in which you earn one-twelfth or less of the yearly limitation ($680 a month if under age 65; $940 between the ages of 65 and 69) and do not perform substantial services in self-employment.

How Social Security Benefits Are Taxed

Depending on the level of your total retirement income, including investment income and earnings, you may be required to pay federal income taxes on up to 85% of your Social Security benefits. The threshold level for determining the taxability of Social Security income takes into account three factors:

1. Your adjusted gross income (including any wages, dividends, interest, and pension benefits).
2. Any tax-exempt income, such as dividends from a municipal bond fund.
3. One-half of the Social Security benefits you (and your spouse if filing jointly) receive during the year.

The amount of your Social Security benefits subject to tax is based on your income as it relates to the two-step rate thresholds of $25,000 and $34,000 for single taxpayers, or $32,000 and $44,000 for couples filing jointly.

Here is an example of how the tax would be calculated for a typical retired couple, Mr. and Mrs. Jones. (You can use the right-hand column in Table 9–3 to determine the projected taxes on your Social Security income.) The Joneses have adjusted gross income totaling $36,000 from a company pension plan, taxable investment income, and wages from part-time employment. They also receive $12,000 in Social Security benefits and

---

Table 9–3
How Your Social Security Income Is Taxed

	Mr. & Mrs. Jones	Your Figures
A. Adjusted gross income (income from wages, dividends, interest, pensions)	$36,000	_____
B. Tax-exempt interest	4,000	_____
C. 50% of Social Security benefits	6,000	_____
D. Total of Lines A, B, and C (modified AGI)	46,000	_____
E. Excess of Line D over first threshold ($32,000)	14,000	_____
F. Excess of Line D over second threshold ($44,000)	2,000	_____
G. 50% of Line E, plus 35% of Line F	7,700	_____
H. 85% of Social Security benefits	10,200	_____
I. 50% of benefits, plus 85% of Line F	7,700	_____
J. Add smallest of Lines G, H, I to Line A (AGI)	43,700	_____

$4,000 in tax-exempt municipal bond interest. Adding one-half of their Social Security benefits plus the $4,000 in tax-exempt income to their adjusted gross income results in a total of $46,000. The Joneses would subtract the $32,000 first threshold amount from this total, resulting in an excess of $14,000 over the threshold. Next, the Joneses would subtract the $44,000 second threshold amount from the $46,000 total, resulting in an excess of $2,000. Finally, they compare the sum of 50% of the excess over the first threshold *plus* 35% of the excess over the second threshold ($7,700), with 85% of their annual Social Security benefits ($10,200), and with 50% of their annual Social Security benefits plus 85% of the excess over the second threshold ($7,700). The Joneses then add the smallest of the three figures to their adjusted gross income, for a total of $43,700 in taxable income. In this case, 64% of the Joneses' Social Security benefits are taxable.

What makes this tax calculation even more foreboding is that the threshold amounts ($25,000 and $34,000 for single taxpayers and $32,000 and $44,000 for joint taxpayers) are not adjusted upward for inflation, meaning that a greater proportion of retired persons will be paying taxes on larger shares of their Social Security benefits (but not more than 85% under present rules) as levels of income and benefits rise over time.

Monitoring Your Social Security Benefits

Before moving on to the next section on Medicare, it is worth noting that you can request at any time an estimate of your Social Security benefits. While doing so makes sense from a retirement planning perspective, it also gives you the opportunity to determine if your earnings have been credited properly with the Social Security Administration for each year that you have worked. You may obtain this information by filling out and returning Form SSA–7004 (*Request for Earnings and Benefit Estimate Statement*) to the Social Security Administration. Forms may be obtained by calling the Administration at 1-800-772-1213.

If you request a Social Security estimate, the earnings and benefit statement you receive will show your credited earnings up to the maximum taxable amount for each year of employment. If there is an error in the total for any year, you should report the error at once to your local Social Security office. The earnings and benefit statement will also give you an estimate of your future retirement, disability, and death benefits.

It's probably not a bad idea to submit a new form SSA–7004 every three years to verify the accuracy of your Social Security records. If an error has been made, it will be much easier to correct if you file Form SSA–7004 periodically during your working years, rather than waiting until you are ready to retire.

The Medicare program has two facets. Part A covers hospitalization and skilled-nursing care and is financed by payroll taxes on employees, employers, and self-employed persons. Part B pays for doctor bills and hospital outpatient services and is financed through a combination of general federal revenues (75%) and monthly participant premiums (25%). For Part B coverage, you will be charged a monthly premium ($46.10 in 1995) that generally increases each year to reflect rising medical costs.

Medicare Enrollment

Everyone who is eligible for Social Security benefits (including nonworking spouses) is also eligible for Medicare, once he or she reaches age 65. Should you retire early—say, age 63—you would be required to wait two years to enroll in Medicare. If you retire at age 65, you will likely enroll in Medicare at the same time that you apply for Social Security benefits. However, if you plan to continue working beyond your normal retirement age, you should still apply separately for Medicare as soon as you reach age 65. Also, persons under age 65 who have been entitled to Social Security disability benefits for at least two years, as well as most persons with kidney failure, are eligible for Medicare.

When you sign up for Part A of Medicare, you will also be enrolled in Part B, unless you decline such coverage. Premiums for Part B coverage are either deducted from your Social Security check or, if you are not receiving Social Security benefits because of employment, billed to you quarterly. If you delay selecting Part B coverage beyond the initial enrollment period, your monthly premiums will be higher, unless you delay enrollment because you have coverage under an employer-sponsored plan based on current employment.

Medicare Coverage

Medicare generally covers your hospital bills for a full 60 days once you have paid an initial deductible ($716 in 1995). After 60 days in

Medicare Benefits

The federal Medicare program offers important benefits for people age 65 and older, covering a large portion of approved charges for doctor bills, hospital stays of up to 150 days, and skilled-nursing care following a hospital stay.

the hospital, you must pay a portion of your bill ($179 a day in 1995) as co-insurance. After 90 days in the hospital, you have the option for 60 more days to pay the lesser of a daily amount set by Medicare ($358 in 1995) or your hospital's charges. The maximum covered hospital stay in any one benefit period is 150 days.

Medicare also pays the full cost of preapproved coverage at a skilled-nursing care facility for up to 20 days following a hospital stay. For the next 80 days you must pay a co-insurance premium ($89.50 per day in 1995), with Medicare paying the remainder of the approved charges. (Your total coverage is limited to 100 days per benefit period.) In addition, Medicare will pay the full cost of approved home care services prescribed by a doctor, such as physical therapy, intermittent skilled-nursing care, and rehabilitation equipment. And Medicare picks up most of the cost of hospice care for terminally ill patients for up to 210 days. Finally, Medicare Part B pays for 80% of approved amounts for doctor bills, medical supplies, diagnostic tests, and outpatient hospital care once you have paid the annual deductible of $100.

Despite the many approved coverages, Medicare is not a complete health insurance plan. The following is a list of some of the treatments and services that do not fall under the Medicare umbrella:

- Treatment or services not considered by Medicare to be reasonable or medically necessary.
- Routine physical examinations, dental care, cosmetic surgery, foot care, eyeglasses, hearing aids.
- Most prescription drugs and medicines taken outside the hospital.
- Private-duty nursing or extra charges for a private hospital room, telephone, or television.
- Custodial nursing care or skilled-nursing care beyond the 100 days per benefit period.
- Health care outside of the United States, with certain limited exceptions in Canada and Mexico.

To fill these and other gaps in Medicare coverage, many retirees purchase Medicare supplement insurance and long-term care insurance.

Plugging the Holes in Medicare Coverage

Medicare supplement insurance pays some of the expenses not covered by Medicare. If you expect to rely on Medicare during retirement and will not have any other health care coverage, you should consider buying a Medicare supplement policy, commonly known as "medigap" coverage. In the past, medigap coverage varied widely among the scores of different policies offered by various insurers, making it difficult for retired persons to fairly assess the relative merits of each plan. As a result, senior citizens often paid too much for medigap insurance and received less-than-adequate coverage.

But the market for medigap insurance became more consumer-friendly in 1992, when the Congress enacted some important health care reforms. Federal law now requires insurers to offer medigap policies in 10 standardized formats, categorized by the letters A through J. The basic policy A covers co-insurance for doctor bills and co-payments for hospital stays in excess of 60 days. The full-featured policy J is designed to meet the entire range of expenses and deductibles not covered by Medicare, including outpatient prescription drugs, at-home care, co-insurance for skilled nursing care, health care abroad, and preventive care. The remaining policies (B through I) offer varying mixes of coverage options. Table 9–4 provides an overview of the basic features of each medigap option.

Of course, the more services your medigap policy provides, the higher your annual premium will be. While rates will vary depending on the insurance company you choose and your state of residence, the new standardization rules enable you to make fair comparisons among the different policies and purchase the

---

Table 9–4

The 10 Standard Medigap Policies (A–J)

Policy Type	A	B	C	D	E	F	G	H	I	J
Basic benefits	●	●	●	●	●	●	●	●	●	●
Part A—hospital deductible	○	●	●	●	●	●	●	●	●	●
Part B—doctor deductible	○	○	●	○	○	●	○	○	○	●
Part B—% of excess doctor bill	○	○	○	○	○	100%	80%	○	100%	100%
Skilled-nursing co-insurance	○	○	●	●	●	●	●	●	●	●
At-home care	○	○	○	●	○	○	●	○	●	●
Prescription drugs	○	○	○	○	○	○	○	●	●	●
Preventive care	○	○	○	○	●	○	○	○	○	●
Health care abroad	○	○	●	●	●	●	●	●	●	●

Policy offers this benefit ●   Policy does not offer this benefit ○

Source: Reprinted with permission: 1995 William M. Mercer, Inc.

right mix of benefits to meet your needs. The most important feature of the medigap plan is that at age 65 you are automatically eligible to buy Medicare supplement insurance, provided that you act within six months of enrolling in Medicare Part B. You cannot be rejected because of illness, existing medical conditions, or prior health-insurance claims history.

The various medigap policies are described in detail in *The Medicare Handbook,* published by the US Department of Health and Human Services. To order a copy call 1-800-772-1213.

Medicare Terminology

You should be familiar with the following terms as you consider the different features offered by the two broad Medicare programs, as well as the 10 medigap options.

Accepting Assignment   An agreement by a doctor or other service provider to accept the Medicare approved amount as the entire fee and to receive payment directly from Medicare.

Approved Amount   The amount that Medicare will pay for a particular treatment or service. Sometimes called *allowable amount* or *recognized amount.*

Benefit Period   A benefit period begins on the first day of hospitalization and ends after the beneficiary has been out of the hospital or skilled-nursing facility for 60 days. After the end of the benefit period, a new deductible must be paid if additional treatment is required.

Co-Insurance   The share of expenses you must continue to pay after you have paid any deductibles. Co-insurance may be a fixed dollar amount or a percentage of the expenses. For example, you pay 20% of physician charges as co-insurance under Part B of the Medicare program.

Deductible   Initial amount of expenses you must pay before Medicare benefit payments begin.

Nonparticipating Provider   Physician or service provider who may not accept assignment and who may charge more than the approved amount. You must pay the difference between the provider's bill and the approved Medicare allowance. As of 1993, it is illegal for a nonparticipating provider to charge you more than 15% above the approved amount.

Participating Provider   Physician or service provider who agrees to accept Medicare approved amount.

Long-Term Care Insurance

One of the major limitations of the Medicare program is that it excludes coverage for basic (or custodial) nursing home care, the cost of which now averages about $30,000 a year. To prepare for this potential liability, many people now buy long-term care insurance. Rather than reimbursing you for expenses actually incurred, these policies pay daily benefits ranging in amounts from $30 to $250. While premium rates vary depending on the level of benefits you desire, such coverage will generally be more expensive if you wait until after retirement to sign up. For example, long-term care premiums for a 70-year-old are roughly four times the level that would be charged to a 55-year-old receiving comparable coverage.

Neither Medicare nor Medicare supplement insurance covers basic nursing home care. Yet more than 40% of people will spend some period of time in a nursing home after age 65.

As a general rule, you should avoid long-term care insurance policies that require a hospital stay before you can qualify for benefits. And be sure to check on the financial strength of the insurance company issuing you the policy. The company should carry a top rating from at least one of the independent rating agencies, such as A.M. Best Co. (A+ or better), Standard & Poor's Corp. (AA or better), Moody's Investors Services (Aa or better), or Duff & Phelps, Inc. (AA or better).

What to Look For in a Long-Term Care Policy

In general, you should consider six primary factors when shopping for long-term care insurance:

1. The policy should be guaranteed renewable for life. This feature ensures that your coverage cannot be canceled by the insurance company.
2. The policy should pay benefits regardless of the level of care. That is, be sure that you are covered not only for care at a nursing home, but for home care and adult day care as well.
3. You can save money by choosing a shorter coverage period. The term of coverage is the number of years for which your policy will pay benefits, with options ranging from one year to a lifetime. You can pay less in premiums and still cover the likely length of a nursing home stay by choosing a three- or five-year term of coverage rather than a lifetime policy.

4. The longer the waiting period (i.e., deductible period), the lower your premium. The waiting period is the length of time between the day you start to need long-term care and the day the policy starts paying benefits. The range available is generally 21 to 365 days. A 60- or 90-day waiting period will reduce your premiums considerably.

5. Benefits should be paid at any time when you are unable to perform two of the activities of daily living (i.e., eating, dressing, or bathing) or if you become mentally impaired. Coverage should specifically include Parkinson's disease and Alzheimer's disease.

6. Inflation protection can help your insurance benefits keep pace with rising health care costs. Many policies offer the option of increasing your benefits (and, of course, your premiums) each year to match increases in the Consumer Price Index.

Final Thoughts

It should be clear that the Social Security system provides a substantial safety net for your retirement years. But it should be equally clear that the level of retirement benefits provided by Social Security may not meet all of your retirement income needs. Nor is the medical coverage provided by Medicare likely to be comprehensive enough to meet the health care demands of the average retired person. So, while it is important that you understand the services and benefits Social Security will provide in your retirement, it is perhaps more important that you recognize the services and benefits that will *not* be provided by Social Security.

This chapter should be a useful guide for factoring in the likely effects of Social Security on your long-term retirement program; however, it should not be considered a comprehensive source of information on Social Security. If you feel that you need more comprehensive information, you might consider purchasing a copy of the *1996 Mercer Guide to Social Security*, a 200-page book providing a thorough description of Social Security benefits and eligibility requirements. The book can be obtained by sending a check for $12.50 ($9.95 plus $2.55 for shipping and handling) to William M. Mercer, Inc., Social Security Division, 1500 Meidinger Tower, Louisville, KY 40202.

Facing Your Retirement

A s you approach your retirement years, you will face some important decisions regarding the disposition of the assets you have accumulated in various retirement plans. The regulations that govern the withdrawal of these assets are complicated, and even a seemingly inconsequential oversight on your part can have serious consequences. Where distributions from your retirement account are concerned, it pays to spend some time learning the rules of the game.

It would be helpful if there were a clear-cut, "best" option for distributing your retirement assets, but that unfortunately is not the case. For example, the idea of receiving your retirement benefits as a fixed monthly payment for the remainder of your life may seem quite attractive, since doing so would not only relieve you of the burden of managing your retirement assets, but also would ensure that you could not outlive your assets. However, the fixed monthly benefit option is vulnerable to inflation, and you would have little recourse in the event of a financial emergency. Alternatively, you may prefer the idea of receiving all of your retirement benefits in a lump sum. This option allows you to control your own retirement destiny, but you may not have confidence in your ability to oversee your investments as you grow older.

The first section of this chapter looks at the many choices you will have to make in managing your assets during your retirement. In many cases, you probably will have to choose between some form of annuity or lump-sum payout from your employer's retirement plan. As you begin to receive these distributions, in whatever form, there will be critical tax considerations that will impact your level of benefits. Thus, the second section of this chapter provides an overview of retirement tax issues, as well as some recommendations for minimizing your tax liability.

While most investors will want to defer taking retirement distributions for as long as possible to maximize the advantages of tax deferral, a minimum annual retirement distribution generally becomes mandatory once you reach age $70\frac{1}{2}$. The third section of this chapter deals specifically with the rather cumbersome issues and calculations involved in complying with this tax regulation. Finally, the chapter concludes by outlining a strategy to determine an appropriate level of annual withdrawals to match your personal financial and lifestyle circumstances. Interspersed throughout the chapter, you will also find seven "tax traps" highlighting common errors investors make as they plan their retirement distributions.

The Annuity Payout Option

Many company pension plans offer only one form of retirement benefit, a monthly payment known as an annuity.

If your company-sponsored retirement plan is a defined benefit plan that offers an annuity payout option, you typically are given the choice of receiving the payment in one of several forms. The first payment plan is known as the single-life annuity option, in which monthly payments either conclude with your death or continue to a designated beneficiary for a given period—say, 10 years—after your death. If you are single, the single-life annuity option likely will be the best choice. However, even if you are married, the single-life annuity might be the better choice in cases where

- Your spouse will receive a separate pension of his or her own. In this case, choosing separate single-life annuities may maximize your combined monthly benefits.
- You think it is likely that you will live much longer than your spouse (e.g., your spouse is much older or in poor health).
- You and your spouse have sufficient assets such that your spouse's standard of living could be maintained even if you were to die and your pension benefits were halted.

Most married persons will select a joint-and-survivor annuity option covering both themselves and their spouse. Indeed, if you are married your employer must offer you a joint-and-survivor pension payout option. What is more, before you may accept any other payout option, your spouse must give his or her written consent in the form of a signed waiver. While the monthly benefit under a joint-and-survivor annuity will be lower than for a single-life annuity, the payments are guaranteed to continue until your spouse dies.

The joint-and-survivor annuity is generally offered in two forms: (1) a 50% joint-and-survivor annuity, which provides a higher level of monthly income during your lifetime, but pays your spouse only 50% of that amount after you die; and (2) a 100% joint-and-survivor annuity, which offers a reduced bene-

---

Table 10–1
Typical Annuity Payment Schedules

$200,000 purchase price; age 65; spouse age 62
Single-Life Annuity
- $1,820 per month for life of pensioner
Single-Life with Guaranty
- 10-year guaranty: $1,710 per month for life or at least 10 years
- 20-year guaranty: $1,560 per month for life or at least 20 years
Joint-and-Survivor Annuity
- 50% survivor benefit: $1,700 per month for life
  ($850 per month for life if pensioner dies first)
- 100% survivor benefit: $1,500 per month for life
  ($1,500 per month for life if pensioner dies first)

---

fit during your lifetime but is not diminished after your death. In general, a joint-and-survivor annuity will be the better choice if your spouse needs income security in retirement. A joint-and-survivor annuity will be especially attractive in the following situations:

- Your spouse has no pension and may not have sufficient life insurance proceeds or other assets after your death to meet daily living expenses. In this situation, particularly if your spouse is likely to outlive you and your pension will not provide cost-of-living adjustments, you should consider the 100% joint-and-survivor benefit.

- Your employer provides medical benefits both to pensioners and to their spouses. If you choose a joint-and-survivor annuity, your spouse may be eligible to maintain any medical benefits after you die. If you choose a single-life annuity, medical coverage for your spouse typically ends upon your death, at the same time that your pension benefits cease.

- You are able to designate someone other than a spouse as your joint annuitant. This option is permissible under some pension plans and may make sense, for example, if you are single and have an aging parent who depends on you for financial support. If your joint annuitant is much older, the benefit reduction for choosing the joint-and-survivor option will be relatively muted.

Table 10–1 illustrates some examples of how the two annuity payout options would work for a 65-year-old worker with a 62-year-old spouse.

The Lump-Sum Payout Option

Lump-sum distributions are usually available to participants in defined contribution plans and sometimes available to participants in defined benefit plans when they retire or leave their jobs.

In many cases, you have the option of receiving your company-sponsored retirement benefit as a single payment, known as a lump sum. Any lump-sum payment offered by your company's defined benefit plan will have an actuarially equivalent value to the monthly benefit you would receive for life under the annuity payout option. For example, if your annuity benefit is $800 per month at retirement, your lump-sum amount might be $100,000. (Your payments, of course, will depend on your age and an anticipated rate of investment return.) In the case of a defined contribution plan, your lump-sum payment will equal your total account balance as of the plan's valuation date. Lump-sum pension distributions of $100,000 to $250,000 or more are not unusual for workers with a lifetime of service to an employer.

For many retirees, the thought of suddenly having the responsibility for such a large amount of money can be intimidating. Nonetheless, there are some advantages in choosing a lump-sum payout option, the most important of which is flexibility. For instance, you have the ability to pay taxes on the lump sum (possibly at a favorable rate) and then spend part of it, say, on a down payment for a new retirement home. Or, you could roll over the lump sum into an individual retirement account, allowing earnings to continue to accrue on a tax-deferred basis, and then take distributions later as needed. You also have the flexibility to select your own investments and perhaps have the opportunity to leave some money behind for your heirs.

As you weigh the trade-offs between a lump-sum payout and an annuity payout, you should keep in mind that an annuity gen-

---

Retirement Tax Trap

If you are eligible for a distribution from your company's retirement plan, your employer is required in most cases to give you the option of having the taxable amount of your distribution transferred on your behalf as a direct rollover to any IRA or other eligible retirement plan of your choice. If you decline this option, your taxable distribution will be assessed 20% federal tax withholding.

The Trap:

If you are planning to roll over your distribution, you must elect the direct rollover option *prior to receiving your distribution* if you want to avoid the mandatory 20% withholding. If you receive the distribution first, the 20% withholding applies even if the distribution is invested in an eligible retirement plan.

Table 10–2
Annuity Payout versus Lump-Sum Payout

Annuity Advantages	Lump-Sum Advantages
You cannot outlive income	Can offer inflation protection
May maintain retiree health benefits	Can provide emergency funds
Better for long life expectancy	Ability to leave money to heirs
	Flexibility to select invest-ments
	Potential for higher returns
	Better for short life expectancy

Annuity Disadvantages	Lump-Sum Disadvantages
Usually no inflation protection	You could outlive your money
No access to principal in emergencies	Temptation to spend, not save
No ability to leave money to heirs	No retiree health care benefits
No flexibility in making withdrawals	

erally provides a level benefit for a specified period of time (such as your life or the joint lives of you and your beneficiary). If you are a particularly healthy individual, the possibility of a longer-than-average life span may make the annuity the most appropriate option. One big disadvantage of the annuity payout versus the lump-sum payout is that most annuity payments are not adjusted for inflation. A lump-sum distribution, on the other hand, can be invested to provide some growth in principal and thus should keep better pace with inflation. Table 10–2 provides an overview of the advantages and disadvantages of these two payment options.

Purchasing an Annuity with Your Lump-Sum Payout

Before you decide between the annuity and the lump-sum payout options offered through your company-sponsored retirement plan, you should compare your employer's annuity with some of the commercial retirement annuities available from insurance companies. If you elect to take the lump-sum distribution from your pension plan, you could use all or part of the proceeds to purchase an annuity on your own. In some cases, you may be able to find a better deal than that offered by your employer. To arrive at an annuity quotation, an insurance agent will need to know the lump-sum value of your pension and your birth date (and your spouse's birth date, if applicable). It is generally best to limit yourself to companies that carry top ratings from several independent rating agencies.

Once you have received several quotations, compare the monthly annuity benefits offered by the various insurance companies with the benefits available under your employer's plan, making sure that all of the annuities are of a comparable type (e.g., all are for a 100% joint-and-survivor). If one of the insurance company annuities offers a better payment rate than your employer-sponsored annuity, consider having all or a portion of your distribution transferred directly to the insurance company in order to purchase an annuity.

For more information on annuities, you may request a free booklet, *A Consumer's Guide to Annuities,* by writing to The American Council of Life Insurance, Consumer Department, 1001 Pennsylvania Avenue N.W., Washington, DC 20004-2599.

Tax Implications for the Retirement Investor

Whether you choose an annuity payout option or a lump-sum payout option, the IRS will take its share.

As a general rule, you must pay taxes on any monies you receive from a retirement plan—including lump-sum distributions, monthly pension checks, and withdrawals from individual retirement accounts—unless you roll over the assets into an IRA or other eligible retirement plan. Any *after-tax* contributions that you make to your retirement plan are not taxed upon withdrawal and are not eligible to be rolled over. The amount of tax you pay on monies that you receive from your retirement plan depends largely on two factors: (1) your age, and (2) the type of distribution or withdrawal you receive.

If you are under age $59\frac{1}{2}$, in addition to paying ordinary income tax on any distributions that are not rolled over into an IRA or other eligible retirement plan, you will face a 10% penalty tax on the taxable portion of your distribution. For example, assuming you are in the 31% tax bracket, if you withdraw $20,000 from an IRA or 401(k) plan at age 45, you will owe $6,200 in income taxes as well as a penalty tax of $2,000, for a total tax payment of $8,200. While regular income taxes will be due in all cases, the 10% penalty will not apply in the following circumstances, even for persons under age $59\frac{1}{2}$:

- If you become disabled.
- If you die and your retirement plan balance is distributed to your beneficiary or to your estate.
- If you receive distributions from your retirement plan as a series of substantially equal payments calculated to last over your lifetime. You must use an IRS-approved method of cal-

---

Retirement Tax Trap

Employees who receive distributions from a qualified plan before age $59\frac{1}{2}$ normally must pay a 10% penalty as well as ordinary income tax on the amount of the distribution. There is an exception, however, for workers who take the distribution after termination of employment in the year they turn 55 or later. In this case, employees must pay ordinary income taxes on the distribution, but not the 10% penalty tax. If they choose to roll over the distribution into an IRA, their money stays tax-deferred.

The Trap

If the 55-year-old first rolls over a distribution into an IRA and then withdraws any of that money from the IRA before age $59\frac{1}{2}$, the 10% penalty once again applies.

---

culating the distributions based on your life expectancy, and the payments must be made at least once a year for five years, or until you reach age $59\frac{1}{2}$, whichever is later.

■ If you take a distribution as a result of termination of employment, either during or after the year you turn 55. This exception does not apply to withdrawals from IRA accounts.

If you are age $59\frac{1}{2}$ or older, you still must pay ordinary income taxes on distributions and withdrawals that are not rolled over into an eligible retirement plan; however, you are no longer subject to the 10% penalty tax. In addition, at age $59\frac{1}{2}$ you become eligible to use forward averaging for any lump-sum distribution you receive from a qualified retirement plan, which may enable you to pay less on your distribution than your current tax rate.

Tax Implications for Lump-Sum Payouts

If you select the lump-sum distribution option from your company retirement plan, you must either pay taxes on the distribution in the current year or effect a rollover into an IRA or other eligible retirement plan and defer taxes until you begin making withdrawals. By rolling over your lump-sum distribution into an IRA, your assets can continue to grow on a tax-deferred basis. You also control how the assets are invested and when withdrawals are made. These advantages almost always make the rollover a more attractive financial option if you have no immediate need for your retirement assets.

If you choose the rollover option, be extremely careful not to run afoul of the 20% withholding tax now required on any rollovers that are not made *directly* into another eligible

Table 10–3
Tax Rates for Forward Averaging

Lump Sum Amount	10-Year Averaging	5-Year Averaging
$ 20,000	5.5%	7.5%
30,000	8.4	11.0
40,000	10.5	12.8
50,000	11.7	13.8
100,000	14.5	15.0
150,000	16.4	18.1
200,000	18.5	20.6
300,000	22.1	23.3
377,000*	25.0	24.8
400,000	25.7	25.2
600,000	31.2	27.4

*Approximate level where five-year averaging becomes more advantageous.

retirement plan. If you are uncertain about how to proceed in effecting your rollover, ask your employer to leave your lump-sum distribution invested in your company plan until you are ready to proceed.

Using Forward Averaging

Forward averaging allows you to pay taxes on a lump-sum distribution as if you had received it over a period of years, rather than all at once. It also allows you to exclude all income from other sources from the forward averaging tax calculation. For example, five-year averaging allows you to calculate your tax liability (using current applicable tax rates) as if your lump sum were distributed over a five-year period and you had no other income. Ten-year averaging treats the distribution as if it occurred over 10 years, using tax rates that were in effect during 1986. In addition, if you were born prior to 1936, you may elect 20% capital gains taxation for the portion of your lump-sum distribution attributable to pre-1974 participation in a qualified plan. (The remaining post-1973 portion is taxed under the ten-year or five-year forward averaging guidelines.) Table 10–3 provides an overview of the applicable tax rates using each forward-averaging option.

Forward averaging is only available on lump-sum distributions that meet six basic requirements:

1. It must be made from a "qualified" retirement plan, not from an IRA or other nonqualified plan.

2. It must be prompted by retirement (or some other separation from service), death, or attainment of age 59½. (For self-employed individuals, it must be prompted by disability, death, or attainment of age 59½.)

3. It must be made to an individual who has been a participant in the qualified plan for at least five years, unless the payment is being made because of death.

4. It must represent the participant's entire balance in the plan.

5. It must be distributed within a single tax year.

6. It must be distributed on or after the participant attains age 59½ in order to be eligible for five-year forward averaging. (Ten-year forward averaging is only available to those born prior to 1936.)

If you elect to use forward averaging with respect to *any* lump-sum distribution you receive during a given tax year, such election must apply to *all* qualifying lump-sum distributions you receive during that same tax year. When you receive a lump-sum distribution, it will be reported to you on Tax Form 1099–R; to calculate your tax liability using forward averaging, you must use Form 4972, *Tax on Lump-Sum Distributions*. You may use forward averaging only once in your lifetime.

Retirement Tax Trap

Forward averaging enables you to pay less than your current tax rate on money you receive as a lump-sum distribution from a qualified retirement plan.

The Trap

When you take a lump-sum distribution from a qualified plan, 20% must be withheld for taxes, even if the amount you will owe is considerably less than 20%. Consider a married 60-year-old employee with $30,000 in income who receives a lump-sum distribution of $50,000. Of that amount, 20%, or $10,000, will be withheld to pay income taxes. By using 10-year forward averaging to compute the tax, the employee would owe only $5,900. Thus, the employee generally will have to wait to receive the difference as a tax refund in the following year.

It is worth noting that Congress voted to abolish five-year averaging in a tax bill that was passed in late 1992 and subsequently vetoed by former President George Bush. Under the terms of the bill, taxpayers who were born prior to 1936 would have retained the right—under a "grandfather" provision—both to 10-year averaging and to 20% capital gains taxation for pre-1974 plan participation. New legislation to abolish five-year

> **Retirement Tax Trap**
>
> The favorable tax treatment known as forward averaging is available for certain distributions from qualified retirement plans. If you change jobs, you can preserve the right to forward averaging by moving your assets from your old employer's retirement plan directly to your new employer's plan. In lieu of transferring the money directly, you can first roll it over to a "conduit" IRA, then roll it again into the new employer's plan.
>
> **The Trap**
>
> If the conduit IRA holds any other money from regular IRA contributions, none of the distribution can be rolled over into the new employer's plan and you lose the right to use forward averaging on the assets.

averaging, presumably carrying the same grandfather provision, may be introduced into Congress again in the future.

Tax Implications for Annuity Payouts

Many pension and other retirement plan distributions include monies that were contributed to the plan on an after-tax basis. The distributions from tax-deferred annuities purchased directly from an insurance company typically fall into the same category. That is, the monies you receive from these distributions include taxable income as well as a return of the after-tax investments that you made to the plan.

There are two methods of figuring the tax owed on these periodic distributions. The first is known as the general annuity rule, or exclusion ratio rule. The second is known as the simplified general rule, or safe harbor rule, and it applies only to an annuity that meets three criteria: (1) it must have commenced after July 1, 1986; (2) it must be either for your life or the joint life of you and your beneficiary; and (3) the payments to you must begin before you reach age 75 or, if they start at 75 or later, must be guaranteed for fewer than five years.

Under the general annuity or exclusion ratio rule, you must use IRS annuity tables to determine what percentage of each distribution is considered a return of your investment. Since these contributions initially were made using after-tax dollars, they would not be taxed again at the time you begin receiving distributions. The remaining portion of each distribution is taxed as ordinary income. The exclusion percentage is applied against each distribution until the total amount of all of the nontaxable payments that you receive equals the total amount of after-tax contributions you made to the plan, also known as your cost basis. For instructions on how to use this "nonsimplified" method, you should consult IRS Publication 939, *Pension General Rule.* You can order this publication at no charge by calling the IRS at 1-800-TAX-FORM.

The simplified general rule, or safe harbor rule, allows you to calculate the nontaxable percentage of each distribution using a simple table. You merely divide the total amount of your after-tax contributions (your cost basis) by the number of expected monthly payments, to come up with the percentage of each payment that is nontaxable. Table 10–4 summarizes the assumed number of expected payments given various age levels.

Table 10–4	
Annuity Tax Calculation	
(Simplified General Rule)	
Your Age	**Number of Payments**
55 and under	300
56–60	260
61–65	240
66–70	170
71 and over	120

To see how the safe harbor calculation works, assume you are 63 years of age, receive a $1,500 monthly annuity payment as a retirement benefit, and have contributed a total of $36,000 in after-tax dollars to your retirement plan. The nontaxable portion of your payment would be calculated by dividing your cost basis by the number of expected payments ($36,000 divided by 240 equals $150). Thus, $150 of your $1,500 monthly benefit would not be taxed, while the remaining $1,350 would be taxable. After you receive your 240th payment, all subsequent payments are fully taxable. If you die before you receive your 240th payment, your estate receives a deduction for the remaining balance of your unrecovered investment.

For more information on how to determine the taxability of your retirement plan distributions using the simplified general rule, you should consult IRS Publication 575, *Pension and Annuity Income.* A copy may be ordered at no charge by calling the IRS at 1-800-TAX-FORM.

Tax Implications for an IRA

If you withdraw money from an individual retirement account and have previously made non–tax-deductible contributions to any IRA you own, a portion of your withdrawal will be considered nontaxable. This nontaxable portion is based on a simple percentage: the total of your nondeductible IRA contributions, divided by the sum of the aggregate year-end balance of all your IRAs (including IRA-SEPs) plus the total amount of your withdrawals during the year. The calculation for determining the nontaxable portion of your withdrawal would be as follows:

$$\frac{\text{Total nondeductible contributions}}{\substack{\text{Aggregate year-end} \\ \text{IRA balance}} + \substack{\text{Any withdrawals} \\ \text{for year}}} = \text{Nontaxable portion}$$

For example, suppose you have made tax-deductible contributions to your IRA totaling $10,000 and non–tax-deductible contributions totaling $8,000. In 1994, you withdraw $5,000, and at the end of 1994 your remaining IRA balance is $27,000. Of the $5,000 you withdraw, what portion is taxable? Using the formula, the answer is 25%, as shown here:

$$\frac{\$8,000}{\$27,000 + \$5,000} = 0.25 \text{ or } 25\%$$

In other words, 25% of the $5,000 distribution, or $1,250, is nontaxable. The remaining $3,750 is fully taxable.

For subsequent tax years, you would complete the same calculation, with one minor modification. You would reduce your non–tax-deductible IRA contributions in the formula by the nontaxable amounts withdrawn previously. Referring back to the previous example, if $1,250 of your distribution was nontaxable in 1994, your non–tax-deductible balance for 1995 will be the original $8,000 minus the $1,250 nontaxable amount, for a total of $6,750.

Required Minimum Distributions

At age 70½ the blanket tax deferral of the earnings in your IRA or qualified retirement plan generally comes to a conclusion.

The IRS regulations mandate that a minimum amount must be withdrawn each year from your tax-deferred retirement savings. This minimum amount is commonly referred to as a required minimum distribution. The rule applies to any retirement plan balances you may have, such as an IRA, Keogh, 401(k), 403(b), or other plans. Of course, you may always withdraw more than the required minimum; however, you receive no "credit" for any additional amounts taken when determining your minimum distribution in future years. Each year, you must always withdraw at least the required minimum from your retirement assets, based on your life expectancy. The penalty for failing to withdraw the required minimum is 50% of the amount you should have withdrawn but did not. And you must still withdraw the correct amount and pay the appropriate taxes.

Generally, you must begin receiving distributions from your retirement plan every year beginning with the year in which you turn 70½. If you turned 70½ prior to 1988 and are still working, you may defer taking distributions from a qualified retirement plan or a 403(b) plan until April 1 following the year in which you retire. In addition, if you are covered under a governmental or church plan, you also may defer distributions from these plans until April 1 following the year of your retirement, provided that you retire later than age 70½.

How do the required minimum distribution rules work in practice? Normally, your distribution must be completed before the end of the calendar year, although your first required distribution for the year in which you reach age 70½ can be delayed until April 1 of the following year. The minimum distribution is based either on your own life expectancy or on the joint life expectancy of you and your primary beneficiary. For example, a 70-year-old has a life expectancy of 16.0 years. A 70-year-old and a 65-year-old spouse who has been designated as the primary beneficiary have a joint life expectancy of 23.1 years. In determining this figure, IRS life expectancy guidelines must be used. These figures are contained in Publication 590, *Individual Retirement Arrangements*, which can be ordered at no charge by calling the IRS at 1-800-TAX-FORM.

Retirement Tax Trap

Once you reach age 70½, you must start withdrawing money from your retirement plans, including IRAs. Withdrawals must be made based on either your life expectancy or the joint life expectancy of you and your primary beneficiary.

The Trap

If you calculate your required distribution incorrectly and withdraw too little, you will pay a penalty equal to 50% of the amount you should have withdrawn but did not. And you must still withdraw the correct amount and pay taxes on it.

Calculating Your Required Minimum Distribution

To determine your required minimum distribution, you should follow these five basic steps:

1. Determine your age on December 31 of the year in which you reach age 70½. That is, if you were born March 1, 1925, you will reach age 70½ in 1995 and will still be age 70 at the end of 1995.

2. Determine the age of the primary beneficiary of your IRA account at year-end. In this example, assume your spouse is your primary beneficiary and will be 65 years old on December 31, 1995.

3. Find the joint life expectancy figure for you and your beneficiary in the life expectancy tables of Publication 590. In this example, your joint life expectancy is 23.1 years based on your ages at year-end.

4. Determine the balance in your retirement plan as of December 31 of the prior year. In this case, assume you have a 401(k) plan and the total balance was $140,000 at year-end 1994.

5. Calculate your required minimum distribution for 1995 by dividing your year-end 1994 asset balance by your life expectancy factor. In this case, $140,000 divided by 23.1 equals $6,061, or 4.3% of your total asset balance.

According to IRS regulations, you would be required to withdraw at least this amount from your 401(k) plan by April 1, 1996. Remember that even though you would not be required to take this distribution until April 1, 1996, it represents your minimum distribution for *1995*. Your required minimum distribution for *1996* will have to be made by December 31, 1996, resulting in two taxable distributions in 1996.

In reality, required minimum distribution calculations can be much more complex than this example. Please be certain to pay careful attention to this matter or consult someone who is qualified when addressing your own personal situation. A more detailed explanation of the minimum distribution rules can be found in IRS Publication 590, *Individual Retirement Arrangements*.

Beware of the "Success Tax"

If you have accumulated substantial assets in tax-deferred retirement plans, you may face a tax penalty if you withdraw too much in any one year. Specifically, there is a 15% excise tax, in addition to the regular income tax, on any retirement distribution in excess of $150,000 in a single year. (These excess amounts must be reported on tax Form 5329.) The 15% levy on these excess distributions is often referred to as the "success tax." But the tax is in no way limited to so-called millionaires. Indeed, financial planners estimate that retirees who earned salaries in the $100,000 range may find themselves subject to this tax if they do not plan their retirement distributions carefully.

The excise tax applies to monies that you receive from *all* tax-advantaged retirement plans, including company-sponsored pensions, IRAs, Keoghs, and employee stock ownership plans. Distributions that you roll over into another qualified plan or distributions that are made from your own after-tax contributions to a retirement plan are not included. Also excluded from the excise tax are distributions resulting from qualified domestic

---

Retirement Tax Trap

Many retirees have accumulated substantial balances in their retirement plans, which could lead to large withdrawals.

The Trap

If, through a combination of pension plan benefits and withdrawals from your IRA, 401(k), or other qualified retirement plans, you receive more than $150,000 in a single year, you must pay a separate 15% excise tax on the "excess" amount over $150,000. When you withdraw a lump sum from a qualified plan that is eligible for forward averaging, you pay the 15% excise tax on any amount in excess of $750,000.

---

relations orders (i.e., divorce settlements) or those made after an individual's death.

Persons most likely to be hit by the tax typically receive a fairly substantial pension, and then unwittingly withdraw a large sum from an IRA or a 401(k) plan. For example, if you receive a $60,000 annual pension and withdraw $100,000 from your 401(k) plan to buy a retirement home, you will face a 15% excise tax on the $10,000 excess distribution ($60,000 + $100,000 = $160,000).

In many cases, planning ahead should help you to avoid the excess distributions tax. For example, assume you are age 70½ and have a $75,000 annual pension. You must begin taking required minimum distributions from all retirement plans by April 1 of the year after you turn 70½, with another withdrawal required by December 31 of that same year. If you were to take both required distributions in the same calendar year and they exceeded $75,000, your *total* withdrawals, including your pension, would exceed the $150,000 maximum and you would owe taxes on the excess amount. You could avoid this situation by taking the first withdrawal before the end of the year when you turn 70½, instead of taking it by April 1 of the following year.

If you have substantial retirement assets, it may be helpful to plan even further in advance. For example, if you retire at age 65, you should estimate the amount you will be required to withdraw each year once you reach age 70½. If it appears that this amount plus any other retirement plan distributions you expect to receive will exceed $150,000, it may be beneficial to begin distributions prior to age 70½. This strategy will reduce the amount of future required minimum distributions and may help you to avoid the excess distributions tax.

The excess distributions tax also applies to lump sums in excess of $750,000, in cases where forward averaging is used. When you withdraw a lump sum from a qualified plan that is eligible for forward averaging, you pay the 15% excise tax on any amount in excess of $750,000. If you made a special "grandfather election" on your 1987 or 1988 tax return, you are subject to different threshold amounts, which should be used to determine any excess distributions.

Planning Your Retirement Withdrawals

This section is designed to help you plan your retirement withdrawals. By completing the worksheet on pages 184–88, you should be able to make a reasonable estimate of the amount you can spend each year from your retirement savings (other copies of the worksheet can be found in the Appendix). To complete the worksheet, you will need to make two basic assumptions:

1. **Your total investment return.** This figure reflects the total return that you expect to earn on your accumulated assets during your retirement.
2. **Your retirement period.** This figure reflects the number of years that you (and your spouse) expect to make withdrawals from your lump-sum savings.

The figures in the worksheet assume that your entire retirement savings will be exhausted by the time you die. This assumption is typical for financial planning purposes since few retired individuals have sufficient assets to support themselves solely from the earnings on their investments. Of course, many people are reluctant to spend too much of their retirement nest egg, and therefore will gradually reduce their spending habits to ensure that some portion of their principal is preserved to cover a financial emergency or to provide money for their heirs.

To avoid depleting your retirement savings prematurely, you should be conservative when making assumptions about your investment return and the length of your retirement. (With this conservatism in mind, the highest total return assumption in Table 10–5 is +10%.) You should also expect to revise your assumptions periodically to reflect your actual investment returns and your changing goals. Of course, no amount of planning can protect you from the risk of outliving your savings, nor can planning assure specific financial results. The goal of this worksheet exercise is more modest: to reduce the risk of being too far off the mark with your withdrawal program and prematurely depleting your retirement assets. Table 10–5 illustrates the number of years your assets should last assuming various rates of return and distribution percentages.

Table 10–5
How Long Will Your Retirement Assets Last?

Annual Percentage Withdrawn	Annual Total Return									
	1%	**2%**	**3%**	**4%**	**5%**	**6%**	**7%**	**8%**	**9%**	**10%**
15%	6	7	7	7	8	8	9	9	10	11
14	7	7	8	8	9	9	10	11	11	13
13	8	8	8	9	9	10	11	12	13	15
12	8	9	9	10	11	11	12	14	16	18
11	9	10	10	11	12	13	14	16	19	25
10	10	11	12	13	14	15	17	20	26	
9	11	12	13	14	16	18	22	28		
8	13	14	15	17	20	23	30			
7	15	16	18	21	25	33				
6	18	20	23	28	36					
5	22	25	30	41						

Years Your Assets Will Last

Level or Rising Withdrawal Payments?

The worksheet allows you to calculate distributions from an accumulated lump sum in two ways:

1. **Level payments.** Under this approach, your accumulated lump sum and any future earnings are converted into a series of fixed payments for the assumed length of your retirement.

2. **Rising payments.** To help provide for rising costs of living, this method projects a series of annually increasing distributions generated by your accumulated lump sum and any future earnings. (The worksheet assumes distributions grow at a 4% annual rate.)

Figure 10–1 illustrates the implications of these two withdrawal strategies using an accumulated lump sum of $250,000. As you can see, the

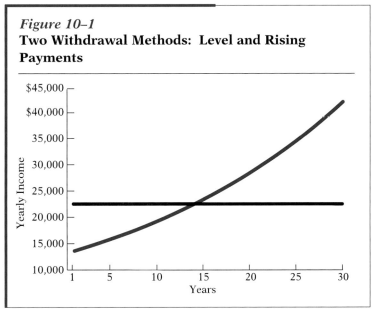

Figure 10–1
Two Withdrawal Methods: Level and Rising Payments

$250,000 lump sum will generate 30 level payments of roughly $20,500 each year, assuming an +8% annual investment return. Alternatively, assuming an +8% annual return and a distribution growth rate of 4% annually, the $250,000 will provide a stream of 30 annual payments beginning at $13,700 in year one and rising gradually to $42,600 in year 30.

Which particular withdrawal method you select will depend on your evaluation of the relative risks involved and your need for current income when you retire. With the level payment method, withdrawals from your lump sum will be higher at the outset; however, the "real" (inflation-adjusted) value of these payments will decline if inflation persists. The rising payment method will provide lower initial distributions, but payments will grow each year to better protect against possible inflation. Of course, a simple compromise might be to withdraw an amount somewhere between the two results shown on the worksheet. Then, every few years during your retirement, recalculate your distributions to determine if you can afford to increase your distributions. This kind of conservative approach is one way to avoid the risk of depleting your savings too early in your retirement, while still enjoying a comfortable standard of living.

Lump-Sum Withdrawal Worksheet

To begin, you should note that this lump-sum withdrawal worksheet does not take into account the impact of taxes on investment earnings or distributions. If your lump sum is invested in a tax-deferred account, such as an IRA, the annual withdrawal amounts will likely be taxable at your current income tax rate. If your lump sum is not invested in a tax-deferred account, you should assume that a portion of your annual investment return will be lost to taxes. For example, if your income tax bracket is 28% and you assume an +8% investment return, your after-tax return will be approximately +6% (100% – 28% = 72%; 72% × 8% = 6%). The worksheet also assumes that inflation will average 4% during your retirement.

Part One: Your Assumptions   Your first step in completing the lump-sum withdrawal worksheet is to specify a future investment return and your expected retirement period.

Line 1   Enter your assumed investment return.

Line 2   Enter your assumed retirement period.

Table 10–6
Part One: Your Assumptions

	Example	Your Own Situation
1. Investment return	8.0%	
2. Retirement period	30	

Part Two: Worksheet Factors   The factors that you will need to complete the worksheet can be found in Table 10–7. You will need to refer to your assumptions in Lines 1 and 2 to determine the appropriate factors from the tables.

Line 3   Enter your level income factor. Assuming a +8% return and a 30-year retirement period, the level income factor from Table 10–7 would be 0.0822.

Table 10–7
Factors for Worksheet

Level Income Factor

Retirement Period	Annual Investment Return						
	6%	7%	8%	9%	10%	11%	12%
15	0.0971	0.1026	0.1082	0.1138	0.1195	0.1253	0.1311
20	0.0822	0.0882	0.0943	0.1005	0.1068	0.1131	0.1195
25	0.0738	0.0802	0.0867	0.0934	0.1002	0.1070	0.1138
30	0.0685	0.0753	0.0822	0.0893	0.0964	0.1036	0.1108
35	0.0651	0.0722	0.0794	0.0868	0.0943	0.1017	0.1092
40	0.0627	0.0701	0.0776	0.0853	0.0930	0.1006	0.1083

Rising Income Factor*

Retirement Period	Annual Investment Return						
	6%	7%	8%	9%	10%	11%	12%
15	0.0759	0.0807	0.0857	0.0907	0.0959	0.1011	0.1065
20	0.0596	0.0646	0.0699	0.0753	0.0809	0.0866	0.0924
25	0.0498	0.0551	0.0606	0.0664	0.0723	0.0785	0.0847
30	0.0433	0.0489	0.0547	0.0607	0.0670	0.0735	0.0801
35	0.0388	0.0445	0.0505	0.0569	0.0635	0.0702	0.0772
40	0.0354	0.0413	0.0475	0.0541	0.0610	0.0681	0.0753

*Assumes a 4% annual distribution growth rate

Line 4   Enter your rising income factor. Assuming a +8% return and a 30-year retirement period, the rising income factor from Table 10–7 would be 0.0547.

Table 10–8
Part Two: Worksheet Factors

	Example	Your Own Situation
3. Level income factor (Table 10–7)	0.0822	
4. Rising income factor (Table 10–7)*	0.0547	

Part Three: Annual Income from Lump-Sum Savings   The third step in the worksheet determines the amount of income you will receive on a monthly basis from the proceeds of your lump-sum investment.

Line 5   Enter your expected aggregate lump-sum savings at retirement. This figure should include any assets that you hold in employer-sponsored retirement savings plans, as well as personal savings that you have accumulated in an IRA or other savings vehicle. Remember that while this worksheet does not take taxes into account, withdrawals from tax-deferred accounts will be taxable at your then-current tax rate. If your retirement savings are invested in both tax-deferred and taxable accounts, you should use a separate worksheet for the tax-deferred and taxable portions. For the taxable savings, assume a lower annual net investment return to reflect the impact of taxes on earnings.

Line 6   Calculate your annual fixed withdrawal amount by multiplying Line 5 by Line 3. If you withdraw this amount each year, and if you meet your investment return assumption, your retirement savings will last for the period you specified in Line 2.

Line 7   Convert your annual fixed withdrawal amount into a monthly amount by dividing Line 6 by 12. In the example above, a fixed annual payment of $20,500 over 30 years translates into $1,700 a month for the same period.

Line 8   Calculate your annual withdrawal amount assuming rising payments by multiplying Line 5 by Line 4. The worksheet assumes a 4% annual distribution growth rate.

Line 9   Calculate your monthly distributions for the first year by dividing Line 8 by 12. In each subsequent year for the next 30 years, this monthly amount will be increased by 4%. Thus, the withdrawal of $1,100 per month in the first year will rise to $1,140 per month in the second year, $1,190 per month in the third year, and so on.

Table 10–9
Part Three: Annual Income from Lump-Sum Savings

	Example	Your Own Situation
5. Your retirement lump-sum savings	$250,000	
6. Level income, annual (Line 5 × Line 3)	20,500	
7. Level income, monthly (Line 6 ÷ 12)	1,700	
8. Rising income, annual (Line 5 × Line 4)	13,700	
9. Rising income, monthly (Line 8 ÷ 12)	1,100	

Part Four: Income Summary   You should use this section to summarize all of the major sources of income you expect to receive during your retirement. The Retirement Savings Worksheet discussed in Chapter 3 illustrates the monthly pension and Social Security benefits you determined previously.

Line 10   Enter your monthly Social Security benefit. You should have estimated this figure in the Retirement Savings Worksheet in Chapter 3.

Line 11   Enter any monthly benefits from an employer-sponsored pension plan.

Line 12   Enter monthly income from lump-sum investments (from Line 7 or Line 9).

Line 13   Enter any other expected retirement income.

Line 14   Add Lines 10 through 13 to determine your total monthly retirement income.

Table 10–10
Part Four: Income Summary

	Example	Your Own Situation
10. Social Security	$1,300	_____
11. Pension	900	_____
12. Income from lump sum (Line 7 or Line 9)	1,100	_____
13. Other income	0	_____
14. Total monthly income (Line 10 + Line 11 + Line 12 + Line 13)	3,300	_____

Final Thoughts

It is probably apparent that taking distributions from your retirement savings is not quite as simple as you might think. There are a number of critical decisions to be made as you approach and enter into your retirement, each of which impacts the level of income you will receive, the taxability of this income, and how long the income will last. So, these decisions should be given serious consideration well before your actual retirement begins.

While the regulations that govern retirement plans are complicated, there is no reason that your transition into retirement should be anything other than a rewarding experience, provided that you follow the basic guidelines outlined in this chapter. That involves, first and foremost, planning ahead and considering carefully how you will handle all of your retirement plan distributions, including any monies you expect to receive over the years from your IRA. You also need to explore your options thoroughly before you move or redeem your retirement assets, and be wary of the tax traps that may snare the unsuspecting investor. If you are ever in doubt along the way about how to proceed, do not hesitate to seek help from a qualified tax adviser or financial planner.

Remember also that each decision you face should be made in the context of your overall financial situation. Nowhere is it written that you must take an "all or nothing" approach to your retirement. For instance, it may make sense to arrange for part of your retirement assets to be paid out as an annuity or systematic installment that you cannot outlive, and to invest the remainder in a diversified portfolio of mutual funds that can provide income and capital growth to keep pace with inflation.

Indeed, just as mutual funds are an ideal investment vehicle for building your retirement savings, they are also an ideal vehicle for managing your accumulated assets during your retirement. The flexibility, diversification, and range of investments available from mutual funds enable you to easily adjust the mix of your retirement assets to meet your changing objectives. Most mutual fund organizations also offer convenient services for distributing your retirement assets. For example, a systematic withdrawal plan allows you to receive regular monthly distributions from your mutual fund. And many fund sponsors will calculate your required minimum distribution for you, so you can be certain of complying with the IRS guidelines.

If you have followed the long retirement road laid out in this guide, you should be looking forward to a comfortable retirement. However, many investors may find that they simply have not accumulated sufficient assets to assure a comfortable retirement. If you are among this group, do not despair. Chapter 11 outlines a number of simple strategies you can employ in your later years to greatly improve your retirement situation.

Retirement Strategies for the Later Years

At each stage in the investment life cycle, you face new challenges and opportunities in your quest for financial security. As you approach your 50s, the final stage of your working years, you may begin to realize that your retirement savings efforts have not been sufficient to meet the retirement lifestyle that you desire. Don't lose heart! Even at this late stage in your retirement savings program, there are quite a few options available to give your savings one final boost.

As you near retirement, your earnings and disposable income are likely to be at their peak, leaving considerable excess resources that can be invested for your retirement. What is more, some major expenses, such as mortgage payments and college tuition, may suddenly cease. And tax breaks, such as the one-time $125,000 exclusion from capital gains taxation on the sale of your residence, will become available. All of these lifestyle changes present opportunities to strengthen your finances and free up additional cash flow for investment purposes.

This chapter presents a series of "final stretch" measures you might consider as you near retirement. If you are fortunate enough to be on sound financial footing as you approach your retirement years, you may wish to give this chapter only a cursory glance. But if you are like many retirees and you could use a few dollars more to enjoy your retirement to its fullest, you will find some invaluable suggestions. In particular, the final section of this chapter on estate planning should be of interest whatever your financial circumstances.

While it is difficult to find new sources of income as you approach the final decade before you retire, it is possible to work within the income that you receive to find new opportunities to add to your retirement savings. This section highlights just a few of the options that may be available to boost your level of savings.

Savings Strategies

As noted in Chapter 1, the key to a comfortable retirement is having the discipline to save. While saving presumes that you have discretionary income, you may find "excess cash" in some surprising places.

Pay Your Mortgage . . . Again

If your monthly mortgage payment is $1,000 and you pay off your loan by, say, age 53, you could continue to make the same payments, but instead of paying the bank you could invest the proceeds in your retirement savings. Assuming a +8% return and a 31% tax rate, doing so would accumulate a balance of $204,000 by the time you reach age 65. By the same measure, if you have been making regular monthly payments for college expenses, continue investing the same amount of money into your retirement savings even after the tuition bills have stopped. In each case, if you haven't had the money available to spend, you won't even miss it.

Of course, to the extent possible, these additional savings should always be directed to tax-advantaged accounts. Using the example above, saving $1,000 each month in a tax-deferred account earning +8% annually would result in your final accumulated balance at age 65 increasing from $204,000 to $241,000. And, if your contributions are tax-deductible, the government is, in essence, making part of the contribution for you. For example, if you are in the 31% tax bracket, the government is providing $310 of each contribution in the form of an interest-free loan until you withdraw the money and pay taxes on it. You should never overlook the compelling mathematics of tax-deductibility.

Save All Pay Raises and Bonuses

During your peak earning years, the pay increases and bonuses you receive are likely to be the highest of your career. Channeling these "windfalls" into your retirement savings will give your retirement investment program a nice boost. For example, say you earn an annual salary of $75,000 and are approaching the five-year mark until retirement. If you receive 5% raises over each of the next five years and save the entire amount of each raise in a tax-deferred account earning an +8% return, you will have added about $72,000 to your retirement nest egg in just five years.

Don't Splurge

When you reach your 50s, you may suddenly find that for the first time in your life you can afford to buy that expensive car you have always wanted. Avoid giving in to this indulgence, unless your retirement nest egg is on solid ground. Otherwise, consider buying a cheaper car and investing the difference in your retirement portfolio.

Cut Your Discretionary Spending

If you can reduce your monthly spending, you will benefit from a higher savings rate, even as you acclimate yourself to the reduced level of income you may receive once your paycheck has stopped. Try cutting your discretionary spending by, say, 5% over the next 12 months and invest the difference. In the following year, cut your spending by an additional 5%, again investing the difference. You may be surprised how quickly some small sacrifices here and there—one less dinner on the town, a few less rounds of golf—can add to your retirement nest egg.

Postpone Your Retirement

As mentioned in Chapter 8, another sure way to augment your retirement savings is to continue to work past age 65. For example, assume you have 20 years of service at age 60 and earn an annual salary of $75,000. If your company allows early retirement at age 60, your annual pension may be about $18,000. At the normal retirement age of 65 you would receive an annual pension of about $28,500. If your company allows, you could continue building your retirement benefits by delaying your retirement until age 70, resulting in an annual pension of about $43,500. (Each of these examples assumes a 5% annual salary increase and a pension benefit equal to 1.25% of average salary in the final three years.)

In the same manner, delaying the receipt of your Social Security benefits past age 65 will also boost the monthly benefits that you receive. If you were born in 1931 or 1932, for example, the increase is 5% for each year that you delay collecting benefits, up until age 70. This credit is being raised gradually so that it will amount to 8% per year for those born after 1942.

When devising their retirement strategy, many retirees do not take into account the most important asset that they own: their home. There are many legitimate options, such as trading down to a smaller home, taking out a reverse mortgage, or arranging a sale-leaseback, that allow you to "have your cake and eat it, too."

Taking Advantage of Your Home Equity

An often overlooked source of capital for retirement is the equity in your home.

"Trading Down" Your Home

The federal tax code offers two highly advantageous preretirement financial planning options to homeowners who have built up substantial equity in their primary residences. If used appropriately, these allowances may enable you to "trade down" to a less-expensive home and at the same time free up cash to add to your retirement portfolio. The first tax code provision allows you to take a one-time exclusion of up to $125,000 in capital gains realized from the sale of your primary residence. The second provision enables you to defer taxes on some or all of any remaining capital gains above the $125,000 exclusion by purchasing a replacement home.

To be eligible for the $125,000 capital gain exclusion, your transaction must meet certain restrictions:

■ You must be age 55 or older at the time of the sale of your residence. If you and your spouse own the residence jointly and file a joint tax return, only one of you must be age 55 or older to be eligible for the exclusion.

■ Neither you nor your spouse can ever have used the exclusion before.

■ The home must have been your primary residence for at least three of the five years prior to the date of the sale.

To be eligible to defer the capital gain on the sale of a primary residence when you buy a new residence, you must meet the following requirements:

■ You must buy and occupy your new residence within 24 months before or after selling your old residence.

■ The price of the new residence must be equal to or greater than the adjusted sales price of your old residence. The adjusted sales price is the selling price less direct selling expenses, any fix-up expenses related to the sale, and, if applicable, the one-time $125,000 exclusion.

■ You must not have deferred a gain on the sale and replacement of your primary residence within the last two years, unless you did so as the result of a job transfer or to accept a new job in another location.

The following example illustrates the tax calculations involved for a 55-year-old selling a principal residence, electing to use the $125,000 one-time exclusion, and buying a lower-cost replacement residence. The example assumes a cost basis of $120,000 and a selling price of $300,000 for the existing residence, and a purchase price of $150,000 for the replacement residence. To determine the portion of the capital gain not covered by the $125,000 exclusion:

Sales price	$300,000
Less: cost basis	(120,000)
Gain before exclusion	$180,000
Less: $125,000 exclusion	(125,000)
Gain after exclusion	$ 55,000

To determine the amount of the capital gain realized and subject to taxation:

Sales price	$300,000
Less: $125,000 exclusion	(125,000)
Adjusted sales price	$175,000
Less: cost of new residence	(150,000)
Gain realized and taxable	$ 25,000

To determine the cost basis of the new residence:

Cost of new residence	$150,000
Less: gain after exclusion	(55,000)
Add: Gain recognized and taxable	25,000
Cost basis of new residence	$120,000

How does the transaction in this example free up cash for investment purposes? The proceeds from selling the old home amount to $300,000, less any sales commission and closing costs. The cash expenses associated with the purchase of the new home consist of a down payment of $30,000 (20% of $150,000) plus the $7,000 tax owed ($25,000 × 0.28, assuming a 28% tax rate) on the recognized capital gain, for a total of $37,000. That leaves net proceeds of $263,000. Even allowing for transaction costs and moving expenses, downsizing in this instance generates a substantial amount of excess cash.

This transaction actually could be made even more attractive. If the cost of the new residence had been $175,000 instead of $150,000, the recognized capital gain from the sale and the replacement of the primary residence would have been zero, leaving no tax liability. A 20% down payment on the new residence would require $35,000, so the available cash would be $265,000. The result, assuming the same transaction and moving costs as in the first example, would be an extra $2,000 available for investment purposes and a house worth $25,000 more. For more information on the mathematics of trading down, you should refer to IRS Form 2119.

Many retirees combine trading down to a less-expensive residence with trading down to a less-expensive community as well. The so-called Sun Belt states offer warm weather as well as a fairly low cost of living, a combination that is difficult to resist if your goal is to live comfortably on a smaller budget. If you are considering such a move, you should give some thought to the following issues.

Become Familiar with the New Location   Before you make any final decisions, you should visit the area at different times of the year. An area that offers a temperate climate during the winter months may not be as appealing during the "dog days" of summer. Be sure to thoroughly investigate health care facilities in the community, particularly if you have a medical condition that may require specialized or emergency treatment. And make sure that the types of recreational and cultural activities you enjoy are available. After you retire, you may find that your interests have increased in the arts, movies, library reading, theater, adult education, and similar activities. Don't simply assume that the new location will offer all of the recreational and cultural resources that you will want.

Consider All Taxes, Not Just Income Taxes   The idea of moving to a state with no income tax may seem like a powerful attraction. But remember that your earned income in the form of salary or wages will either disappear altogether or decline substantially during your retirement. So, the absence of a state income tax may not be the advantage that you thought it was. What is more, states with no income taxes typically have relatively high sales taxes, and may also levy taxes on both tangible personal property (e.g., automobiles) and intangible property (e.g., stocks and bonds).

In considering whether to relocate, you should determine what these taxes will amount to each year based on the property that you own. Keep in mind that your consumption of goods and services will probably increase during your retirement, so you should estimate any tax increase that will result from higher sales taxes.

Compare Costs Carefully   In addition to estimating taxes, you should prepare a budget outlining what you expect to spend on housing, food, utilities, taxes, auto insurance, medical care, recreation, and the like. While your heating costs may be lower at a new location, your air conditioning costs may be higher. If your move will result in extra traveling costs to visit friends and family, include these expenses in your budget for the new location.

Be Prepared to "Disengage" from Your Old Location

Individuals who buy a retirement home in another state may find themselves contacted by the tax authorities of the state they left. To avoid the risk of being taxed as a resident of both states, you must abandon your domicile in the old state. Evidence that you have done so might include taking the following steps: (1) obtaining a new driver's license and relinquishing your old one; (2) moving your bank and brokerage accounts; (3) renting a safe deposit box at the new location and moving your valuables; (4) changing your voter registration; and (5) electing nonresident status or resigning from business and social organizations at your old location.

Consider Personal and Family Issues

Many retirees are reluctant to pull up stakes and move away from relatives, life-long friends, and their home communities. Carefully weigh the importance of these factors in your relocation decision. If you have friends and acquaintances who live at the new location, your move obviously will be much easier. In all, even if you have no reservations about your new location, you might consider renting for at least a year before purchasing a new home.

Reverse Mortgages

Reverse mortgage loans are a new form of mortgage that allow you to convert the equity in your home into installment payments that could provide you with monthly income for life. By taking out a reverse mortgage, you borrow against your property but, instead of getting the proceeds in a lump sum, they are paid to you in installments. As an alternative, you may have the option of getting the proceeds in the form of regular payments for a predetermined period of time (say, 10 years) or in the form of a credit line against which you can withdraw money when you want it. When you die or move from your house, your reverse equity loan immediately becomes due.

Since there are no monthly payments due for a reverse mortgage, you do not need a salary or other earnings to qualify. The amount of monthly income you can obtain from a reverse mortgage depends on several factors, including your age, prevailing interest rates, and the value of your property. Although reverse mortgages are available to borrowers age 62 and older, the monthly income is much higher for older borrowers. An 85-year-old taking out a reverse mortgage, for example, might expect roughly five times the monthly payment that would be available to a 65-year-old borrower on property valued at the same amount.

While available in most states, reverse mortgages are relatively new and are not widely used. A program authorized by Congress will make guarantees from the Federal Housing Administration available for 25,000 reverse mortgages through September 1995. Reverse mortgages are expected to become more common as private lenders gain experience with them and as a secondary market emerges to enable lenders to sell reverse equity mortgages to investors.

Sale-Leaseback Arrangements

A sale-leaseback transaction is typically arranged between retiree-parents and their children. The parents sell their home to the child (or a partnership of two or more children), and then arrange to lease the home and continue to live in it. In a sale-leaseback transaction, the parents often will use their $125,000 capital gain exclusion and finance the transaction by taking back a mortgage. The sales price, mortgage interest, and monthly rental fee must be at market rates for the transaction to meet Internal Revenue Service approval. One caveat: Sale-leaseback transactions between parents and children involve important tax and estate planning issues. They may or may not be appropriate for your individual circumstances, so you should consult a qualified attorney or tax adviser before taking any action.

As you are probably aware, you may leave an unlimited amount of assets to your spouse free of federal estate tax. And each individual has a $600,000 lifetime exemption from federal gift and estate taxes, meaning that there is no tax on the first $600,000 in your estate. But above that amount, federal taxes begin at 37% and rise to a steep 55% on estates above $3 million. State levies on estates may significantly increase the total tax bill. Even estates that would be considered moderate in size today face a substantial tax bite at these rates.

Estate planning issues can be exceedingly complex; thus, you should probably seek the advice of an attorney or some other qualified professional in this area before making any changes to your estate. This section presents a quick overview of five basic estate planning considerations that will be important to virtually every investor.

A Few Words about Estate Planning

Whatever your financial circumstances, you should be using some basic estate planning techniques to ensure the orderly, tax-minimized transfer of your property to your designated beneficiaries after your death.

Prepare and Execute a Will

Most Americans still die without a will. Yet having a will is the most common way to ensure that assets held in your name are distributed according to your intentions. You may intend, for example, to leave your assets to your spouse. But if you die without a will, your property will likely be split among your spouse and your children by a court according to state law. A will also carries out the important functions of naming a guardian to oversee the interests of minor children and an executor to administer your estate. Without a will, a court would also make those choices for you. The absence of a will is also likely to mean significant delays in settling your estate, possibly delaying the distribution of assets to your heirs at a time of financial need.

Consider a Living Trust

When you establish a living trust, also known as a revocable trust, you transfer title of assets in your name to the trust. You select the beneficiaries in the event of your death, just as you would in a will. If state law permits, you can also designate yourself as trustee to manage the trust assets. Living trusts provide few tax advantages, but in states where probate is costly and time-consuming they may be an attractive alternative. Living trusts also avoid the public disclosure that usually accompanies probate proceedings in court. And if you own real estate in more than one state, a living trust will allow your heirs to avoid multiple probate proceedings.

Consider a Power of Attorney and Living Will

A durable power of attorney is a document used to designate someone as your guardian in the event you become incompetent. Normally, this person would handle your financial and business affairs in your place. A living will is a document declaring that you do not want artificial medical steps taken to prolong your life in the event of a terminal illness. As an alternative to a living will, you may want to execute a separate power of attorney for health care. This document would appoint someone as your agent to make health care decisions for you if you become incapacitated. You can establish the extent of the agent's powers and include instructions about what medical treatment would be acceptable or unacceptable to you. Laws covering living wills and powers of attorney for health care vary by state, so check with an attorney before relying on one of these arrangements.

Take Advantage of the $10,000 Gift-Tax Exemption

You can give up to $10,000 each year to as many people as you like, free of federal gift or income taxes. Couples filing joint tax returns can give up to $20,000. By giving money each year to your intended heirs in this fashion, you will reduce your estate and avoid taxes. For example, a couple with three married children and six grandchildren could give $20,000 each to the children, their spouses, and the grandchildren, or a total of $240,000 in one year, all free of tax.

Don't Waste Your $600,000 Gift/Estate Tax Exemption

Many people incorrectly assume that because each individual is entitled to the $600,000 exemption, a married couple can avoid taxes on an estate up to $1.2 million. That is true, but only if you plan carefully. Say Mr. and Mrs. Jones have $2.2 million in assets. Mr. Jones dies first and leaves everything to Mrs. Jones. His $1.1 million in property is covered by the unlimited spousal deduction, so no federal estate tax is due. But when Mrs. Jones dies, her estate—now valued at $2.2 million—is subject to $700,000 in taxes, so the Jones children inherit $1.5 million.

With careful planning, Mr. Jones could have left $600,000 of his $1.1 million in trust for his wife and children, with the trust income going to Mrs. Jones for the remainder of her life and the principal going to the children upon her death. Mr. Jones's remaining $500,000 would be left to his wife and would be covered by the spousal deduction. Upon her death, Mrs. Jones's estate would total $1.6 million and would pay estate taxes of $425,000. As a result, the Jones children would inherit $1.775 million, almost $300,000 more than they would have received under the first example.

You may find some of the strategies highlighted in this chapter worthwhile whether you are in retirement, near retirement, or just starting to plan for a distant retirement. However, the issues and strategies can be quite complex depending on your individual situation, and you should not hesitate to contact a qualified financial planner or attorney when it comes to the actual implementation stage.

Final Thoughts

A t this point, you probably have a good appreciation of how uncertain your retirement will be if you do not determine now to take responsibility for your own financial security. The future of the Social Security system is tenuous, and it is unlikely that the promises made to today's generation of wage earners can be kept if the system remains in its present state. What's more, the private pension system has evolved in ways that may weaken retirement security for many employees. And the tradition of career employment, capped by a guaranteed pension, has become somewhat fractured as a result of the economic dislocations of recent years. Rather than spend their working careers with one company, employees today tend to switch jobs frequently, often losing critical pension benefits along the way.

In this dynamic and challenging environment, we all must start early in our working lives to establish a retirement investment program. To be successful, such a program must entail considerable savings discipline and should take advantage of all available tax deferrals and tax exemptions. In addition to maintaining a regular monthly savings program, you probably will need to save in larger amounts than you are currently. The exceptional investment returns of the 1980s are unlikely to be repeated, and investors today seeking to accumulate retirement benefits for tomorrow will find that they must set aside considerably more of their yearly income to build the same size nest egg as their parents.

For example, if, during the decade of the 1980s, you wanted to accumulate, say, $100,000 in a balanced portfolio (one-third in each asset class) through a program of regular monthly savings, you would have needed to make contributions of about $400 each month to meet your objective, based on an aggregate annual rate of return of +13%. If the rate of return on a similarly balanced portfolio falls to, say, +8% in the coming decade, you will need to make contributions of $540 each month to reach the same final asset objective. As you can see, even though your monthly contributions are some 35% higher in the second instance, your accumulated asset total remains unchanged.

With lower returns in prospect for financial assets, it is even more critical that you establish and follow a thoughtful investment plan for your retirement. By way of summary, the following eight "rules" for retirement investing nicely encapsulate the major themes of this guide.

Be Knowledgeable You should develop a basic familiarity with the workings of the economy and the financial markets—both at the outset of your investment program and on an ongoing basis. Think about your investments from an historical perspective and consider the likely long-term trade-offs between reward and risk. When considering a mutual fund investment, evaluate the fund on the basis of its investment objectives and policies, its continuity of management, the reputation of its sponsor, and its costs.

Be Steadfast You must develop a basic financial plan for your investments and "stay the course," allowing nothing to distract you from your long-term goals. When financial markets turn against you, as they inevitably will, remember your long-term investment plan and avoid the temptation to abruptly change course. Remember that you *cannot* time the movements of the financial markets with any degree of consistency. In particular, periods of market pressure or weakness generally tend to be the worst times to shift the assets in your portfolio. Your ability to remain steadfast in the face of market challenges will be a significant determinant of the long-term results of your retirement investment program.

Be Consistent It is generally better to build your retirement portfolio by contributing on a systematic basis (i.e., dollar-cost averaging) rather than making large, all-at-once investments. While a regular investment program will not entirely insulate you from portfolio losses, dollar-cost averaging provides a disciplined investment approach that will serve you well. Any IRA, 401(k), or 403(b) retirement plan provides an easy-to-use investment vehicle for systematic—and tax-advantaged—retirement investing.

Be Balanced Holding a balanced portfolio of stocks, bonds, and short-term reserves is the most sensible way to hedge against the vagaries of the financial markets. Overseas securities and real estate holdings may also be appropriate to further diversify your portfolio, but these investments should be considered in the light of the incremental risks they entail. When in doubt, a single balanced mutual fund would be the best course of action. Remember also that the portfolio allocation you maintain during your accumulation years probably will not be appropriate for your retirement years, when you likely will require a generous and sustainable current income stream. The life cycle approach to investing should be your guide to portfolio allocation.

Be Diversified   Diversification is simply common sense. Whatever investment balance you select, you should spread your investments among a large number of stocks and bonds. The easiest—and typically least expensive—way to accomplish this objective is through mutual funds. In a single portfolio, you can achieve a level of diversification that likely could never be attained by investing in individual securities.

Be Risk-Aware, Not Risk-Avoiding   While you should carefully analyze the potential risks of every prospective investment—and measure that risk against your personal financial circumstances—be wary of stockpiling your retirement portfolio with "risk-free" investments. Many investors view risk primarily as the chance that they will lose money, and therefore hold money market instruments or certificates of deposit to eliminate the possibility of principal losses. But on a long-term basis, risk is more accurately thought of as the possibility that your accumulated assets (adjusted for inflation) will be insufficient to meet your financial goals. In this light, while stocks clearly have had the highest risk in terms of short-term price volatility, they have had the lowest risk in terms of long-term protection of your assets against the erosion of inflation.

Be Cost Conscious   When choosing among mutual funds, sensible investment analysis demands that you consider all three aspects of investing—risk, return, and cost. The basis for this "investment triangle" is simple: the sales commissions and annual management and administrative fees paid by fund investors reduce, dollar for dollar, the gross returns that they earn. In other words, *other factors held equal,* the investment program with the lowest cost (including any sales charges, management fees, operating expenses, etc.) will provide the highest return. That is not to say that you should never buy a high-cost fund or a fund with a sales charge. But you should recognize that these funds have a built-in disadvantage relative to their low-cost, no-load counterparts. The difference between an expense ratio of 2.0% and 0.5% may not have seemed all that significant during the past decade, when the returns on financial assets averaged about +13% annually. But this cost differential takes on greater importance if returns on financial assets move considerably lower. A 2.0% expense ratio consumes only about one-seventh of a + 13% return; it consumes one-fourth of an +8% return. Adding in a modest inflation rate of 3%, an investor's real return would barely be in positive territory.

Be Skeptical   Do not succumb to the common pitfalls of inexperienced investors: (1) making investment decisions based on crowd psychology, (2) following the lead of "market gurus," or (3) giving in to the allure of market timing. Never forget that past returns only indicate how an investment performed yesterday and rarely indicate how an investment will perform tomorrow. There are no easy answers in the complex world of investing, and you should be skeptical of any financial advice that you receive, including the advice offered in this guide.

If you take nothing else away from this guide, remember that financial security can only be accomplished through careful and deliberate planning—and then action! In the words of Benjamin Franklin, "He that lives upon hope will die fasting." While Mr. Franklin probably did not intend that somewhat grim assessment to apply to retirement planning, the message could hardly be more appropriate. You cannot simply wait for your retirement to happen and hope for the best. Plan carefully, act decisively, and the success of your retirement investing program is virtually assured.

Glossary of Terms

A

Accumulation Period   The period during your working years when you make regular contributions to a deferred annuity or retirement plan account. See **payout period.**

Active Investing   An investment approach that seeks to exceed the returns of the financial markets. Active managers rely on research, market forecasts, and their own judgment and experience in making investment decisions.

Actuarial Equivalence   Two annuity payout options that have the same actuarial value. For example, a lifetime monthly benefit of $67.60 starting at age 60 has an actuarial equivalence to a monthly benefit of $100 beginning at age 65. The value of annuity payout options will vary depending on the assumed interest rate and life expectancy.

Advisory Fee   See **management fee.**

Annuitant   A person covered by an annuity contract.

Annuity   In general, a series of payments continuing until death. A commercial annuity is a contract issued by an insurance company that provides some level of payments for the life of the annuitant. Fixed annuities guarantee a particular rate of interest for a certain period of time, after which the guaranteed rate is reset. Variable annuities permit you to allocate your money among a group of mutual funds with different investment objectives. See also **single life annuity, joint-and-survivor annuity, accumulation period,** and **payout period.**

Annuity Payout Option   A pension plan benefit that is paid in the form of a monthly distribution for life.

Ask Price   See **offering price.**

Automatic Investment Plan   An arrangement that permits regular investments in a mutual fund through payroll deductions, automatic transfers from a checking account, or automatic exchanges from another mutual fund.

Automatic Reinvestment   An arrangement whereby distributions of mutual fund dividends or capital gains are used to purchase additional fund shares.

B

Back-End Load   A sales commission paid at the time mutual fund shares are sold. May also be called a redemption fee or contingent deferred sales charge. In some cases, back-end loads may be gradually phased out over a period of years.

Beneficiary   The person designated to receive the proceeds of a pension, retirement account, annuity contract, or insurance policy in the event of the holder's death.

Broker-Dealer   A securities firm that sells mutual funds or other securities to the public.

C

Capital Gains Distribution   Payment to mutual fund shareholders of any gains realized during the year on securities that have been sold at a profit. Capital gains are distributed on a "net" basis, after subtracting any capital losses for the year. When losses exceed gains for the year, the difference may be carried forward and subtracted from future gains. Capital gains distributions are usually made annually.

Closed-End Fund   A closed-end investment company that pools money from individuals to establish a portfolio of stocks or bonds. Unlike an open-end fund, a closed-end fund issues a fixed number of shares, which then trade as an individual stock.

Conduit IRA   An individual retirement account established for the purpose of receiving a rollover of a lump-sum distribution. By using a conduit IRA, you preserve the right to roll over the balance into a new employer qualified retirement plan.

Contingent Deferred Sales Charge   See **back-end load.**

Custodian   A bank, trust company, or other organization responsible for safeguarding financial assets.

D

Defined Benefit Plan   A retirement plan that guarantees a certain benefit, usually based on average salary in the period before retirement and on the number of years of service. Employers bear the investment risk with defined benefit plans. Benefits in most cases are guaranteed up to a certain monthly limit by the Pension Benefit Guaranty Corporation, a federal agency.

Defined Contribution Plan   A retirement plan offering a benefit that is dependent on total contributions made by the employer and the employee and on the investment returns earned by those contributions. Employees bear the investment risk with defined contribution plans. See also **profit-sharing plan, 401(k) plan, money purchase plan,** and **employee stock ownership plan.**

Direct Transfer   Moving tax-deferred retirement plan money from one plan or custodian directly to another. A transfer is not a withdrawal and does not incur any taxes or penalties.

Dividend Distribution   Payment to mutual fund shareholders of income from interest or dividends generated by the fund's investments. Dividends may be paid on a quarterly, semiannual, or annual basis.

Dollar-Cost Averaging   Investing equal amounts of money at regular intervals on an ongoing basis. This technique reduces average share costs over time because more shares are acquired during periods when prices are lower, and fewer shares when prices are higher.

E

Early Withdrawal Penalty A 10% penalty (in addition to ordinary income taxes owed) on money withdrawn from a tax-advantaged retirement plan before age 59½. Penalty does not apply in special circumstances.

Employee Retirement Income Security Act of 1974 (ERISA) The primary federal law governing private pension plans. ERISA sets standards for funding and administering pension plans and governs investment practices. The ERISA law also established a federal program to guarantee benefits from defined benefit plans under the Pension Benefit Guaranty Corporation.

Employee Stock Ownership Plan A qualified retirement plan that invests in the employer's company stock on behalf of employees.

Excess Distribution Any amount over $150,000 withdrawn from retirement plans by an individual in a single year. The excess amount is subject to a 15% excise tax.

Exchange Privilege The right to exchange shares in one fund for shares in another fund within the same fund family, typically at no charge but sometimes for a nominal fee.

Ex-Dividend Date The date when a distribution of dividends or capital gains is deducted from a mutual fund's assets or set aside for payment to shareholders. See also **record date** and **payable date.**

Expense Ratio The percentage of a fund's average net assets used to pay fund expenses. The expense ratio takes into account management fees, administrative fees, and any 12b–1 fees.

F

401(k) Plan A defined contribution plan that allows employees to contribute pretax dollars through salary deferral. The contribution limit is $9,240 in 1994. Many plans offer a variety of investment options, including stocks, bonds, short-term reserves, and company stock.

403(b) Plan A type of tax-sheltered annuity available to employees of the government and nonprofit organizations. Employees can make pretax contributions up to an annual limit (generally $9,500 in 1994).

Fee Table A table, included at the front of a mutual fund's prospectus, illustrating expenses and fees charged by the fund.

Fixed-Income Securities Investments, such as bonds, that have a fixed payment schedule. While the level of income offered by these securities is predetermined, they may fluctuate in price.

Forward Averaging A method of calculating taxes on a lump-sum distribution from a qualified retirement plan that enables you to pay less than your current tax rate.

Front-End Load A sales commission paid at the time shares of a mutual fund are purchased.

Fund Family A group of mutual funds sponsored by the same organization, often offering exchange privileges between funds and combined account statements for multiple funds.

I

Individual Retirement Account (IRA)   A tax-deferred retirement account for workers that allows annual contributions of up to $2,000, or $2,250 for a spousal IRA established by a worker and nonworking spouse. IRA contributions are fully deductible for single persons with income up to $25,000 and married couples making up to $40,000. Deductibility is phased out for single persons with incomes between $25,000 and $35,000 and for married couples with incomes between $40,000 and $50,000 who participate in employer-sponsored retirement plans.

In-Service Withdrawal   A withdrawal from an employer-sponsored retirement plan by a participant who remains employed.

Investment Adviser   An individual or organization that manages a portfolio and makes day-to-day investment decisions regarding the purchase or sale of securities.

Investment Objective   A mutual fund's performance goal, such as long-term capital appreciation, high current income, or tax-exempt income.

J–K

Joint-and-Survivor Annuity   An annuity covering two people and paying benefits until the last survivor dies. A 100% joint-and-survivor annuity pays the same benefit to both annuitants. A 50% joint-and-survivor annuity pays the surviving annuitant only 50% of the amount paid to the first annuitant.

Keogh Plan   See **self-employed pension.**

L

Load Fund   A mutual fund that charges a sales commission.

Low-Load Fund   A mutual fund that charges a sales commission of 3% or less.

Lump-Sum Distribution   Payment(s) representing an employee's interest in a qualified retirement plan. The payment must be prompted by retirement (or other separation from service), death, disability, or attaining age $59\frac{1}{2}$ and must be made within a single tax year. Lump-sum distributions are eligible for forward averaging or rollover.

M

Management Fee   The fee paid by a mutual fund to its investment adviser.

Money Purchase Plan   A type of defined contribution plan in which employer contributions are based on a percentage of the employee's pay.

Mutual Fund   An open end investment company that pools money from individuals and uses it to purchase securities such as stocks, bonds, and money market instruments. Mutual funds issue and redeem shares on a daily basis at net asset value, less any applicable sales commissions.

N

Net Asset Value (NAV)   The value of a mutual fund's total assets, less its liabilities, divided by the number of shares outstanding.

No-Load Fund   A mutual fund that charges no sales commission.

Nominal Return   The return on an investment before adjustment for inflation. See **real return.**

Nonqualified Plan   A retirement plan that does not meet the IRS requirements for favorable tax treatment.

O

Offering Price   The purchase price per share of a mutual fund, determined by adding any applicable sales charge to the fund's net asset value (NAV) per share. Also known as **ask price.** See **redemption price.**

Open End Investment Company   See **mutual fund.**

P

Part B Prospectus   See **statement of additional information.**

Passive Investing   An investment approach that seeks to mimic the return and risk characteristics of a discrete market segment by holding all the securities that compose the market segment, or a statistically representative sample. See also **active investing.**

Payable Date   Date on which distributions of dividends or capital gains are paid to shareholders who do not reinvest. See also **record date** and **ex-dividend date.**

Payout Period   The time period during which you make withdrawals from a deferred annuity or retirement account.

Portfolio   All the securities that are held by a mutual fund.

Portfolio Manager   See **investment adviser.**

Portfolio Transaction Costs   The costs associated with buying and selling securities, including commissions on stocks, dealer markups on bonds, bid/ask spreads, and any other miscellaneous expenses.

Profit-Sharing Plan   A defined contribution plan in which contributions can be varied and no minimum contribution is required.

Prospectus   A legal document providing pertinent information about a mutual fund, including discussions of the fund's investment objectives and policies, risks, costs, past performance, and other information useful to prospective investors.

Q–R

Qualified Plan   A retirement plan approved by the IRS and eligible for favorable tax treatment. Employer contributions are deductible as business expenses and earnings on plan assets are not taxed until they are distributed.

Real Return   Investment return adjusted for inflation. For example, if the nominal investment return for a particular period is +8% and inflation is 3%, the real return is +5%.

Record Date   The deadline for owning shares for the purpose of receiving the next distribution of dividends or capital gains.

Redemption Fee   See **back-end load.**

Redemption Price   Also bid or sell price. The price at which a mutual fund's shares can be redeemed, determined by deducting any applicable sales charge from the net asset value (NAV) per share. See also **offering price.**

Required Minimum Distribution   The amount that must be withdrawn annually from all your retirement plans once you reach age 70½. Withdrawals can be made based on the single or the joint life expectancy of you and your primary beneficiary.

Rollover   Moving all or part of the balance of a tax-deferred retirement plan into an individual retirement account or other eligible plan without incurring any tax liability.

S

Salary Reduction Simplified Employee Pension Plan (SARSEP)   A low-cost, no-frills version of a 401(k) employee savings plan that is available only to companies with 25 or fewer employees. Also known as a 408(k) plan. SARSEPs have the same annual contribution limit ($9,204 in 1994) as 401(k)s but do not allow for plan loans or hardship withdrawals. Employer contributions to SARSEPs must be immediately vested.

Securities and Exchange Commission   The federal government agency that regulates mutual funds, registered investment advisers, the stock and bond markets, and securities broker-dealers.

Self-Employed Pension   A qualified retirement plan for the self-employed, including sole proprietors and partners. Also known as a Keogh plan. Can be structured as a defined benefit plan or as defined contribution plan.

Short-Term Reserves   Short-term, highly liquid interest-bearing investments such as US Treasury bills, bank certificates of deposit, and commercial paper.

Simplified Employee Pension (SEP-IRA)   A no-frills version of the self-employed pension, or Keogh plan.

Single Life Annuity   An annuity covering one person. There are two types of single life annuities. A straight life annuity provides payments until death. A life annuity with a guaranteed period provides payments until death or continues payments to a beneficiary for a guaranteed term, such as 10 years.

Statement of Additional Information   Separate document provided as a supplement to a mutual fund's prospectus. Contains more detailed information about fund policies, operations, and investment risks. Lists all officers and directors of the fund and their compensation. Also known as **Part B** of the prospectus. Available on request from the mutual fund sponsor.

T

12b–1 Fee   An annual fee charged by some mutual funds to pay for marketing and distribution activities.

Tax-Deferred Retirement Plan   Any retirement plan in which earnings are not currently taxable.

Total Return   A measure of investment performance during a particular period, including income and any change in price.

Turnover Rate   A measure of a mutual fund's trading activity. Turnover is calculated by taking the lesser of the fund's total purchases or total sales of securities (not counting securities with maturities under one year) and dividing by the average monthly assets.

V–Y

Vesting   The right to receive retirement plan benefits. Employers can use either of two vesting timetables. The first, known as *cliff vesting*, permits zero vesting for the first five years if 100% is conferred by the end of the fifth year. The alternative timetable, *graded vesting*, requires at least 20% vesting after three years, with an additional 20% provided each year afterward, so that participants are fully vested at the end of the seventh year.

Withdrawal   Taking money out of a tax-advantaged retirement plan, which makes it subject to tax and possible penalty if you are under age 59½.

Withdrawal Plan   A method of gradually converting a mutual fund balance into income by arranging for regular (usually monthly) redemptions of a predetermined dollar amount. Also known as a systematic withdrawal plan.

Yield   The annualized rate at which an investment earns income.

APPENDIX

Worksheet: How Much Should I Save for Retirement?
(See Chapter 3 for complete instructions.)

	Example	Your Own Situation
Your Retirement Income Goal and Benefits		
1. Your current income	$80,000	_____
2. Your retirement income goal (70% to 80% of line 1)	$56,000	_____
3. Social Security benefits	$24,000	_____
4. Pension	$10,000	_____
5. Annual shortfall (Line 2 — Line 3 — Line 4)	$22,000	_____
6. Current retirement savings	$34,000	_____
7. Current annual savings	$7,200	_____
Your Assumptions		
8. Investment return	8%	_____
9. Years until retirement	20	_____
10. Retirement period (in years)	25	_____
Retirement Factors		
11. Inflation factor (Table A)	2.19	_____
12. Capital needed for retirement (Table B)	16.49	_____
13. Inflation adjustment for pension (Table C)	4.96	_____
14. Investment growth (Table D)	4.66	_____
15. Current retirement savings factor (Table E)	.0150	_____
Your Income Needs		
16. Annual income goal at retirement (Line 2 × Line 11)	$123,000	_____
17. Annual income shortfall at retirement (Line 5 × Line 11)	$48,000	_____
18. Savings needed for retirement (Line 17 × Line 12)	$792,000	_____
Inflation Adjustment		
19. Value of pension at retirement (Line 4 × Line 11)	$22,000	_____
20. Inflation adjustment for pension (Line 19 × Line 13)	$109,000	_____
Value of Current Savings at Retirement		
21. Current savings at retirement (Line 6 × Line 14)	$158,000	_____
Your Retirement Savings Goal		
22. Net savings needed for retirement (Line 18 + Line 20 − Line 21)	$743,000	_____
23. Percentage of annual income needed to meet retirement goal (Line 22 × Line 15 ÷ Line 1)	14%	_____
24. Current annual savings rate (Line 7 ÷ Line 1)	9%	_____
25. Required increase in annual savings rate (Line 23 − Line 24)	5%	_____

Note: Figures in example are rounded and assume a 4% annual rate of inflation.

Factors for Worksheet
Table A
Inflation Factor (Line 11 of Worksheet)

Years Until Retirement	Factor	Years Until Retirement	Factor
1	1.04	21	2.28
2	1.08	22	2.37
3	1.12	23	2.46
4	1.17	24	2.56
5	1.22	25	2.67
6	1.27	26	2.77
7	1.32	27	2.88
8	1.37	28	3.00
9	1.42	29	3.12
10	1.48	30	3.24
11	1.54	31	3.37
12	1.60	32	3.51
13	1.67	33	3.65
14	1.73	34	3.79
15	1.80	35	3.95
16	1.87	36	4.10
17	1.95	37	4.27
18	2.03	38	4.44
19	2.11	39	4.62
20	2.19	40	4.80

Table B
Savings Needed for Retirement (Line 12)

Retirement Period	Investment Return							
	5%	6%	7%	8%	9%	10%	11%	12%
15	14.04	13.17	12.39	11.67	11.02	10.43	9.89	9.39
20	18.29	16.79	15.47	14.31	13.28	12.36	11.55	10.82
25	22.34	20.08	18.15	16.49	15.06	13.82	12.75	11.80
30	26.20	23.07	20.47	18.30	16.47	14.93	13.61	12.48
35	29.88	25.79	22.48	19.79	17.59	15.76	14.24	12.95
40	33.39	28.26	24.23	21.03	18.47	16.39	14.69	13.28

Table C
Inflation Adjustment for Pension (Line 13)

Retirement Period	Investment Return							
	5%	6%	7%	8%	9%	10%	11%	12%
15	3.14	2.88	2.64	2.43	2.23	2.06	1.91	1.76
20	5.20	4.63	4.13	3.71	3.33	3.00	2.71	2.45
25	7.54	6.53	5.68	4.96	4.35	3.84	3.40	3.02
30	10.06	8.48	7.19	6.14	5.27	4.56	3.96	3.46
35	12.69	10.42	8.63	7.20	6.07	5.15	4.41	3.79
40	15.37	12.31	9.97	8.15	6.74	5.63	4.75	4.05

Note: Factors assume a 4% annual rate of inflation.

Factors for Worksheet

Table D
Investment Growth (Line 14)

Years Until Retirement	Investment Return							
	5%	6%	7%	8%	9%	10%	11%	12%
1	1.05	1.06	1.07	1.08	1.09	1.10	1.11	1.12
2	1.10	1.12	1.14	1.17	1.19	1.21	1.23	1.25
3	1.16	1.19	1.23	1.26	1.30	1.33	1.37	1.40
4	1.22	1.26	1.31	1.36	1.41	1.46	1.52	1.57
5	1.28	1.34	1.40	1.47	1.54	1.61	1.69	1.76
6	1.34	1.42	1.50	1.59	1.68	1.77	1.87	1.97
7	1.41	1.50	1.61	1.71	1.83	1.95	2.08	2.21
8	1.48	1.59	1.72	1.85	1.99	2.14	2.30	2.48
9	1.55	1.69	1.84	2.00	2.17	2.36	2.56	2.77
10	1.63	1.79	1.97	2.16	2.37	2.59	2.84	3.11
11	1.71	1.90	2.10	2.33	2.58	2.85	3.15	3.48
12	1.80	2.01	2.25	2.52	2.81	3.14	3.50	3.90
13	1.89	2.13	2.41	2.72	3.07	3.45	3.88	4.36
14	1.98	2.26	2.58	2.94	3.34	3.80	4.31	4.89
15	2.08	2.40	2.76	3.17	3.64	4.18	4.78	5.47
16	2.18	2.54	2.95	3.43	3.97	4.59	5.31	6.13
17	2.29	2.69	3.16	3.70	4.33	5.05	5.90	6.87
18	2.41	2.85	3.38	4.00	4.72	5.56	6.54	7.69
19	2.53	3.03	3.62	4.32	5.14	6.12	7.26	8.61
20	2.65	3.21	3.87	4.66	5.60	6.73	8.06	9.65
21	2.79	3.40	4.14	5.03	6.11	7.40	8.95	10.80
22	2.93	3.60	4.43	5.44	6.66	8.14	9.93	12.10
23	3.07	3.82	4.74	5.87	7.26	8.95	11.03	13.55
24	3.23	4.05	5.07	6.34	7.91	9.85	12.24	15.18
25	3.39	4.29	5.43	6.85	8.62	10.83	13.59	17.00
26	3.56	4.55	5.81	7.40	9.40	11.92	15.08	19.04
27	3.73	4.82	6.21	7.99	10.25	13.11	16.74	21.32
28	3.92	5.11	6.65	8.63	11.17	14.42	18.58	23.88
29	4.12	5.42	7.11	9.32	12.17	15.86	20.62	26.75
30	4.32	5.74	7.61	10.06	13.27	17.45	22.89	29.96
31	4.54	6.09	8.15	10.87	14.46	19.19	25.41	33.56
32	4.76	6.45	8.72	11.74	15.76	21.11	28.21	37.58
33	5.00	6.84	9.33	12.68	17.18	23.23	31.31	42.09
34	5.25	7.25	9.98	13.69	18.73	25.55	34.75	47.14
35	5.52	7.69	10.68	14.79	20.41	28.10	38.57	52.80
36	5.79	8.15	11.42	15.97	22.25	30.91	42.82	59.14
37	6.08	8.64	12.22	17.25	24.25	34.00	47.53	66.23
38	6.39	9.15	13.08	18.63	26.44	37.40	52.76	74.18
39	6.70	9.70	13.99	20.12	28.82	41.14	58.56	83.08
40	7.04	10.29	14.97	21.72	31.41	45.26	65.00	93.05

Note: Factors assume a 4% annual rate of inflation.

Factors for Worksheet

Table E
Current Retirement Savings Factor (Line 15)

Years Until Retirement	Investment Return							
	5%	6%	7%	8%	9%	10%	11%	12%
1	0.9524	0.9434	0.9346	0.9259	0.9174	0.9091	0.9009	0.8929
2	0.4557	0.4492	0.4429	0.4368	0.4307	0.4248	0.4190	0.4134
3	0.2907	0.2852	0.2799	0.2747	0.2696	0.2646	0.2598	0.2550
4	0.2086	0.2037	0.1989	0.1943	0.1898	0.1854	0.1811	0.1770
5	0.1597	0.1552	0.1508	0.1466	0.1425	0.1385	0.1346	0.1309
6	0.1274	0.1232	0.1191	0.1152	0.1114	0.1077	0.1042	0.1008
7	0.1045	0.1005	0.0967	0.0931	0.0896	0.0862	0.0830	0.0798
8	0.0875	0.0838	0.0802	0.0768	0.0735	0.0704	0.0674	0.0645
9	0.0744	0.0709	0.0675	0.0643	0.0613	0.0584	0.0556	0.0529
10	0.0641	0.0607	0.0576	0.0546	0.0517	0.0490	0.0464	0.0439
11	0.0557	0.0526	0.0496	0.0468	0.0441	0.0415	0.0391	0.0368
12	0.0489	0.0459	0.0431	0.0404	0.0379	0.0355	0.0332	0.0311
13	0.0432	0.0403	0.0376	0.0351	0.0327	0.0305	0.0284	0.0265
14	0.0384	0.0357	0.0331	0.0307	0.0285	0.0264	0.0245	0.0226
15	0.0343	0.0317	0.0293	0.0270	0.0249	0.0230	0.0211	0.0194
16	0.0307	0.0283	0.0260	0.0238	0.0219	0.0200	0.0183	0.0168
17	0.0277	0.0253	0.0232	0.0211	0.0193	0.0176	0.0160	0.0145
18	0.0250	0.0228	0.0207	0.0188	0.0170	0.0154	0.0140	0.0126
19	0.0227	0.0205	0.0186	0.0168	0.0151	0.0136	0.0122	0.0110
20	0.0206	0.0186	0.0167	0.0150	0.0134	0.0120	0.0107	0.0096
21	0.0188	0.0168	0.0151	0.0134	0.0120	0.0107	0.0095	0.0084
22	0.0171	0.0153	0.0136	0.0121	0.0107	0.0095	0.0083	0.0073
23	0.0157	0.0139	0.0123	0.0109	0.0096	0.0084	0.0074	0.0064
24	0.0144	0.0127	0.0112	0.0098	0.0086	0.0075	0.0065	0.0057
25	0.0132	0.0116	0.0102	0.0089	0.0077	0.0067	0.0058	0.0050
26	0.0122	0.0106	0.0092	0.0080	0.0069	0.0060	0.0051	0.0044
27	0.0112	0.0097	0.0084	0.0073	0.0062	0.0053	0.0046	0.0039
28	0.0103	0.0089	0.0077	0.0066	0.0056	0.0048	0.0040	0.0034
29	0.0095	0.0082	0.0070	0.0060	0.0051	0.0043	0.0036	0.0030
30	0.0088	0.0075	0.0064	0.0054	0.0046	0.0038	0.0032	0.0027
31	0.0082	0.0069	0.0059	0.0049	0.0041	0.0034	0.0029	0.0024
32	0.0076	0.0064	0.0054	0.0045	0.0037	0.0031	0.0026	0.0021
33	0.0070	0.0059	0.0049	0.0041	0.0034	0.0028	0.0023	0.0019
34	0.0065	0.0055	0.0045	0.0037	0.0031	0.0025	0.0020	0.0016
35	0.0061	0.0050	0.0042	0.0034	0.0028	0.0023	0.0018	0.0015
36	0.0056	0.0047	0.0038	0.0031	0.0025	0.0020	0.0016	0.0013
37	0.0053	0.0043	0.0035	0.0029	0.0023	0.0018	0.0015	0.0012
38	0.0049	0.0040	0.0032	0.0026	0.0021	0.0017	0.0013	0.0010
39	0.0046	0.0037	0.0030	0.0024	0.0019	0.0015	0.0012	0.0009
40	0.0043	0.0034	0.0028	0.0022	0.0017	0.0013	0.0010	0.0008

Note: Factors assume a 4% annual rate of inflation.

Worksheet: Lump-Sum Withdrawal
(See Chapter 10 for complete instructions.)

	Example	Your Own Situation
Your Assumptions		
1. Investment return	8.0%	_____
2. Retirement period	30	_____
Worksheet Factors (See Table on Page 185)		
3. Level income factor (Table 10–7)	0.0822	_____
4. Rising income factor (Table 10–7)	0.0547	_____
Annual Income from Lump-Sum Savings		
5. Your retirement lump-sum savings	$250,000	_____
6. Level income, annual (Line 5 × Line 3)	$20,500	_____
7. Level income, monthly (Line 6 ÷ 12)	$1,700	_____
8. Rising income, annual (Line 5 × Line 4)	$13,700	_____
9. Rising Income, monthly (Line 8 ÷ 12)	$1,100	_____
Income Summary		
Use this section to summarize your monthly retirement income from all sources.		
10. Social Security	$1,300	_____
11. Pension	$900	_____
12. Income from lump-sum (Line 7 or Line 9)	$1,100	_____
13. Other income	$0	_____
14. Total monthly income (Line 10 + Line 11 + Line 12 + Line 13)	$3,300	_____

Note: Figures in examples are rounded.

INDEX